Eduard Bernstein and Marxism

It was one of Bernstein's fundamental convictions that violence for its own sake was barbarian; his bitter and unremitting campaign against Bolshevism testifies to his devotion to liberal parliamentarism. Bernstein was the antithesis of the dogmatic revolutionists; he would have refused to impose the will of his party upon a hostile country, and he was anxious to arrive at the desired end—Socialism—only with the proper means—democracy. In other words, he was unwilling to kill for the sake of logic.

—from *The Dilemma of Democratic Socialism*

PETER GAY

THE DILEMMA
DEMOCRATIC

OF
SOCIALISM

Eduard Bernstein's
Challenge to Marx

OCTAGON BOOKS

A DIVISION OF FARRAR, STRAUS AND GIROUX

New York   1979

Reprinted 1979
by special arrangement with Columbia University Press

OCTAGON BOOKS
A DIVISION OF FARRAR, STRAUS & GIROUX, INC.
19 Union Square West
New York, N.Y. 10003

LIBRARY OF CONGRESS CATALOG CARD NUMBER: 78-24820
ISBN 0-374-93017-1

Manufactured by Braun-Brumfield, Inc.
Ann Arbor, Michigan
Printed in the United States of America

To my mother and to
the memory of my
father

Preface

A DEMOCRATIC SOCIALIST MOVEMENT that attempts to transform a capitalist into a Socialist order is necessarily faced with the choice between incompatibles—principles and power. Socialist parties that are dedicated to democracy proceed on the fundamental assumption that their enemies are human, too, an assumption that limits the range of their weapons. Discussion, vote-getting, parliamentarism—rather than terrorism, violence, revolution—constitute the arsenal of the democratic Socialist. Again, the Socialist who is also a democrat will eschew dictatorship to maintain himself in power and rely, instead, on persuasion.

But a democratic Socialist movement that remains faithful to its principles may never achieve power. Or, if an accident should put control into its hands, it may soon lose it to less scrupulous adversaries. Is democratic Socialism, then, impossible? Or can it be achieved only if the party is willing to abandon the democratic method temporarily to attain power by violence in the hope that it may return to parliamentarism as soon as control is secure? Surely this second alternative contains tragic possibilities: a democratic movement that resorts to authoritarian methods to gain its objective may not remain a democratic movement for long. Still, the first alternative—to cling to democratic procedures under all circumstances—may doom the party to continual political impotence.

The dilemma is real enough, and it has repeatedly plagued all great democratic Socialist movements, particularly the British Labour Party and the German Social Democrats. In 1935 Harold Laski dealt in arresting fashion with the dilemma of principles vs. power, which his party was confronting. "A capitalist democracy," he wrote, "will not allow its electorate to stumble into Socialism by the accident of a verdict at the polls." [1] Laski feared that even the British genius for compromise would break down before an electoral triumph of the Labour Party, and he predicted that the victori-

[1] *Democracy in Crisis* (Chapel Hill: University of North Carolina Press, 1935), p. 77.

ous Socialists would encounter determined sabotage from the opposition party, the House of Lords, the Crown, the Army, the bureaucracy, and the financial community. "A party which, in effect, is attempting a revolution by constitutional means is bound at least to consider whether in fact the means of the constitution are at its disposal." [2]

History has shown that Laski's apprehensions were in large measure unfounded and that the commitment to democracy (or, to say the least, the timidity) of a defending class may be stronger than its commitment to the old social order. The British experience suggests not so much that the dilemma is imaginary but that generalizations are impossible: historical circumstances peculiar to each country will help to determine what political methods will lead a party to success. The only general statement open to us may be a tautology: democratic Socialism is possible only in those countries in which it is possible.

British Socialism has been the subject of many valuable studies. Other forms of Socialist thought have also received their share of critical attention: Marxism has been canvassed thoroughly ever since the first volume of *Capital* appeared eighty-five years ago. Leninism and Stalinism have been propelled to the foreground in recent years, owing not to their intrinsic merit but to political developments with which we are all too familiar. But, as any student of Socialism knows, there are some curious gaps in the literature. Most notable is the neglect of German constitutional Socialism, a theory and movement which, in many respects, surpasses in significance its British counterpart.

This book is an attempt to close this gap. It is a study of the origins, the meaning, and the impact of German Revisionist Socialism. Revisionism, too, was confronted with the dilemma of power, and it is this dilemma that underlies the analysis presented here.

Since Revisionism originated and received its finest expression in the writings of Eduard Bernstein, this book contains—in addition to a theoretical and historical analysis—Bernstein's intellectual biography. Bernstein was one of those men

[2] *Ibid.*, p. 107.

who eminently deserve, yet rarely get, a biography. The story of his life is the story of his party, but Bernstein was a great man in his own right: fearlessly honest and scrupulous, he rose above expediency and party loyalty when truth demanded it. His dedication to truth was as unfailing as his devotion to democracy. Furthermore, the modifications which he introduced into Marxism struck at the heart of the problem of social change and of the development of capitalism. If his Revisionism failed, it was, ultimately, not the failure of Bernstein but the failure of Germany. It is a failure that offers eloquent testimony as to the kind of country Germany really was, and that becomes all the more striking when we contrast it with the success of the British Labour Party.

It is a pleasant duty to record my debts of gratitude. I am deeply indebted to the Social Science Research Council for a generous grant which permitted me to spend a year in full-time research and writing. The International Institute for Social History at Amsterdam allowed me complete access to the Bernstein Archives, which throw much light on Bernstein's career and on the genesis of his thought. My special thanks are due to Herr W. Blumenberg, chief of the German section of the Institute, whose guidance was most helpful. Here in New York, the Buttinger Library kindly permitted me to use books not elsewhere available.

Above all, I want to thank Professor Franz Neumann, under whose direction this study was undertaken, for his unfailing support at all times and for the careful readings which immensely benefited the work. It is not extravagant to say that but for his aid (in these and many other matters) this volume might never have been published. I am grateful to my friend Professor Henry Roberts for his critical readings of the manuscript. It owes much to his keen sense of style and proportion. Dr. Otto Landsberg, a personal friend of Eduard Bernstein's and one of the six members of the German provisional government formed in November 1918, was kind enough to grant me a most enlightening interview. Professors Robert Lynd, Robert MacIver, Reinhold Neibuhr, and Lindsay Rogers all went over the manuscript and suggested improvements. A number of my friends—Justus Buchler, Fred

Burin, Martha Salmon, Paul Seabury, Fritz Stern, Lenoir Wright—read chapters of this book and helped with encouragement and criticism. Finally, I wish to thank my editor, Mr. Christopher Herold, for his invaluable assistance.

PETER GAY

New York
June 1, 1952

Acknowledgments

I WISH to acknowledge permission to quote brief passages from the following books: *Actuelles,* by Albert Camus, published by Gallimard, Paris; *Der Revisionismus,* by Erika Rikli, published by Dr. H. Girsberger, Zurich; *Hammer or Anvil,* by Evelyn Anderson, published by Victor Gollancz, Ltd., London; *The School for Dictators,* by Ignazio Silone, published by Harper and Brothers, New York, and Jonathan Cape, London; *Selected Correspondence, Karl Marx and Frederick Engels,* edited by V. Adoratzky, *The Communist Manifesto,* by Karl Marx and Friedrich Engels, and *What is to be Done?* by V. I. Lenin, all published by International Publishers, New York; *The Class Struggle,* by Karl Kautsky, published by Charles H. Kerr & Co., Chicago; *An Essay on Marxian Economics,* by Joan Robinson, published by the St. Martin's Press, Inc., New York, the Macmillan Company of Canada, and Macmillan & Co., Ltd., London; *A Theory of the Labor Movement,* by Selig Perlman, published by the Macmillan Company, New York; *Karl Marx's Capital,* by A. D. Lindsay, published by Oxford University Press, London; *Reason and Revolution,* by Herbert Marcuse, and *The Theory of Capitalist Development,* by Paul Sweezy, both published by Oxford University Press, Inc., New York; *Capital,* Vol. I, by Karl Marx, published by Random House, New York; *Imperial Germany,* by Thorstein Veblen, published by The Viking Press, Inc., New York.

P. G.

New York
June 1, 1952

Contents

BOOK ONE / THE MAN

Chapter 1

Education of a Socialist: Berlin

From 1850 to 1872

> *On n'a pas la mérite de sa naissance, on a celui de ses actions.*
>
> ALBERT CAMUS

EDUARD BERNSTEIN, the outstanding reformist theoretician of German Social Democracy in the twentieth century, was born in Berlin on January 6, 1850, at a desperate time for the German working class. The great liberal awakening of but two years before, which had swept across Europe in a series of revolutions, had left little but disillusionment in its wake. The "Fundamental Rights of the German People," proclaimed by the German National Assembly in Frankfurt in December 1848, was to remain nothing more than a catalogue of aspirations.

The intellectuals who had written this impressive liberal charter represented what was best in the urban nationalist bourgeoisie. They were rich in ideas but not arms—and in the dangerous arena of politics ideas are weapons only if they are backed by physical power. The liberals did not possess this power and they soon found that the old society was too strong for them. The landholders, supported by the peasants, were against them. So were the Church, the military, and, in most cases, the bureaucracy. Worse, the liberals, strongly imbued with the religion of property rights, considered the proletariat too dangerous to make it an ally. Wherever workers claimed the fruits of the revolution, as in Paris in June of 1848, they were massacred in the streets by the very men who had proclaimed the end of tyranny and corruption.

The counterrevolution set in before the "Fundamental Rights of the German People" had been signed. By 1849 reaction ruled most of Europe once more, and the king of Prussia had repudiated the Frankfurt charter. A year later,

Frederick William IV proclaimed a constitution for Prussia which was almost a caricature of the liberal program: ministers were responsible only to the king, royal ordinances issued when the parliament was not in session had the force of law. Moreover, the three-class voting system made a farce of universal suffrage: the wealthiest 5 percent of the voters controlled a third of the seats, 15 percent the next third, and the remaining 80 percent the last third. These provisions gave firm control over the legislature (feeble as it was) to rich bourgeois and owners of large landed estates.[1]

In Berlin, the March Revolution of 1848 had failed. Its only result was a decade of reactionary rule in Prussia, and by 1850 hope had given way to despondency among the German proletariat. Rudimentary labor organizations were ruthlessly suppressed by the police. Large numbers of workers were deported from the Prussian capital and other cities; democratic and radical newspapers were subjected to the strictest supervision or had to suspend publication altogether. "The 'powers that were' before the hurricane of 1848," Marx wrote gloomily in 1851, "are once more the 'powers that be.' "[2]

The life of Eduard Bernstein, which began at a time so inauspicious for European Socialism, spans the growth and near-triumph of the German labor movement. The *Communist Manifesto* was published two years before Bernstein's birth; he was a school boy in Berlin when Lassalle founded the first independent workers' party; when the first volume of *Capital* appeared in 1867 he was employed as an apprentice in a bank; in 1885, the year the second volume of *Capital* came out, he was in exile—the editor of the official party newspaper of German Social Democracy; shortly after the death of his friend Engels in 1895 he began the publication of those articles that made him an internationally known figure in Socialist theory; during the World War his defection from

[1] Johannes Ziekursch, *Politische Geschichte des neuen deutschen Kaiserreiches*, I, 61.
[2] Karl Marx, *Revolution and Counter-Revolution*, p. 1. Cf. also Eduard Bernstein, *Geschichte der Berliner Arbeiterbewegung*, I, 69–92.

his beloved party, which was supporting a war he despised, put him once more into the limelight; an aging man during the Weimar Republic, he observed with anguish the failure of the Social Democrats to use the power that was theirs; he died just in time, on December 18, 1932 at the age of 82, six weeks before Adolf Hitler became chancellor of the Reich.

The significance of Revisionist Socialism, a theory for which Bernstein was almost solely responsible, is unquestioned. It is the only important challenge to Marxism that developed within German Social Democracy, and it takes its place beside Fabianism as one of the major modern philosophies of peaceful change towards Socialism.

When Bernstein rebelled against the system of Marx and Engels in the late 1890s, his own party was officially committed to the recently adopted Erfurt Program. In spite of its professions, however, the Social Democratic Party rapidly lost its revolutionary character and turned into a constitutional, reformist organization. This metamorphosis, which had been well under way at the time the Marxist Erfurt Program was under debate, was effected not only by favorable economic and political circumstances; it was materially advanced by a small group of theorists within the party. These men were early characterized by their opponents as "Revisionists";[3] Eduard Bernstein was their intellectual leader and chief publicist.

Bernstein was born in a lower middle-class section of Berlin, the son of Jakob Bernstein who had started out as a plumber and later became a railway engineer. The income from the latter profession was barely sufficient to keep a sizable family within the pale of genteel poverty that is inhabited by what is known as the "petty bourgeoisie." Eduard was the seventh of fifteen children. "This was the only wealth to which my father attained," Bernstein ruefully noted later.[4]

The Bernstein family were Jewish but, like many German Jews of that time, did not practice their religion. They celebrated Christmas, regarding it as a German rather than a spe-

[3] Eduard Bernstein, *Der Revisionismus in der Sozialdemokratie,* pp. 4–8.
[4] Eduard Bernstein, *Von 1850 bis 1872,* p. 7.

cifically Christian holiday. In this atmosphere young Eduard grew up half believer, half skeptic. He recounts an occasion on which he prayed for a dying relative, "Dear God, *if you exist,* please help my cousin." [5]

Eduard was a sickly child and a fairly good student, but he never finished Gymnasium. At the age of sixteen he left school to begin an apprenticeship in a Berlin bank. This ended his formal education. From then on he studied on his own, but his lack of a university training did not prevent him from becoming one of the outstanding intellectuals in a movement richly supplied with university graduates.

Upon completing his apprenticeship late in 1869, he obtained a post as a bank clerk with another Berlin firm and remained there until the fall of 1878, when he left Germany.[6]

There is little in Bernstein's youth before his entrance into politics that need detain us. He has given us a detailed report of his early years which, along with his older autobiographical works, reveals his character to us. These books, like his other publications, bear above all the stamp of integrity. His honesty, thoroughness, and intelligence are apparent everywhere. If Bernstein's writings lack dramatic power, we may compare the man to the hero of Karel Capek's remarkable novel, *An Ordinary Life,* who leads an outwardly placid existence that conceals tensions and ambitions not easily noticed by outsiders.

In his younger years Eduard Bernstein dabbled in poetry. For a while he harbored a strong desire to work in the theatre, either as an actor or as a playwright. No one can read his accounts of his travels and deny him a certain romantic imagination.[7] He admired Schiller and liked to quote

[5] *Ibid.,* p. 164.

[6] V. Adoratsky, paying the usual Stalinist courtesies to an opponent, describes him in a biographical note as follows: "Eduard Bernstein, German Social Democrat, bank clerk." *Selected Correspondence, Karl Marx and Frederick Engels,* p. 378. That is about equivalent to characterizing Engels as a ghostwriter: Bernstein's bank job was a source of livelihood for a number of years, but never anything more. Once he had turned to political journalism and serious writing, he never returned to his earlier pursuit. Even when he was working for the bank his chief interests lay elsewhere.

[7] Cf. Eduard Bernstein, *Aus den Jahren meines Exils,* pp. 10–30.

from his poems.[8] His middle-class tastes in poetry were coupled with a faultlessly bourgeois attitude towards women, typical of most Socialists. His recollection of a pleasant evening in Switzerland is characteristic: "Although my companion was really pretty, I would not then have dreamed of beginning a love affair with a young girl without 'serious intentions.' My views concerning free love as applied to myself were purely theoretical." [9]

Undoubtedly, his solidity and safe emotionalism aided Bernstein in his life task. He was not fated to originate a powerful theory but to suggest significant modifications in a great tradition. That required the very virtues and the very failings which Bernstein possessed. It took a man who could understand greatness without reaching it himself, a man capable of admiration but unwilling to be cowed by a name or a reputation.

Bismarck's aggressive policy of the 1860s had no extraordinary effect on the young Bernstein. Like most other adolescents, he was a patriot. His change of attitude (it was too rational to be called a "conversion") came during the Franco-Prussian war. Late in 1871 his ready sympathies were enlisted on the side of Bebel, Liebknecht, and other Socialists when his reading of radical newspapers convinced him that the government's charge of treason against these men was trumped up. He began to study the principles which the defendants professed since he agreed with their opposition to the late war.[10]

At about this time, Bernstein and several friends had formed a small discussion group called "Utopia." The name had been adopted to characterize the club as "an idealist association that would stand *above* everyday pursuits"—truly

---

[8] *Ibid.,* p. 18. Also, Eduard Bernstein, *Sozialdemokratische Lehrjahre,* p. 22.

[9] *Aus den Jahren meines Exils,* p. 59.

[10] Bernstein, *Von 1850 bis 1872,* pp. 212–17. It had been "heavenly music" in his ears to hear of the stand taken by Bebel and his comrades early in the Franco-Prussian conflict. Not that they had been pacifists; they had called on the members of their party to rise above mere patriotic allegiance to recall that men are brothers.

a far cry from Scientific Socialism.[11] One evening Bernstein made the acquaintance of F. W. Fritzsche, and invited that well-known union organizer and Social Democrat to address a "Utopia" get-together. Fritzsche complied and told the small group about the two Socialist parties that were at that time engaged in bitter combat: the Lassalleans and the so-called Eisenachers. The second, which was under the leadership of Bebel and Liebknecht, was more closely allied to Marxism than the first. Eduard Bernstein joined the latter group in February of 1872. His theoretical preparation consisted of the reading of two books, Lassalle's *Herr Bastiat Schulze von Delitzsch* and Dühring's *Kritische Geschichte der Nationalökonomie und des Sozialismus.*[12]

This is how Eduard Bernstein entered the Social Democratic movement at the age of twenty-two. He was to serve it well for sixty years. But in 1872 he was ill-informed although full of good intentions. His real education in Socialism was only beginning.

Apprenticeship

> *My interest in the fight for my party, and in our skirmishes with the Lassalleans, kept me so busy that a deeper concern with the theory of Socialism· could not compete with it for a long time.*
>
> EDUARD BERNSTEIN

Eduard Bernstein liked to reminisce about his early years as a Social Democrat. One evening in 1873, he tells us, he was addressing a public meeting in Berlin on the general topic of Socialism. In the debate following his lecture, a Lassallean rose to heckle the speaker. He tried to disconcert Bernstein,

[11] *Ibid.,* p. 208.

[12] Lassalle's volume was of special interest to Bernstein. It contained a vehement attack on Aaron Bernstein, Eduard's uncle, a Liberal and a passionate opponent of Social Democracy. Eduard found Lassalle's charges "distorted" and "unjust" and showed but little understanding of Lassalle's thought at that time. This was to change in later years.

called him *ehrlich* ("honest"—an ironic epithet applied to
the Eisenachers by their Socialist rivals), and appealed to the
audience to support the Lassallean party as the only true
Reds in Germany. An excited Eisenacher came to Bernstein's
aid: "Don't you believe him, gentlemen!" he shouted. "We're
much redder than they are!" [13]

From the time he joined the Eisenacher party in early
1872 to the time that he left Germany in late 1878, Eduard
Bernstein went through many such experiences. He was later
to call these six years his "Social Democratic apprenticeship."
His political education proceeded in several areas simultane-
ously. The versatility of his training was due largely to the
peculiar nature of continental parties, which—unlike their
American counterparts—are doctrinal and tend to adhere
more or less strictly to a particular ideology. Bernstein not
only acquired skill as a public speaker: he found himself exposed to the influence of the more experienced party leaders,
and he began to read social theory.

The two books that had the greatest impact on the young
Socialist in these early years were Marx's famous address to
the General Council of the First International, *The Civil War
in France,* which he obtained shortly after its publication in
1871, and Dühring's *Cursus der National- und Sozialökonomie,* which had come out late in 1872.

Marx's long speech, which (in opposition to near-universal
condemnation) exalted the short-lived Paris Commune, was a
masterful conglomerate of dialectical materialist analysis of
history and of propaganda for Marxism in general. Bernstein
found it thrilling reading. He wrote a small drama based on
Marx's pamphlet and performed it at a workers' festival with
great success. Spectacles such as these gave Bismarck grave,
although unwarranted, concern for the safety of the new
Reich against a proletarian revolution in Germany on the
Paris model.[14]

Bernstein's enthusiasm for Dühring's book proved con-
tagious. He communicated his delight with the *Cursus* by
spreading it widely among his associates, including Bebel. For

[13] Bernstein, *Sozialdemokratische Lehrjahre,* pp. 21–22.
[14] *Ibid.,* pp. 13–14; August Bebel, *Aus meinem Leben,* II, 283;
Arthur Rosenberg, *The Birth of the German Republic,* p. 22.

a while it exerted considerable influence, and it took Engels's celebrated reply, the *Anti-Dühring*, to exorcise this demon completely.[15]

His activities as a public speaker soon won Eduard Bernstein a respected place among the Eisenach Socialists. The speaking tours were a rough school: generally they began on a Saturday night and continued through Sunday. They consisted of the delivery of three talks, or participation in three debates, in as many different localities—truly a grueling schedule. The suburbs of Berlin were Bernstein's proving grounds. When he had been a success there, he transferred his attention to the capital itself. Occasionally there were fist fights, but usually violence confined itself to the language used.

With increasing recognition of his talents by the party, Bernstein widened his circle of acquaintance among the top leadership. He was only in his middle twenties, but youth was an attribute of most of his colleagues: Bebel was ten, Ignaz Auer, long-time party secretary, but four years older. Among the leaders of the Eisenachers, only Wilhelm Liebknecht belonged to Marx's generation. Bernstein continued his bank job but used his free time almost exclusively to further the interests of his party. He visited Bebel in prison and welcomed him home upon his release, "making a special trip from Berlin to Leipzig for that purpose," as Bebel notes in his autobiography.[16] The two men soon became fast friends. Ignaz Auer, who held many important party posts, was another early intimate.[17]

In spite of feverish activity, neither the Eisenachers nor the Lassalleans made much headway in Bismarck's Germany. The founding of the Reich had been accompanied by a speculative and largely fraudulent boom which resulted in a serious depression in 1873. A series of strikes, caused by the sharp rise in the cost of living since 1871, was crushed by drastic measures. Labor organizations and left-wing publica-

[15] For a detailed analysis of Dühring's influence, cf. pp. 94–103.
[16] Bebel, *Aus meinem Leben,* II, 278.
[17] Cf. Eduard Bernstein's memorial volume, *Ignaz Auer.*

tions suffered systematic and arbitrary interference. Bismarck, as yet unsuccessfully, advocated special anti-Socialist legislation.[18]

This constant harassment did not prevent the Socialists from scoring minor successes. In the Reichstag elections of January 1874 the two Socialist parties polled 351,670 votes—over 6 percent of the total vote cast. Even with this considerable showing, they were represented in the Reichstag by only nine men, including Hasenclever (the Lassallean leader), Bebel, Liebknecht, and Most.[19]

While repression was a fairly effective means of limiting Socialist activities and curtailing the Socialist vote, the greatest ally of the bourgeois and reactionary parties was division within Socialist ranks. The German government, suspicious and fearful of any united labor or Socialist movement, did not need to apply the maxim, *Divide et impera*: the Socialists were splitting their ranks of their own accord and needed no outside aid.

The fratricidal conflict between the Lassalleans and the Eisenachers was carried on with much bitterness, but the 1874 elections demonstrated the absurdity of the fight. The former had polled 180,319 votes, the latter, 171,351. Nothing could be more convincing testimony of their equal hold on the working class and on the radical members of the bourgeoisie. In some election districts, in which a run-off election had proved necessary, candidates of the bourgeois parties were pitted against a member of either Socialist body. Whom were the other Socialists to support in the run-off? Who, in other words, was their true enemy? The very fact that there could be discussion on this point proved—if proof was needed—that it was high time for the parties to unite if they were not to annihilate each other.[20]

Bismarck's policy was clear for all to see, and Bismarck was unquestioned dictator of German policy. The Iron Chan-

[18] Franz Mehring, *Geschichte der deutschen Sozialdemokratie,* IV, 39–48.

[19] *Ibid.,* IV, 71–72.

[20] For an example, cf. Bernstein, *Sozialdemokratische Lehrjahre,* pp. 33–34. To a large extent, both groups overcame their mutual animosity long enough to vote for a fellow-Socialist in the run-off elections.

cellor had created his Reich by forming an alliance between Prussia's military aristocracy and the German bourgeoisie. In this alliance the role of the bourgeoisie was not wholly fixed, except that it was to be secondary to the aristocracy. What *was* determined in this scheme was the role of the working class: it was to work hard and be obedient.[21] With rapidly advancing industrialization, the question of working-class organization was becoming acute. In the early 1870s German labor unions were immature and presented a vastly different picture from their British counterparts.[22] The trade unions that had sprung up in the 1860s and early 1870s were rarely grass-roots organizations. Most of them had been founded by the bourgeois Progressive or the Lassallean party to act as semidependent branch organizations.[23] But this state of affairs was not likely to persist. German industry, cleverly borrowing British techniques, was making rapid strides. The upper middle class, as represented chiefly by the industrialists, was anxious to push its way forward. How Bismarck would solve the growing conflict between the military aristocracy and the dynamic bourgeoisie was not then clear. But there was no doubt that the working classes were to be assigned the lowly role of the producer possessing only a token voice in the determination of policy. The ruling classes were willing

[21] This point has been brilliantly developed by Rosenberg, *Birth of the German Republic,* pp. 1–8. Cf. also Gustav Mayer, *Friedrich Engels,* II, 264 ff.

[22] The young Mehring sadly noted: "German labor associations do not even approach the grandeur of English trade unions; they . . . have never shown that tenacious patience in accumulating gigantic funds for the preparation of strikes, or that prudent timing for the inception of these strikes, or that iron energy for carrying them through, as have the British." *Zur Geschichte der deutschen Sozialdemokratie,* pp. 83–84. But such a comparison is hardly fair. Great Britain was the most highly industrialized country in Europe; Germany in 1870 was still comparatively backward. Great Britain had a long-enduring tradition of voluntary associations interrupted only in consciously recognized periods of reaction; German clubs and trade unions were hampered by *Vereinsgesetze* which put associative activity under constant police scrutiny. As Thorstein Veblen noted in his perceptive book *Imperial Germany,* the very fact of Germany's late entrance into the industrial race brought with it special problems.

[23] Mehring, *Zur Geschichte,* p. 17.

to use force to maintain this power relation. The liberal bourgeoisie could be left out of consideration entirely. Defeated in 1848 and 1862, it commanded little assent and less power. Therefore Bismarck's hands were relatively free, and he and the men around him proceeded to reorganize the Prussian bureaucracy as the mainstay of reaction, to erase all traces of liberalism from the army, and to convince the owning classes that cooperation among them was essential.[24]

For these reasons, thoughtful Socialists were anxious that the two radical parties should establish a common front before the government took even more repressive measures. But doctrinal differences, which in the course of time had hardened into personal conflicts, stood in the way of unity.

Lassalle *vs.* Marx: A Digression

> *It seems that every workers' party in a great country can grow only through internal strife, and this is based on the general law of dialectical development. The German Party became what it is in the struggle between the Eisenachers and the Lassalleans.*
>
> ENGELS TO BERNSTEIN

The unification of the German labor movement was accomplished in 1875. The significance of this event can be appreciated only if the origins and divergences of the two strands of German Social Democracy which were now woven together are fully understood.

The Allgemeiner Deutscher Arbeiterverein was the direct outcome of a magnificent *tour de force,* probably unparalleled in the history of political parties. It was created by Ferdinand Lassalle, almost out of thin air, near the end of his brief and adventurous life.

In February 1863, a Leipzig workingmen's association sent a letter to Lassalle, whose speeches had caught their imagination, asking his opinion of the possibilities of organizing a national workingmen's congress. Lassalle's prompt answer,

[24] This point has been taken from Franz Neumann's *Behemoth,* pp. 3–7, where it is developed in detail.

the famous "Open Letter of Reply," was published in March. It advised workers to form a political party for the "purpose of legal and peaceful but untiring agitation for the introduction of universal and direct suffrage in all German lands." [25] In his enthusiasm he predicted that the proposed new party would quickly grow to massive proportions: "From the moment that this association contains but 100,000 members, it will be a power to be reckoned with." [26]

On May 23, 1863, the Allgemeiner Deutscher Arbeiterverein was founded at the Pantheon in Leipzig, Lassalle presiding. It was an intensely personal creation which could come to life only with the touch of the master: Lassalle was President, the name of the organization was the one he had proposed in his "Open Letter of Reply." Its stated single purpose—to fight for universal suffrage—was directly copied from Lassalle's letter.[27] Like the Chartists in Great Britain, then, the Lassalleans hoped to gain economic ends by the pursuit of purely political aims; the course of events soon forced them to expand their demands gradually and to move to the left.

The young party was in serious trouble from its very inception. Lassalle's confident dream of scores of thousands of members never materialized. His efforts were prodigious; he addressed uncounted workers' meetings and exploited his numerous courtroom appearances as publicity for his party. But membership remained insignificant. "Well, we have about

[25] Eduard Bernstein, ed., *Ferdinand Lassalles Reden und Schriften,* II, 444.

[26] *Loc. cit.*

[27] Paragraph 1 of the by-laws read: "The undersigned herewith found an association for the German federated states under the name Allgemeiner Deutscher Arbeiterverein. It pursues the purpose of working toward the creation of universal, equal, and direct suffrage with peaceful and legal methods, especially through persuasion of public opinion. It is convinced that sufficient representation of the social interests of the German working class and a true abolition of class distinctions (*Klassengegensätze*) in society can be brought about only through establishment of universal, equal, and direct suffrage." Quoted in Wilhelm Schröder, *Geschichte der sozialdemokratischen Parteiorganisation,* p. 5.

one thousand members," he wrote glumly in August 1863. ". . . This apathy toward a movement which is solely for them, which is being carried on purely in their interest! . . . When will this obtuse people shake off its lethargy!" [28]

This was a cry of despair of which the volatile Lassalle was fond, but it also represented a deeper historical truth than he himself realized. The German working class was not by nature dull or apathetic, but it lacked experience and training for effective organization. Lassalle's outcry, like William Morris's plaint against "the damned wantlessness of the poor" overlooked the fact that it is necessary to educate people in discontent; to create historical circumstances in which the lower classes obtain standards of comparison by which they can judge their deprivation. More is required—the realization is needed that oppression and poverty amidst plenty are neither God-given nor a necessary part of the order of nature, but are man-made and therefore amenable to change. The German working class had little schooling in independent action and, what was more, most of its potential leadership had been forced to emigrate after 1848.

The Verein remained an insignificant organization after Lassalle's death in a duel on July 31, 1864. For several years it was plagued by a succession of incompetent presidents; it was further weakened by ugly feuds within the membership. It began to improve its fortunes only after the capable but authoritarian journalist von Schweitzer was elected its president in 1867. Schweitzer took over a bankrupt, disorderly party and welded it into an effective instrument within a short time. In 1866, Bismarck had granted universal suffrage to the North German Reichstag as part of his "Revolution from Above." Under the Schweitzer regime, the Verein began to send several delegates to the new Reichstag.

Lassalle's state-Socialist doctrines were strongly impressed upon the party program. It called for a free people's state, condemned the domination of labor by capital, and urged that the European state system should be reconstituted in greater accord with popular needs. In December 1866 the

[28] Quoted by Mehring, *Zur Geschichte*, p. 23.

Verein added Lassalle's well-known panacea for the "solution of the social question"—the creation of producers' cooperatives with state help.[29]

In the years 1867 to 1871, when Schweitzer's "dictatorship" came to a close, the Verein established a number of trade unions. But these unions were intended merely as convenient organizations that could serve as adjuncts to the party; the Lassalleans never overcame their marked hostility to trade unionism.[30]

While the Verein slowly moved away from pure Lassalleanism, it never found itself close to the Marxist camp. Lassalle had been a true Hegelian; the state played a critical role in his philosophy. Socialism, Lassalle taught, was to be imposed by the existing state system. Marx, on the other hand, had turned the Hegelian philosophy of the state on its head. The state, Marx held, must be destroyed before Socialism can be realized.

Further, Lassalle had been a patriot.[31] From a Marxist point of view this was bad enough, but his version of the class struggle was worse. Marx contemptuously called it Realpolitik, which he defined as the attempt to adapt policy to circumstances without trying to reshape them.[32] True, Lassalle had urged independent political action of the workers—it was the signal merit of his party to have been the first to foster it—but it was to be action within the present state structure.

Lassalle's political tactics followed from this world view. They called for collaboration of the workers with the nobility (including the Junkers) against the liberal middle class. Since Lassalle favored industrial concentration, he could well ally himself with the captains of industry in open opposition to

[29] Wilhelm Schröder, ed., *Handbuch der sozialdemokratischen Parteitage*, p. 460.

[30] During that time, the Verein grew more radical and on several occasions declared its concurrence with the demands of the First International, especially regarding the communal ownership of land. Mehring, *Zur Geschichte*, p. 93.

[31] It has been pointed out that Lassalle was a "good" nationalist à la Mazzini. A. Joseph Berlau, *The German Social Democratic Party, 1914–1921*, p. 20n. But to the Marxists this was a distinction without a difference.

[32] Adoratsky, *Selected Correspondence*, pp. 193–97.

liberalism.[33] His correspondence with Bismarck shows how far he was prepared to go.[34]

There were other than theoretical grounds for disillusionment with the Verein. Its nationalist, pro-Prussian policies (another Lassallean legacy) alienated large numbers of workers from South and Central Germany. August Bebel belonged to these men who were to be the backbone of the rival Eisenach party.[35] Furthermore, Schweitzer's heavy hand caused much resentment. No doubt some centralization of party business was necessary, but Schweitzer went too far and created personal enemies who were only too glad to join a competing group.[36]

This rival party, the so-called Sozialdemokratische Arbeiterpartei Eisenacher Programms, was formed in August 1869. Its leaders were August Bebel, who carried several important labor organizations with him, and his close ally Wilhelm Liebknecht.[37] Both men were enthusiastic Marxists whose theoretical understanding was, to say the least, inadequate.

Their party offered a program that was a strange mixture of Marxism and of bourgeois radicalism. Its great advantage, not sufficiently recognized by Marx and Engels, lay in its independence from Lassalle: the new Eisenach party could found its program on specifically different assumptions. True, it did not present a purely Marxist platform to the public. Its first point demanded a "free people's state." But that was a concession to the South German particularists, the democrats whose Socialism was, at best, an appendage to their anti-Prussian republicanism.[38]

[33] For a more detailed treatment of Lassalle, cf. pp. 89-94.
[34] Cf. Gustav Mayer, *Bismarck und Lassalle, passim.* On Lassalle's career and philosophy, cf. Hermann Oncken, *Lassalle.*
[35] Mehring once derisively said that the chief motive animating these men was *Preussenhass*—hatred of Prussia. *Zur Geschichte,* pp. 67, 70.
[36] Cf. Bebel, *Aus meinem Leben,* II, 1-2, and Robert Michels, *Political Parties,* p. 190. Curiously enough, Marx had a high opinion of Schweitzer.
[37] Mehring, *Karl Marx,* p. 421. Cf. Gustav Mayer, *Johann Baptist von Schweitzer,* pp. 330-59.
[38] This group was powerful enough to exact theoretical concessions. Its pressure was frequently a source of embarrassment to

But the rest of the program sounded very different:

> The struggle for the liberation of the working classes is not a struggle for class privileges and prerogatives but for equal rights and duties and the abolition of all class rule. . . . The economic dependence of the worker on the capitalist is the foundation of serfdom in every form, and therefore the Sozialdemokratische Arbeiterpartei endeavors to obtain the full produce of his labor for every worker by cooperative labor (*genossenschaftliche Arbeit*) and abolition of the present-day mode of production, the wage system. Political liberty is the essential prerequisite for the economic emancipation of the laboring classes. The social is inseparable from the political question; its solution depends on the latter and is possible only in the democratic state.[39]

At the beginning, the doctrinal differences between the Eisenachers and the Lassalleans appeared of small significance. A cursory reading of party statements would make it difficult for the reader to decide which of the two parties was "redder" than the other. But soon there were strong indications that, while Lassalle's party could not take this step, the Eisenachers were on the road to adopting a Marxist program. As Liebknecht wrote in 1869 after the Eisenach Congress, "The last consequences of Communism lie hidden in our program." [40] And when on June 19, 1870, the North German Reichstag voted credits for the war against France, the Lassalleans stood with the majority, while the Eisenachers, Bebel and Liebknecht abstained. This was a graphic demonstration that the two parties were not identical. Abstention was a radical move; Napoleon III represented the epitome of reaction to most German Liberals and Socialists, and failure to support the campaign that would destroy him seemed to them

---

the leaders. For example, the South Germans made it impossible for Liebknecht to put his young party behind the Basel Resolution of the First International, which had called for the abolition of private ownership of land.

[39] Schröder, *Handbuch,* pp. 464–65.

[40] Quoted in Mehring, *Zur Geschichte,* p. 89. Needless to say, the statement was an exaggeration.

stupid and unpatriotic. But the government's annexationist pronouncements soon enlightened Socialist opinion and brought it into line with Bebel's and Liebknecht's opposition to the war.[41] It will be remembered that it was these events and their aftermath that directed Eduard Bernstein's attention to Social Democracy.

The Gotha Program and Beyond

> *The program is no good, even apart from its sanctification of the Lassallean articles of faith.*
>
> MARX TO BRACKE

When Eduard Bernstein entered the political scene early in 1872, the two Socialist parties were kept apart mainly by personal rancor. Unity was a crying necessity, but either group recalled bitterly the insults it had had to suffer from the other. Disputes rarely were confined to theoretical differences. Usually they degenerated into personal quarrels, in which one impugned the honesty, political "purity," and even sexual habits of the other. Von Schweitzer was called a "traitor" and a "government Socialist." Becker, Lassalle's immediate successor as president of the Verein, advised Marx to "pickle himself with his international association and hang himself in the chimney as a mad herring." A colorful, if somewhat obscure invitation, which caused Liebknecht to submit a resolution to the Berlin chapter of the Verein demanding that "Becker be excluded from the Verein as a liar, infamous slanderer, and hopelessly incurable idiot." [42] In his speaking tours, Eduard Bernstein experienced a large number of incidents which showed great hostility between the two groups.[43] It is hardly surprising, therefore, that the rival factions approached unity skeptically: aware of the inevitable

[41] Mehring, *Geschichte,* IV, 5–6.
[42] This exchange is quoted in Mehring, *Zur Geschichte,* pp. 56–57.
[43] Bernstein, *Sozialdemokratische Lehrjahre,* pp. 23–25, 28–30, 31–35.

outcome but anxious to force the other side to take the first step.

At first, Bernstein and most of his fellow Eisenachers shared this cautious view. But at its Coburg Congress in 1874, which Bernstein attended as a delegate, the Sozialdemokratische Arbeiterpartei made definite overtures to its rival. Bernstein spoke briefly in favor of a unity congress: "The opinions of the Lassalleans are now wavering. In any case, not all of them are opposed to fusion." [44]

Once the Reichstag elections of 1874 had demonstrated the practically equal strength of the two parties, the bothersome question as to which of the two was to swallow the other simply evaporated. On January 19, 1875, Eduard Bernstein reported to Bebel, who was once more in prison, on a public meeting in Berlin which had debated unification:

> I don't know how you feel about fusion, but I believe that we agree to the extent that the idea of unity should be kept before us as long as possible. I have no illusions, but I know that the need for unity is also very great for members of the Verein. Unfortunately, these people are such obdurate Lassalleans that we will have to grant concessions in that respect.[45]

Events bore out this prediction to the full.

Finally on February 14 and 15, 1875, a conference took place in Gotha. One of the Eisenacher delegates was the young Eduard Bernstein, who may have been chosen because some of the party leaders were then in jail. He was just twenty-five years old, and participation in this conference was his first important contribution to Social Democratic politics.

Liebknecht was the only one ready with a draft program. The Lassalleans hastily put together a counterdraft to oppose some Eisenacher points. A definite program was finally drawn up, and a unity congress was called for May of the same year. It, too, took place in Gotha, from May 22 to 27. At that congress, the long-drawn-out hostilities were ended, a pro-

[44] *Ibid.,* p. 41. Cf. Schröder, *Handbuch,* p. 124.
[45] Quoted in Bebel, *Aus meinem Leben,* II, 315.

gram was agreed upon, and a united Sozialistische Arbeiter-partei Deutschlands emerged.

But the results of the congress were by no means universally applauded. Bebel had looked upon the unification attempts with deep misgivings.[46] Engels, who shared this opinion, wrote Bebel a detailed letter after seeing the draft program of the February conference, cautioning against unity on terms that would endanger Marxist principles.[47] But Engels's warnings were ignored by the party, and the Gotha Congress accepted the draft program substantially as written. Liebknecht himself was one of its principal proponents.[48]

Marx entered the debate with a critical analysis of the draft which he sent to Bracke for circulation among the Eisenachers on May 5, two weeks before the congress. It had no effect on the Gotha Program itself, but the critique, which was published by Engels in 1891, since then has had considerable influence on Marxist thought.

A reading of the program as finally adopted will show a fairly even balance between Marxist and Lassallean elements. It called for the establishment, "with all legal means," of a "free state and of the Socialist society"; it demanded the "breaking of the iron law of wages through the abolition of the wage system"; the destruction of "exploitation in all forms; the removal of all social and political inequalities." [49]

The specific demands were taken largely from the Eisenach program of 1869: universal, equal, direct suffrage, abolition of all combination and press laws, general and equal public education, a progressive income tax, a normal working day, abolition of child labor, and the ubiquitous producers' cooperatives.

Marx's criticism, important though it is in its constructive part, underestimates the difficulties standing in the way of the fusion of the two Socialist parties. His conclusion that the

---

[46] Schröder, *Handbuch,* pp. 126–27.

[47] Bebel, *Aus meinem Leben,* II, 318–24.

[48] Schröder, *Handbuch,* p. 467; Bernstein, *Sozialdemokratische Lehrjahre,* p. 46. Lenin considered Engels's letter to Bebel as very important. Cf. Karl Marx, *Critique of the Gotha Programme,* Appendix II.

[49] Schröder, *Handbuch,* pp. 468–69.

Lassalleans overwhelmed the Eisenachers is certainly too strong.[50]

Later, Bernstein made some perceptive comments on the intellectual equipment of German Social Democratic leaders of that time which deserve quotation:

> The delegates of both parties, Lassalleans and Eise-nachers, did not act at the [February] conference as fixed groups. On both sides, within each camp, there were differences of opinion. . . . Liebknecht was . . . only to a limited extent the interpreter of Marx's theory. Some of the sentences of the draft program which were vehemently condemned by Marx stemmed, if I am not very much mistaken, from Liebknecht. . . .
>
> Generally, the deeper meaning of the basic ideas of Marx's theories of history and society were at that time inadequately grasped by the Eisenachers. The majority was theoretically more deeply influenced in their Socialism by Lassalle than by Marx. True, they rejected certain of Lassalle's demands and proposals, but founded their Social-ist reasoning on statements which derived from the pre-Marxist epoch of the Socialist movement, and which could be found in Lassalle. Thus, the Gotha draft program was not, as Marx supposed, a victory of the Lassallean delega-tion over the Eisenacher, but it was the result of insuffi-cient theoretical insight among the latter.[51]

In spite of Marx's scolding, then, the new party stood closer to his teachings than had both old groups, and its evolution towards complete adoption of Marxism was only a question of time.

The new party prospered in spite of persecution and chi-canery. Its first real test came in the 1877 elections to the Reichstag. The results exceeded all expectation: the party polled 493,447 votes, which amounted to more than 9 per-

[50] Cf., on this point, Mehring, *Karl Marx*, pp. 533–34.
[51] *Sozialdemokratische Lehrjahre*, pp. 45–46. The point seems to me well taken and is borne out by reports on the Gotha Congress. Cf. also Mehring, *Geschichte*, IV, 89–90.

cent of the total number of votes cast, and made the Social
Democratic Party the fourth strongest party in the country.[52]

The actual number of seats which the party gained in the
Reichstag—twelve—was disappointing, but this showing was
the result of the existence of rotten boroughs as well as of
the skillful gerrymandering of electoral districts, which
heavily favored agrarian at the expense of urban, industrial
areas.[53] Bismarck, who recognized and feared the strength of
the awakening German proletariat, determined to take drastic
steps; he did not find a pretext for them until well over a
year after this important election.

At this time, the growing party was involved in a disease
of adolescence—theoretical confusion. Some prominent members sought to cure disunity by a strong dose of "German
Socialism," largely Dühring's brand. But that stage was soon
overcome by Engels's vigorous critique, and the theoretical
struggles were presently replaced by a more elemental contest—the fight for survival.

Meanwhile, Eduard Bernstein was active. He continued his
work as a bank clerk, participated in the labors of the party
control commission (*Ausschuss*), and did his part in the
1877 elections by campaigning in Berlin. Early the following
year he helped to found a discussion club, the Mohren Club,
of which the Socialists Karl Höchberg and C. A. Schramm
were also members, and from which sprang a project in adult
education—a night school for workers. Schramm taught a
course in political economy; Bernstein, with characteristic
modesty, felt himself "insufficiently schooled in the theory of
Socialism" and therefore taught a bookkeeping course.[54]

Eduard Bernstein's Berlin education was now drawing to a
close.[55] The Social Democratic Party was about to enter upon

---

[52] A breakdown of the vote shows, not unexpectedly, that the
Social Democrats were at their strongest in urban centers, especially Berlin and Hamburg.

[53] Cf. Walter Koch, *Volk und Staatsführung vor dem Weltkriege*,
pp. 7–10.

[54] Bernstein, *Sozialdemokratische Lehrjahre*, p. 57.

[55] It is in this period that Bernstein formally abandoned Judaism.
German Social Democracy, following Marx's lead, had always
been anticlerical. When, in 1877–78, a Social Christian movement

a period of crisis in which Bernstein would play a far more prominent role than he might have imagined. This period, later known in German Socialist circles as the "heroic years," was initiated by two attempts on the life of Emperor William I. Both of them, Hödel's attack on May 11, 1878, and Dr. Nobiling's on June 2 of the same year, were *attentats* by two psychotic personalities, neither of whom belonged to Social Democracy and neither of whom expressed Social Democratic policies with his nonsensical act of terrorism against an octogenarian.[56]

Bismarck's immediate reaction was determined and brutal. He drew up a stringent bill to outlaw Social Democracy; this was, however, defeated by an overwhelming majority. The second attempted assassination gave him another chance. On the night of the shooting, an *official* communique reported that Nobiling had admitted to "membership in German Social Democracy," and to "accomplices." [57] This statement was a complete fabrication, but the deliberate lie had its desired effect. It marked the beginning of a white terror which inflicted severe blows on the already handicapped Social Democracy. Socialist meetings and congresses were outlawed, newspapers confiscated, members arrested. Mehring reports the activity of the police in the closing of gatherings: they were ordered to disband because "one window was open, which made is an open-air meeting . . . because one person in the audience had shouted 'ridiculous' during a speech . . . because a dog had strayed into the hall." [58] A novel form of pressure was being exerted by many employers: employees were compelled to sign papers stating that they did not belong to Social Democratic organizations or would abandon them immediately. Eduard Bernstein successfully coun-

---

was initiated by conservative sources, Social Democracy countered it by agitating against church membership. Johann Most led the drive which resulted in the official severance of bonds with their respective churches of several hundred Social Democrats. Bernstein was among them, ratifying an existing fact.

[56] Hödel had at one time been a member of the party but had been expelled.

[57] Bernstein, *Sozialdemokratische Lehrjahre*, p. 62.

[58] *Geschichte*, IV, 140.

tered this move by publishing an appeal to all workers to sign
such papers wherever they were required; he argued that
such falsehoods were justifiable in the face of economic
oppression.[59]

The Reichstag had meanwhile been dissolved and the elections of July 30 gave Bismarck his desired majority.[60] His
anti-Socialist bill became law on October 19, 1878, after a
heated six-week debate.[61] It remained in force for twelve
years and was applied with varying degrees of harshness. In
Berlin a minor state of siege was declared in November 1878,
and 78 Social Democrats were banished from the capital. Of
47 Social Democratic newspapers, 45 were banned, and only
two of them managed to stay in existence by changing their
names and moderating their politics.[62] In most parts of Germany the police far overstepped the express limitations of the
law and proceeded ruthlessly and arbitrarily. To a cynical
twentieth century, used to far more effective persecutions,
these tribulations of the German Socialists might seem mild
enough—not even the mandates of the Social Democrats in
the Reichstag were annulled. But to the nineteenth-century
Socialists the hardships were very real, and they should not
be underrated by a century far more callous toward mass-
suffering.

Initially the party was thrown into confusion, but it soon
recovered to plan countermeasures. German Social Democracy converted the period of suppression into an ultimate
triumph. Eduard Bernstein, who had moved to Switzerland
in October 1878, most effectively aided his comrades in arms
from his new vantage point.

[59] Bernstein, *Sozialdemokratische Lehrjahre,* pp. 64–65.
[60] In spite of the weeks of police terror, the Socialists salvaged
nine seats in the new Reichstag, and their vote did not decline
drastically. They polled 437,158 votes.
[61] The law was not nearly Draconian enough for Bismarck. He
wanted to disfranchise all those who voted Socialist, deprive
Socialists of the right to hold office and enjoy the privileges of
members of the Reichstag. Cf. his letter to Tiedemann, quoted
in Otto von Bismarck, *Gedanken und Erinnerungen,* II, 218. Cf.
also Rosenberg, *Birth of the German Republic,* pp. 30–31.
[62] Mehring, *Geschichte,* IV, 5, 156.

Chapter 2

The Education Continued: Zurich

Exile

> *This is open season on Social Democrats; justice and law do not exist for us.*
>
> BEBEL TO VOLLMAR, 1878

LATE IN THE SUMMER of 1878, while Bismarck's repressive legislation was being debated in the Reichstag, Eduard Bernstein had a tempting offer: would he leave his bank job in Berlin to go to Switzerland? He would become secretary to Karl Höchberg, a wealthy young Socialist whose poor health forced him to live in a mild climate. Bernstein succumbed after some hesitation and left his native city on October 12, 1878, shortly before the anti-Socialist bill became law. He little realized as he boarded the train to Lugano that he would not see Germany again for over twenty years.

Karl Höchberg, Bernstein's new employer, was a controversial figure. Only two facts stand undisputed—he was sincere, and prodigal with the considerable funds at his disposal. Engels, who never trusted Utopians, said of him, "If Höchberg can be called a 'plus' at all, it's his money; otherwise he's a negative quantity." [1] He had little theoretical understanding of economics and history. In the semimonthly journal, *Die Zukunft,* which he had founded and was publishing himself, he concentrated on abstract discussions of the "socioeconomic ideal." Harsh expressions, such as economic exploitation or the class struggle, rarely penetrated into this refined realm.

During Bernstein's first winter in Switzerland, which he spent at Lugano, *Die Zukunft* became a victim of the new anti-Socialist legislation. Then, in April 1879, Höchberg, anxious to do his part in spreading the Socialist gospel, moved

---

[1] *Karl Marx-Friedrich Engels Gesamtausgabe,* Third Division, IV, 487. Marx acknowledged his good intentions. *Ibid.,* p. 470. Mehring called him a "self-sacrificing idealist." *Geschichte der deutschen Sozialdemokratie,* IV, 119.

his headquarters to Zurich. With Bernstein's assistance he now undertook to reprint and distribute Schäffle's *Quintessence of Socialism*. Nothing could have demonstrated Höchberg's lack of realism more clearly than this enterprise—to bring about Socialism by converting the intelligentsia to it.[2] Naturally, Marx, who had once described Schäffle as an "ordinary, vulgar economist," had the most profound contempt for such methods.[3]

While the distribution of the Schäffle volume to German intellectuals was proceeding, Bernstein obtained a copy of Engel's powerful *Anti-Dühring*, which had just been published in book form after serialization in the *Vorwärts*. Its impact on him was decisive. "It converted me to Marxism," he recalled.[4] This book, which Engels had not wanted to write, had a profound effect on others as well and became the best propagandist the Marxist cause was to have for many years.[5]

In this same year in which Bernstein became a faithful disciple to the Marxist gospel he also managed to get into serious personal differences with Marx and Engels, whom he had never met. It all began with another of Höchberg's ill-conceived schemes. "We are planning, or really are in the process of publishing, a Yearbook for Social Science," Bernstein wrote to Engels on June 13, 1879, in the first letter he ever addressed to Marx's collaborator.[6] Exactly two months later he notified Engels that a copy of the Yearbook was on its way to Engels. "We would very much like to hear your opinion of the book." [7]

The opinion—not only of Engels, but of Marx, Liebknecht, and Bebel as well—was as unfavorable as possible. The first issue had contained a foolish article, signed with three asterisks, which listed the purported errors committed by German Social Democracy.[8] It criticized the Socialists for relying too

[2] This is similar to the early Fabian tactics of "permeation."
[3] *Marx-Engels Gesamtausgabe*, Third Division, IV, 384.
[4] *Sozialdemokratische Lehrjahre*, p. 72.
[5] Cf. Gustav Mayer, *Friedrich Engels*, II, 283–95; 347–48.
[6] Bernstein Archives.
[7] Letter of August 13, 1879, Bernstein Archives.
[8] "Rückblicke auf die sozialistische Bewegung in Deutschland," *Jahrbuch für Sozialwissenschaft und Sozialpolitik*, I (1879), 75–96.

strongly on proletarian members and for refusing to maintain close relations with the liberal bourgeoisie. "The young party," ran one typical passage, which was

> attacked, scoffed at, and slandered as no other party, had cause (more than the others) to look for able allies, to win over people with intelligence and knowledge and thus to assure the means and the possibilities for progressive development. But it preferred to style itself a "labor party" in the most onesided fashion, and thus kept its best friends from joining it.[9]

The article concluded in a most unfortunate *mea culpa*: "We must admit: Yes! [Our party] is not totally innocent of the creation of the October law, for it unnecessarily fanned the hatred of the bourgeoisie." [10]

The authorship of this strange piece of work was not known and caused much wrong guessing both in London and in Germany.[11] In actuality, the ill-fated article had been written by Karl Flesch, who was later to become a well-known reformer and city councilor of Frankfurt. He had sent it to his friend Höchberg, who then revised it with Schramm's aid. Bernstein's share was slight; [12] he only added a few thoughts on Höchberg's insistence. He had "stood only too deeply in the midst of party agitation," he wrote, "not to find an excuse for most of the matters now being criticized." [13]

The incident assumed far greater proportions than it deserved because it took place when a central party newspaper

[9] *Ibid.*, pp. 85–86.
[10] *Ibid.*, p. 96.
[11] Engels thought that the asterisks represented "Höchberg, and probably Bernstein and Lübeck." *Marx-Engels Gesamtausgabe*, Third Division, IV, 495. Bebel believed that the article had been "jointly authored" by Höchberg, Schramm, and Bernstein. Bebel, *Aus meinem Leben*, III, 58.
[12] In spite of this fact, the myth of Berstein's active participation in the article has been deliberately kept alive. Cf. V. Adoratsky, ed., *Selected Correspondence, Karl Marx and Frederick Engels*, p. 377.
[13] Bernstein, *Sozialdemokratische Lehrjahre*, p. 79. This is Bernstein's own account of the affair, which has been given full credit by Mayer, *Engels*, II, 334, and Mehring, *Geschichte*, IV, 168.

was to be founded. The outlawed party needed a strong voice. Karl Hirsch, a German Socialist in exile in Belgium, had been publishing a small sheet, *Die Laterne*, since December 1878, which proved insufficient for the needs of a large albeit illegal party. Johann Most, formerly a close friend of Bernstein's, started a newspaper in London in January 1879, *Die Freiheit*. But Most soon spent his time fighting the party leadership, printed little but gossip, and, in the bargain, embraced anarchism and terrorism.

Bebel and Liebknecht then turned to the German Socialist contingent in Zurich and suggested that the paper be started there. Höchberg offered to finance the venture. But Marx and Engels, always suspicious of Höchberg, were now certain—after the publication of the Yearbook—that any newspaper with which he was connected would cause positive harm to Social Democracy. Engels told Bebel that a man like Höchberg should be expelled from the party; in the midst of delicate negotiations the well-meaning Höchberg visited London and had a most painful interview with Engels. He is *"au fond"* a "good but appallingly naive fellow," Engels reported after the meeting.[14] Höchberg had been "thunderstruck," Engels wrote to Becker, "when I explained to him that we could never think of lowering the proletarian banner which we have held aloft for nearly forty years." [15]

Bebel insisted that Höchberg exerted no real influence in the party, but Engels remained unimpressed.[16] After protracted wrangling, Hirsch, publisher of the *Laterne*, was chosen editor of the newspaper upon Liebknecht's suggestion. When Hirsch declined, the Bavarian Socialist von Vollmar accepted the post, and the first issue of the *Sozialdemokrat* appeared in Zurich on September 28, 1879.

In this comedy of errors, Eduard Bernstein played anything but a happy role. As Höchberg's trusted aide he re-

---

[14] Quoted in Mayer, *Engels*, II, 338.
[15] Adoratsky, *Selected Correspondence*, p. 348.
[16] Bebel, *Aus meinem Leben*, III, 55. For Marx's uncompromising attitude, cf. *Marx-Engels Gesamtausgabe*, Third Division, IV, 446–47. Engels wrote a long memorandum concerning the party newspaper which is still worth reading for its remarks on party tactics. Cf. Adoratsky, *Selected Correspondence*, pp. 362–77.

garded himself very much as part of the negotiations and Engels irritably accused him of acting as if he were editor.[17]

Fortunately for the party, these prolonged misunderstandings did not prevent the publication of the *Sozialdemokrat*. The opening number stated its purpose: it was to be an international organ of German-speaking Social Democracy wherever it might find itself, basing itself firmly on the Gotha Program.

Eduard Bernstein was active in the *Sozialdemokrat* from the very beginning, but he remained anxious to efface the bad impression he had made on the Londoners. In May 1880, Wilhelm Liebknecht had gone to London at Höchberg's expense, but his visit was by no means the complete success which he later assumed it to be.[18] Therefore Bernstein and Bebel decided to visit Marx and Engels themselves. After careful preparation they started on their trip in December 1880.[19] It was designed to serve a dual purpose: to make peace between London and Zurich and to choose a new editor for the *Sozialdemokrat*, since Vollmar was determined to give up his post on January 1, 1881. While Liebknecht had put forward Hirsch once more, Bebel held his private hope that Bernstein could be placed in that responsible position.

But if this plan was to be carried through, it was necessary for the party leaders to change their mind about Bernstein. "I . . . wished to take Bernstein with me to the lions' den," Bebel wrote in his reminiscences. "Marx and Engels . . . were strongly hostile to him, and I wanted to show them that he was not the terrible fellow that the two old ones believed him to be." [20]

The trip to London was a striking success. Though neither visitor had ever met Marx or Engels, they now secured the full confidence of the Londoners. Bernstein has written of his London visit with his usual modesty, but a glow of satisfaction still pervades these pages.[21]

[17] *Marx-Engels Gesamtausgabe*, Third Division, IV, 487.
[18] Bernstein, *Sozialdemokratische Lehrjahre*, pp. 113–14.
[19] For a detailed account, cf. Bebel, *Aus meinem Leben*, III, 165 ff.
[20] *Ibid.*, III, 165.
[21] Bernstein, *Aus den Jahren meines Exils*, pp. 162–70; *Sozialdemokratische Lehrjahre*, pp. 113–16. For corroboration cf. Mayer, *Engels*, II, 347–48.

The way to Bernstein's editorship was now open. Hirsch proved troublesome and vacillating, and Bernstein was named provisional editor of the *Sozialdemokrat* in January 1881. It was the beginning of a great career.

Bismarck's anti-Socialist law had transformed Bernstein's temporary residence abroad into enforced exile. At the beginning he was lonely. He had never before been separated from his family, and his first year abroad was tinted darkly by feelings of strangeness and solitude. But these sentiments gradually wore off. He was fortunate in the friendship and approval of his equals, success attended his journalistic endeavors, and the scenery was beautiful. Always open to the attractions of nature, Bernstein never fails to inform his readers of the charms of the landscape, or the view that presented itself from the windows of his lodgings in Zurich:

> Directly below us was the Zurichberg, largely overgrown with vines, a little further down it had beautiful trees to delight the eye, then to the right a considerable part of the town of Zurich, to the left an equally large section of the enchanting Zurichsee, and beyond both the beautifully overgrown chains of the Utli mountains. . . .[22]

Then, too, life in Zurich had much to offer. As a center for the international Socialist movement it was second only to London. Bernstein took full advantage of the presence of Socialists of many countries, and the names of radicals from all over Europe make their brief appearance in his autobiographical pages. Like Great Britain, Switzerland was a good place for Socialist activity. Its Social Democratic movement was legal and active. Swiss workers' associations had played an important part in the First International, and exiles, such as the group around the *Sozialdemokrat*, thrived in this free atmosphere.[23]

But in spite of happy activity and a diverting existence,

[22] *Sozialdemokratische Lehrjahre*, p. 97.
[23] Cf. Mario Gridazzi, *Die Entwicklung der sozialistischen Ideen in der Schweiz bis zum Ausbruch des Weltkrieges, passim,* esp. pp. 138–40.

Bernstein and the other Zurich exiles were oppressed by an incubus which they could not escape—the German anti-Socialist law. After the scattering and crippling of Social Democratic clubs and associations and after the closing-down of Socialist newspapers, the Zurich group bore the grave responsibility of keeping the party alive—let alone well-informed—through the publication of as effective a party organ as they could put before the public. The task weighed heavily upon them and lent a seriousness to their life which no entertainment could dispel.

The Heroic Years

> *Men must either be caressed or else annihilated; they will revenge themselves for small injuries, but cannot do so for great ones; the injury therefore that we do to a man must be such that we need not fear his vengeance.*
>
> NICCOLÒ MACHIAVELLI

The chief problem of the outlawed German Socialist Party was survival. It resorted to two methods: secret party congresses conducted surreptitiously on foreign soil, and the publication of a newspaper.

The Reichstag mandates of the Social Democrats had not been revoked, but since it was impossible for the party as a whole to meet anywhere in Germany, the danger of a rift between the parliamentary party and the rest of the Social Democrats was increasing. The Reichstag session of 1880 had prolonged the anti-Socialist law until September 1884. The rigor with which the law had been enforced had increased the bitterness and intransigeance of the Social Democrats, and a party congress that would outline a determined policy for these dangerous times was imperative. New Reichstag elections were to be held in 1881, and election agitation in these difficult circumstances would have to be carefully planned. Furthermore, the party leadership was anxious to facilitate the distribution of the *Sozialdemokrat* in Germany and to articulate an official position vis-à-vis two dissident members. Most's vindictive anarchist sheet, *Die Freiheit,* was completely out of hand, and Hasselmann, a Social Democratic member of the Reichstag and former Lassallean, had openly disavowed his party by aligning himself with the Russian Nihilists.

After some negotiations and postponements, the first secret congress of the Social Democratic Party was held in romantic but primitive surroundings at Castle Wyden in Switzerland, from August 20 to 23, 1880. This was four months before the Bebel-Bernstein pilgrimage to London.

The report of the Wyden Congress, issued in Switzerland as a small booklet, still makes interesting reading today. It differs from other reports in two ways—it summarizes rather than reproduces speeches; and, for obvious reasons, it does not give the names of any of the German speakers. The meetings proved of inestimable value to the party and served to reunite all prominent Social Democrats—Bebel, Liebknecht, Auer, Kautsky, Fritzsche, Hasenclever, Motteler, and Bernstein. The resolutions left the Gotha Program unaltered, except for striking out the word "legal" from the phrase, "the Social Democratic Party endeavors to obtain the free state and the Socialist society . . . by all legal means." A reading of the report shows this emendation to be less a call to revolution than the recognition of an existing fact: since the outlawry of the party had made *all* its activities illegal, it would be absurd and hypocritical for the party to insist on the legality of its procedure. With this explanation, the resolution was carried unanimously, amidst general acclamation.[24]

The congress also strengthened the morale of the party by expelling Most and Hasselmann. The delegates were embittered against both men. At one point the presiding officer declared that even though he did not wish to appear opposed to the epithet in principle, he thought that in the interest of orderly debate the expression *Lump* (scoundrel) should not be applied to Hasselmann.[25]

One resolution, of special interest to the Zurich exiles,

[24] *Protokoll des Kongresses der deutschen Sozialdemokratie, 1880,* pp. 27–29.
[25] *Ibid.,* p. 33.

declared the *Sozialdemokrat* the "only official organ of the party." [26]

This was the first of three clandestine congresses held under the anti-Socialist law. The second took place in Copenhagen in 1883, when Bernstein was editor of the *Sozialdemokrat*. He traveled to the Danish capital along devious routes, using a false name like any romantic conspirator. The third was held near St. Gall in 1887. Eduard Bernstein has expressed the chief motive and result of all three congresses in describing the spirit of the first: "All were filled with the thought, 'We belong together and must stick together.' " [27]

Important as these congresses were to him, Eduard Bernstein's editorship of the party newspaper, which he assumed early in 1881, was of far greater significance. From the beginning he proved to be the right man for the job. Engels entered into a lively correspondence with him, criticizing, suggesting, praising. After three months in the editor's chair, Bernstein asked to be relieved of the post because he felt unready for such a responsible position.[28] Engels, writing for himself and Marx, opposed the move with a highly flattering letter:

We were very disagreeably surprised to receive your note that you wish to leave the paper. We can see absolutely no reason for it, and it would be *very agreeable* to us if you would reconsider. You have edited the paper skillfully from the very beginning, you have given it the right tone and developed the necessary wit. In editing a newspaper, erudition is not nearly so important as a quick understanding of matters in the right spirit (*die Sachen gleich rasch von der Seite auffassen*) and you have always done that. . . . I just don't see who could take your place at present, as long as Liebknecht is in jail.[29]

Since similar praise came from Liebknecht and Bebel,

[26] *Ibid.*, p. 47.
[27] Bernstein, *Sozialdemokratische Lehrjahre*, p. 110.
[28] *Ibid.*, p. 121.
[29] Eduard Bernstein, ed., *Die Briefe von Friedrich Engels an Eduard Bernstein*, p. 22.

Bernstein not only did not leave the *Sozialdemokrat* but soon became its permanent editor. He was now in his early thirties, and one of the key members of his party. The sages in London had forgiven him, his correspondence with Engels was growing more intimate, Bebel and Leibknecht were his close friends. These years represent the height of Bernstein's journalistic career. He did not then suspect that the time of his crucial contribution and most decisive influence was a decade away and would lie in social theory rather than militant journalism.

Among the regular contributors to the *Sozialdemokrat* was a brilliant young Austrian intellectual five years Bernstein's junior, Karl Kautsky. His erudition had impressed Liebknecht and Bebel, and Höchberg invited the young Socialist to Zurich as a collaborator on terms that allowed Kaustky sufficient free time to pursue his own work—an arrangement typical of Höchberg's generosity.[30] Bernstein and Kautsky respected each other and collaborated closely on such projects as translating Marx's *Misère de la philosophie* into German. They soon inaugurated a lifelong friendship which was seriously disrupted only during the great Revisionist debate at the turn of the century.[31]

Bernstein edited the *Sozialdemokrat* to the nearly unanimous applause of his party comrades. He was to develop it to such a point that Engels could later say of him that he had made the paper into "unquestionably the best newspaper this party has ever had." [32]

Bernstein's editorial position was not an easy one, for the party which he served was passing through times of trial, its "heroic years." When Marx died on March 14, 1883, Engels remained as the chief adviser to the party as well as to the youthful editor of the official organ.[33]

[30] Bernstein, *Sozialdemokratische Lehrjahre*, pp. 96–97.
[31] For Engels's interesting estimate of Kautsky, cf. Bernstein, *Die Briefe von Friedrich Engels*, p. 22.
[32] Quoted in Mayer, *Engels*, II, 348. It is from a brief article Engels contributed to the last issue of the newspaper of September 27, 1890.
[33] For Engels's letter advising Bernstein of Marx's death, cf. Bernstein, *Die Briefe von Friedrich Engels*, p. 119.

The first elections to the German Reichstag since the passing of the anti-Socialist law took place in October 1881, a year after the Wyden Congress. They were held in an atmosphere of strengthened repression. States of siege were imposed upon Hamburg-Altona late in 1880 and upon Leipzig in June 1881. They resulted in the exile of such outstanding figures as Bebel, Liebknecht, and Hasenclever from these vital areas.[34] But despite such actions by the state machine, the Social Democrats polled 311,961 votes and, when all the run-off elections had been fought, the Socialists had twelve members in the new Reichstag. It was a major victory on all counts: an illegal party, prohibited from meeting, electioneering, and publishing had managed to live through three years of persecution with only a small decrease of adherents. It was early proof that the Bismarckian legislation was a failure.

If repression alone could not kill the Socialist enemy, it might be possible to render it harmless by buying its cooperation. This, in bald terms, was the burden of Bismarck's new policy of social legislation, which was formally initiated by an Imperial Message to the new Reichstag on November 17, 1881. It emphasized the state's interest in the welfare of the worker, which was to be safeguarded not only by the outlawing of Social Democratic excesses, but by positive legislation as well. The general program was embodied in several statutes: a sickness insurance act became law in 1883, accident insurance acts in 1884 and 1885, and an old age insurance act in 1889.[35]

Bismarck's own motivation in pushing these compulsory insurance schemes—the most comprehensive in Europe at that time—was purely political. He had managed to keep the liberals docile by showing his superior strength in the constitutional conflict of 1862 and by introducing franchise reform from above; he was now going to weaken the working class by doing for the proletariat what he would not permit it to do for itself. Social insurance which conferred limited benefits without granting full political rights seemed the ideal cure for

---

[34] Cf. Bebel, *Aus meinem Leben*, III, 178–85.
[35] W. H. Dawson, *Bismarck and State Socialism*, p. 109.

what was called the proletariat's "hatred against the state." [36]
Bismarck as well as the realistic leaders of German Social
Democracy were perfectly aware of the consequences of such
a policy, and their awareness necessarily dictated opposite
courses of action. Liebknecht had called the Reichstag "the
fig leaf of absolutism"; with equal justice we could call the
social legislation of that period "the fig-leaf of the rule of
property." [37]

Engels and Bebel never hesitated in the slightest in their
reaction to the new legislation, which they regarded as crude
blackmail. But their certainty could not prevent a deep split
within the party. The left wing was determined to resist all
attempts of the government to draw the party into the
Bismarckian system; the right wing wanted to vote for
legislation which, it believed, would aid the workers in the
amelioration of their hard lot. This is, of course, an old
dilemma of Socialist strategy. In Germany it first arose with
the vexing question of social insurance; later, it was to plague
Social Democrats when the country embarked upon imperialist ventures. Franz Neumann has formulated it briefly: "The
question was really whether the German worker should
actively support, or at least tolerate, Germany's expansion in
order to share in the material benefits that might possibly be
derived from it." [38]

Engels was anxious to clarify the problem and repeatedly
advised Bernstein to take a firm stand. But the editor of the

[36] In 1884, Bismarck said of the workingman: "Assure him care
when he is sick; assure him maintenance when he is old. If you do
that, and do not fear the sacrifice, or cry out at State Socialism
directly the words 'provision for old age' are uttered—if the
State will show a little more Christian solicitude for the working
man, then I believe that the gentlemen of the Wyden programme
will sound their bird-call in vain, and that the thronging to them
will cease as soon as working-men see that the Government and
legislative bodies are earnestly concerned for their welfare."
Quoted by Dawson, *ibid.*, p. 35.
[37] "The only form of state organization which met with Bismarck's
approval, and which he held to be sane and prudent, was one in
which the propertied classes, grouped around a monarchy, held all
power in their own hands." Arthur Rosenberg, *The Birth of the
German Republic*, p. 22.
[38] Franz Neumann, *Behemoth*, p. 211.

Sozialdemokrat was by now safely orthodox, and in this conflict he found himself unqualifiedly on Engels's and Bebel's side. Accordingly, his newspaper opposed the conciliatory attitude of the right wing and took the line that a policy of anti-Manchesterism was by no means identical with Socialism.[39]

The second secret Socialist congress at Copenhagen endorsed this uncompromising radicalism. It spoke boldly:

> Regarding the so-called *social reform* in Germany, the congress declares that it does not believe in the honest intentions . . . of the ruling classes after their behavior up to the present. The congress is, quite to the contrary, convinced that the so-called social reform is being used only as a tactical maneuver to divert the workers from the correct path. . . . It demands that the party proceed ruthlessly.[40]

The congress backed up this declaration by expressing full support of the policy of the *Sozialdemokrat*.

This congress took place in 1883. The Reichstag elections of the following year were another triumph for the Social Democrats. In May of 1884 the anti-Socialist law had been renewed once more, this time for two years. But in the October elections the illegal party gained both in the number of votes and number of mandates; it polled 549,990 votes (almost 10 percent of the total) and sent twenty-four members to the Reichstag. "The anti-Socialist law stands condemned," wrote Engels gleefully to Bernstein. "State and bourgeoisie stand hopelessly discredited before us." [41] The parliamentary bloc of the Social Democrats could now, under some conditions, function as the balance of power, and it was an unwonted spectacle to see the Socialist deputies courted by parties that so far had barely acknowledged their existence.

In spite of this victory, or possibly because of it, the right-left-wing split within the party became more marked less than

[39] Cf. Mayer, *Engels*, II, 362.
[40] Wilhelm Schröder, ed., *Handbuch der sozialdemokratischen Parteitage*, pp. 518, 534.
[41] Bernstein, *Die Briefe von Friedrich Engels*, p. 159.

a year after the 1884 elections. The ensuing contest, in which Bernstein became deeply involved, revolved around an issue that has cut across all modern history—imperialism.

Germany had been a late-comer to the race for colonies. In the first period of imperialism it had not participated at all. But this new wave, beginning after 1870, found Germany united and ready for expansion. Big industry, already growing monopolistic in structure, was solidly based upon the foundations of the new Reich. At first, Bismarck had opposed the acquisition of colonies, but, as with protection to which he became converted in mid-career, political pressures changed his mind. In the spring session of the Reichstag in 1885, the government brought in a bill which was to grant subsidies to German steamship lines. These public funds were to be used for the creation and extension of existing steamship routes to Africa, Samoa, East Asia, and Australia. While the new colonial policy was not mentioned in the bill, it clearly entered into consideration—particularly in the lines to Africa, where Germany had acquired holdings. The Social Democratic parliamentary party (which, it will be recalled, continued active during the anti-Socialist law) was split: the majority wanted to vote against the subsidies to African ships but *for* those directed elsewhere on the grounds that such subsidies would further world communications and give employment to German workers. The minority, which included Bebel, Liebknecht, Vollmar, and others, was opposed to *all* subsidies.

The *Sozialdemokrat,* under Bernstein's capable direction, lent vigorous editorial support to the minority, and published letters from other party members that took an even sharper tone. The Reichstag Social Democratic majority was annoyed. On March 20, it issued a declaration criticizing the *Sozialdemokrat:* "The paper does not determine the attitude of the parliamentary party, it is the parliamentary party which must control the attitude of the paper." [42] This statement was sent to Bernstein with orders to publish it without comment. The editor, who felt his independence menaced, refused to insert it in the paper, since, as he said, "the *Sozialdemokrat* is in no way the organ of the parliamentary delegation, but that of the

[42] Mehring, *Geschichte,* IV, 267.

party." [43] He offered to resign. But the conflict was smoothed over; the Social Democrats voted against all subsidies to a man, and Bernstein retained his post, his independence untouched. Letters from both Engels and Kautsky (who was now in London, editing the *Neue Zeit*) show that Bernstein had won an important victory.[44]

Mehring believed that the issue created more uproar than it was worth.[45] Generally, even by Engels, it was treated as an organizational problem involving the relations of the parliamentary group to the rest of the party, and the relation of the party newspaper to both. But in retrospect, the short-lived quarrel appears in another light—as the first instance of the profound disagreement that imperialism would later cause within the ranks of German Social Democracy.

While Bernstein retained his independence and freedom of action as editor, he lost it in another field in August of 1886 —he married. He wrote to Engels:

> She is a good comrade and willing to shoulder all obligations which my position imposes upon me. The Kautskys know her and can tell you more about her. In any case there is no danger that she will make a bigger philistine of me than I already am.
>
> We have liked each other for years, but that damned feeling that I might have to be off at any time made me suppress all my wishes. In addition, the thought oppressed me that I might, as a married man, be forced into a situation in which I would cling to my post for *material* reasons. But the little woman fortunately thinks even more harshly than I do on this point, and would prefer to bear all hardships rather than see me prostitute my convictions.
>
> Well, that's off my chest, and now back to more general matters. . . .[46]

His wife, a widow with two children, was a quiet, well-educated woman who tended to remain in the background.

[43] *Sozialdemokratische Lehrjahre,* p. 159.
[44] Bernstein, *Die Briefe von Friedrich Engels,* pp. 164–72.
[45] Mehring, *Geschichte,* IV, 266–70.
[46] Bernstein to Engels, Sept, 17, 1886, Bernstein Archives.

Bernstein lived happily with her for thirty-seven years until her death in 1923. Among the many congratulatory messages was one from Engels who scolded Bernstein for postponing his marriage because of possible financial insecurity: "If all proletarians were as delicate as you, the proletariat would either die out or propagate itself through illegitimate children, and we will get to the latter stage *en masse* only when there will be no more proletariat." [47]

Meanwhile, several mild years of the anti-Socialist law had been replaced by another period of harsh repression. A number of outstanding party leaders, among them Auer and Bebel, received jail sentences for illegal activities such as aiding in the distribution of the *Sozialdemokrat*. Many such prosecutions were initiated by the government in the years 1886-87. It was the year of an election campaign, which featured a French scare along with these renewed efforts to wipe out the Socialists. The new wave of persecution was, however, doomed to failure: in the Reichstag elections of February 1887 the Social Democrats polled 763,128 votes—10 percent of the total and more than ever before—but found the number of its mandates reduced to eleven. The anti-Socialist campaign was now on its last legs, but its last efforts netted it one of its most notorious achievements: [48] Bismarck managed to dislodge the seemingly secure Zurich center of German Social Democracy. By putting pressure on the Swiss ambassador in Berlin, by making repeated representations in Berne, by promising more favourable terms to Switzerland in the forthcoming renewal of the German-Swiss trade treaty, the German government finally persuaded the Swiss to expel the staff of the *Sozialdemokrat* from its territory. The official

[47] Bernstein, *Die Briefe von Friedrich Engels*, p. 182.
[48] While Bismarck and Puttkamer urged the strengthening of the law, Bebel and his colleagues presented to the Reichstag—and thus to the public—revelations of the police machinations of the government, its misuse of the law, its employment of *agents provocateurs*. Especially the last accusation hit the regime in a vulnerable spot: its honor. The Bismarck-Puttkamer regime had pretended to use only legal and honorable methods in the tracking down of dangerous radicals. This pretense was easily exposed, and the law was renewed without sharpening amendments for two and a half years, rather than five years as the government had requested.

reason was the manner in which the newspaper attacked public personages.

The April 28, 1888, issue carried the bad news. Along with it, the newspaper ran a statement addressed by Eduard Bernstein to the Swiss government somewhat earlier, explaining the reasons for the behavior of the *Sozialdemokrat*. It is a sensible and straightforward document:

The sharp language, that is, the attacks against highly placed persons in Germany, about which there are now complaints, is not by any means of recent origin. As organ of a party under exceptional legislation, the *Sozialdemokrat*, from the very beginning, could not help but give expression to the temper of the victims of this law. The bitterness of the circles involved mounted, naturally enough, to the degree that the persecutions increased. The anti-Socialist law was used arbitrarily to destroy not only the political but also the purely trade-union organization of German workers, and to make it nearly impossible for the Socialists of Germany to engage even in the most legal activities (such as election campaigns). Who can be surprised that this bitterness found an echo in the party organ? . . . A fight against the system without a fight against its leaders is hardly conceivable in Germany. . . . Compare the style of the *Sozialdemokrat* with that of the fighting organs of any other party, from the conservative People's Parties to the most radical bourgeois groups, and you will not find that we have misused the right to carry on controversies and to criticize, especially when you remember that we represent a suppressed party.[49]

But the Swiss Bundesrat used articles which had been published by the *Sozialdemokrat* merely as illustrations of ways of thinking to which it was *opposed* in order to show that the newspaper advocated such terrorist practices as the assassination of public personages. When Bernstein refused to alter the basic character of his paper, he and three of his colleagues

[49] Quoted in Bernstein, *Sozialdemokratische Lehrjahre,* pp. 187–88.

were exiled.[50] The four men left Switzerland on May 12, 1888, to continue the publication of the newspaper in London. A chapter had come to an end.

Eduard Bernstein departed from Switzerland with the same fears and uncertainties with which he had entered it. When he had left Germany ten years earlier to join Höchberg he had felt the insecurity of the young man for the first time away from home. But his loneliness had soon been dissipated by friendship and productive work. It had been a successful and satisfying decade, and Bernstein could truly say to himself that he had gone far in the party and done well in his private life. Now he was to break camp and move on. True, he was not a stranger to London, but it was a new life he faced, and he looked toward it more with sorrow than with hope.

[50] Along with Bernstein as editor, Motteler was exiled as chief distributor of the newspaper, Schlüter as director of the closely connected People's Bookstore, and Tauscher as chief printer.

Chapter 3

The Education Rounded Out: London

The Erfurt Program

> *Kautsky's draft, supported by Bebel and my-*
> *self, will be the basis of the Program. . . .*
> *We have the satisfaction of seeing Marx's cri-*
> *tique completely victorious.*
>
> ENGELS TO SORGE, OCTOBER, 1891

ONCE SETTLED in London, Eduard Bernstein continued to edit the *Sozialdemokrat,* but a series of stirring events, initiated by the dismissal of Bismarck, soon made it unnecessary for German Social Democracy to publish its official newspaper abroad.

Bismarck's position under William I had been well-nigh impregnable. After William's death in 1888, however, the Iron Chancellor was no longer the indispensable man. Frederick's reign was but an interlude, cut tragically brief by cancer of the throat. And the young William II, ambitious to rule in fact as well as in theory, proved a difficult master. William's devotion to conservative ideas of social reform engineered by the ruling classes clashed with Bismarck's avowed intention of perpetuating the anti-Socialist legislation. The law was allowed to lapse in 1890—the same year that saw Bismarck's dismissal.

German Social Democracy could now publish its newspaper at home, but Bernstein, who was still under indictment for his seditious editorial activities had to remain abroad. The end of the *Sozialdemokrat,* therefore, meant the end of his fruitful career as an editor.[1] He now began to make his living

[1] Mehring sums up Bernstein's contribution: "Bernstein well understood how to maintain the sheet as an organ of the whole party and to give it, at the same time, a certain, firm, clear direction which adjusted itself to all tactical demands without violating

as London correspondent of the Berlin *Vorwärts* and as regular contributor to Kautsky's theoretical periodical, *Neue Zeit*. The early 1890s, during which he published occasional pieces for journals, were critical for his development as a theorist. In the first place, the articles he wrote during that time prepared him for bigger and better things. Moreover, writing for the *Neue Zeit* undoubtedly led to a change in the direction of his interests. The magazine was a thoughtful journal with emphasis on history and theoretical discussions, and Bernstein now became engrossed in more theoretical subjects. As a free-lance writer, he spent more and more time in the famous reading room of the Library of the British Museum, where Marx had sat and brooded for so long. There, Eduard Bernstein rounded out his education.

The end of the most important piece of repressive anti-Socialist legislation on the statute books raised some difficult questions. The consequences of the law had been most unexpected. Bismarck had wanted to destroy the workers' party, but in the twelve years in which the legislation had been operative, Social Democracy had tripled its popular vote and the number of its mandates in the Reichstag. The ruling classes had confidently expected that the combination of this law with Bismarck's social legislation would make German labor docile and insure its acquiescence in the social order. Instead, Social Democracy had grown more militant and gained valuable experience in the era of repression, experience which it would now use to expand and press its demands. What is more, Bismarck had hoped to cripple the young Free Trade Union movement permanently. But while he succeeded in

principle. In almost no issue raised by the political struggles of a decade—certainly in no decisive one—did the *Sozialdemokrat* wander off on a side path. From his activities as an agitator, Bernstein was much too familiar with the conditions of the proletarian class struggle ever to misunderstand the issues. He worked thoroughly and slowly; a thoughtful nature, with a slight touch of skepticism which tended to overestimate the merits of opponents, he loved the struggle not for the sake of struggle, and was always ready for fruitful discussion. With Engels as adviser, Bernstein contributed at least as much to the theoretical enlightenment of the German working class as to its practical schooling." *Geschichte der deutschen Sozialdemokratie*, IV, 227.

staving off its phenomenal growth until the early 1900s, labor union membership increased more than fivefold during the period of anti-Socialist legislation.

But the law had another unforeseen consequence: it placed the Social Democracy in a false position. The party gave the appearance of being strictly devoted to revolutionary ends (it even rewrote its program in 1891 to underline its intransigeance) while, in reality, it was becoming parliamentary and reformist. This split between thought and action should be kept in mind; it helps to explain much subsequent history.[2]

The newly legal party was undergoing a confusing period of theoretical reconsideration while, at the same time, it increased its following. In the Reichstag elections of February 1890 the Social Democrats ran up the impressive score of 1,427,298 votes—nearly 20 percent of the total—and thirty-five mandates. Symptoms of the restiveness of party membership were the so-called Revolt of the Young Ones—a small group of hyperradicals who attempted to "save" the party from its "bourgeois" tactics—and several speeches by von Vollmar which took a surprisingly reformist tone and advocated a "circumspect policy of negotiation." We may regard Vollmar's talks of 1891 as the first sign of Revisionism in German Social Democracy.[3] Bebel managed to ward off both "deviations" at the important party congresses of Halle in 1890 and Erfurt in the following year. At Halle the party repaired its battered organization and established an official newspaper, the *Vorwärts,* in Berlin. At Erfurt, Social Democracy adopted a new party program which eliminated much of the Lassalleanism that remained. Kautsky was responsible for the theoretical, Bernstein for the tactical sections of the Erfurt Program. Behind both stood Engels who watched over the proceedings closely and was somewhat critical of the results. However, the view of capitalist development which the program enunciated was unmistakably Marxist:

Production on a small scale is based on the ownership of the means of production by the laborer. The economic

[2] Cf. Evelyn Anderson, *Hammer or Anvil,* p. 9.
[3] Gustav Mayer, *Friedrich Engels,* II, 488–89.

development of bourgeois society leads necessarily to the overthrow of this form of production. It separates the worker from his tools and changes him into a propertyless proletarian. The means of production become more and more the monopoly of a comparatively small number of capitalists and landholders.

Productivity increases, but so do monopolies, and for both proletariat and the disappearing middle class this means growing insecurity, "misery, oppression, servitude, degradation and exploitation." The proletariat constantly grows, and so does the reserve army of labor; the class struggle becomes ever more bitter as the abyss between propertied and propertyless is further widened by industrial crises caused by the capitalist system. Private property in the means of production, which had once been used to secure a living to the producer, is today employed as a means of expropriating these producers. Only by the transformation of capitalist private property in the means of production into social property, and by the transformation of commodity production into Socialist production, can the steadily growing output of industry be used to benefit all. This transformation, the program pointed out, means the liberation not only of the proletariat but of mankind as a whole; however, it is only the working classes which can effect this liberation. "The struggle of the working class against capitalist exploitation is necessarily a political battle." Since the interests of the workers in all capitalist countries are identical, the program went on, the German Social Democratic Party fights at the side of all class-conscious workers in all countries. The Erfurt Program ended with a ringing paragraph:

The Social Democratic Party of Germany thus struggles not for new class privileges and advantages but for the abolition of class rule and of classes in general as well as for equal rights and equal duties for all without regard of sex or birth. Beginning with these views, the party fights not only the exploitation and suppression of wage laborers in present-day society but against any kind of exploitation and suppression, be it of class, party, sex, or race.[4]

This, in brief, was the platform on which the party leadership was to make its stand during the Revisionist assault of only a few years later.

Writing History

> *Anybody can make history; only a great man can write it.*
>
> OSCAR WILDE

Eduard Bernstein's London years are remarkable not only for his revision of Marxism, which gained him international notoriety, but also for his publication of a truly extraordinary historical work on the English Civil War in the seventeenth century.

Bernstein's highly original contribution to scholarship represented his share in a large-scale collective project which was designed to cover the "Vorläufer des neueren Sozialismus" (Precursors of Recent Socialism) from a Socialist point of view. His book, *Sozialismus und Demokratie in der grossen englischen Revolution* (Socialism and Democracy in the Great English Revolution),[5] originally published in 1895, came at a time in which general interest in the English Civil War was reviving. These were the years in which British historians published volumes of documents, papers, and interpretative studies on the great struggle between Charles I, Parliament, and the Cromwellian Army. C. H. Firth brought out the famous Clarke papers in installments from 1891 to

[4] Quoted and paraphrased from Wilhelm Schröder, ed., *Handbuch der sozialdemokratischen Parteitage*, pp. 470–71. The first quotation is taken from William E. Bohn's translation of Karl Kautsky, *The Class Struggle*, pp. 7–8.

[5] It was published as a section of Volume I, Part 2 of *Die Geschichte des Sozialismus in Einzeldarstellungen*. The second edition, of 1908, bore the title *Sozialismus und Demokratie in der grossen englischen Revolution*. The English translation, of 1930, is entitled *Cromwell and Communism*.

1901; during the same decade appeared the influential writings of S. R. Gardiner, who published a number of books on that period in English history and edited the *Constitutional Documents of the Puritan Revolution.*

To the extent that these books were interpretations of the 1640s and 1650s, they saw these years in terms of late-Victorian scholarship. Their approach was almost exclusively potitical, and the contest between the Crown, Parliament, and the Army was depicted solely as a fight to the death between constitutionalism and absolutism.[6]

Not that radicalism was totally neglected; the democratic Leveller movement was known to historians as early as Clarendon, whose great Royalist history of the Civil War, written in the 1660s, contained a brief account of the movement which John Lilburne had headed. With the passage of time, the Levellers gained in importance for students of British history. Ranke did not omit them from his general history of England, and Gardiner gave them considerable space in his *History of the Great Civil War,* the epitome of the liberal interpretation. But the emphasis was on constitutional radicalism, and this point of view could not take sufficient account of the social changes which had found violent expression in the civil conflict.

Bernstein's approach to history equipped him to study the Civil War as a social and economic phenomenon. He focused attention on the growth of a dynamic and aggressive upper middle class and its conflicts with both nobility and workers. Commercial financiers and industrial capitalists, Bernstein pointed out, were transforming the old order, and the social philosophies of the age, from Hobbes and Harrington to the Levellers and the Diggers, were born of the clash between a dying feudalism and a youthful capitalism. His book, Bernstein wrote later, was the "only large-scale attempt on my part to discuss historical events on the basis of Marx's and Engels's materialist interpretation of history." [7]

[6] Cf. David Petegorsky, *Left-Wing Democracy in the English Civil War,* pp. 14 ff.
[7] Bernstein, "Entwicklungsgang eines Sozialisten," in *Die Volkswirtschaftslehre der Gegenwart in Selbstdarstellungen,* I, 19. For this paragraph cf. Petergorsky, *loc. cit.*

The study not only painted a picture that differed significantly from that of other writers, but it also presented the philosophy of an English Communist of that period who had been completely overlooked by all other historians—Gerrard Winstanley. Bernstein had found his way through the complexities of the 1640s and 1650s with deftness and intelligence. His account of the Leveller movement had been among the first to do justice to those pioneers of democratic political theory. But his discovery of the leader of the Communist Diggers, Gerrard Winstanley, was probably Bernstein's most important contribution. While Winstanley does not belong with the giants of political theory and is overshadowed in his century by the impressive figures of Hobbes, Harrington, Milton, and Locke, no history of modern Socialism would be complete without a chapter devoted to his doctrines and his party.[8]

It is to Bernstein's great credit that he understood the Civil War more deeply than most contemporary historians, and this is all the more remarkable when we realize that this area was essentially outside his own field. But while the book has had lasting influence, it was not widely reviewed at the time of its appearance, and its true impact seems to have been underrated. Firth and Gardiner received the book well, and Bernstein found British historians exceedingly kind and free from any jealousy.[9] He gratefully noted their helpful attitude as an

[8] Bernstein's book appeared in Germany in 1895. G. P. Gooch wrote his well-known essay, *English Democratic Ideas in the Seventeenth Century*, about four years later and acknowledged Bernstein's original contribution. "Though it was unlikely that in any age where the soil was so deeply ploughed some form of communism should not appear, it is too little known that the English Revolution presents some of the most remarkable Communistic speculation in history" (p. 175). A footnote to this remark completes the story: "The honour of the discovery of Winstanley belongs to Bernstein." Cf. also Petegorsky, *Left-Wing Democracy*, p. 121.

[9] Gardiner sent a note to Bernstein on October 23, 1895, praising the book (Bernstin Archives). Firth wrote him in a similar vein in February, 1896 (Bernstein Archives). That he was regarded as an expert on seventeenth-century English can be seen from the fact that no less a man than Max Weber consulted Bernstein while he was writing *The Protestant Ethic and the Spirit of Capitalism*.

example of the noncompetitive spirit of British scholars which, Bernstein felt, compared most favorably with the pettiness of German university professors.[10]

Making History

> *Un certain aspect critique du Marxisme me paraît toujours valable. . . . Il y avait dans Marx une leçon de modestie qui me semble en passe d'être oubliée. Il y avait aussi dans Marx une soumission à la réalité, et une humilité devant l'expérience qui l'auraient sans aoute conduit à reviser quelques uns des points de vue auᵉ ses disciples d'aujourd'hui veulent désespérément maintenir dans la sclérose du dogme.*
>
> ALBERT CAMUS

The 1890s were the crucial decade of Bernstein's life. During these London years he developed his theory of Revisionism in detail, and nearly all the work he accomplished after his return to Germany in 1901 was in the nature of elaboration and exposition.

To be a German Socialist in the London of that time was to be in Engel s shadow. Bernstein was no exception. His historical studies, his theoretical articles, his edition of the complete works of Lassalle for the party—all these were carried forward under Engel s eye.[11] While such things are impossible to prove, it appears likely that Bernstein's close friendship with the older man postponed his lapse into the

[10] German learned journals generally ignored Bernstein's book. One exception was a highly interesting review by G. Jellinek in the *Historische Zeitschrift.* Jellinek thought little of Kautsky's study of Thomas More and of Lafargue's chapters on Campanella and the Jesuits in Paraguay. On the other hand, "Bernstein's contribution on Communist and radical Socialist streams of thought in the English Revolution, which embraces almost half of the total volume, deserves greater attention." *Historische Zeitschrift,* LXXXI (XLV, new ser.) (1898), 118.
[11] Mayer, *Engels,* II, 393–94, 483.

Revisionist heresy. It can hardly be an accident that the first articles which revealed Bernstein's break with orthodox Marxism appeared in 1896, about a year after Engels's death.[12]

Even during Engels's lifetime, however, Bernstein established close relations with English Socialists. These were exciting years for British radicalism. The Fabian Society was about ten years old, and its major contribution to Socialist literature, the *Fabian Essays in Socialism,* had proved a popular success. The leaders of English Socialism—Graham Wallas, Bernard Shaw, Sidney and Beatrice Webb, Stewart Headlam, Keir Hardie, John Burns, Ramsay MacDonald—were personalities of talent and promise. Bernstein knew them all and was on close friendly terms with several. These connections did not remain hidden from Engels, who was displeased with what he called Bernstein's "Fabian-enthusiasm" (*Fabian-Schwärmerei*).[13] But apparently he did not take too dim a view of Bernstein's friendships; when he died on August 5, 1895, his last will stipulated that Bernstein was to be one of the executors. Further, Bernstein and Bebel were jointly entrusted with Engels's literary remains—surely a sign of complete confidence.

The change which was to culminate in Bernstein's defection from Marxism was gradual and, at first, imperceptible.

[12] This speculation gains at least partial confirmation by Bernstein's attitude towards Lassalle. The preface to the collected works, written in 1891, was highly critical. Another study of Lassalle, which Bernstein wrote in 1904, when he was an avowed Revisionist, is far more favorably inclined. Bernstein has this to say in his preface to the latter work: "The judgment of Lassalle which is expressed in this book differs in several points from the opinions I held in the introduction to the collected works of Lassalle. Please do not ascribe this to the fact that the present study is a sort of memorial. Where there are differences, they are the consequence of more thorough study of Lassalle, as well as of the fact that my own theoretical development has led me spiritually closer to Lassalle. . . ." Bernstein, *Ferdinand Lassalle und seine Bedeutung für die Arbeiterklasse,* Preface.
[13] Mayer, *Engels,* II, 405. This phrase appears in a letter Engels sent to Bebel on Aug. 20, 1892. It is clear from this letter that Engels attributed Bernstein's "overestimation of the Fabians" to a nervous illness which he had recently undergone.

The early 1890s, during which it occurred, were peaceful years for Europe. This antirevolutionary climate of opinion touched off sympathetic vibrations in Bernstein's temperament. In Germany it was becoming ever more evident that reformism, anathema though it was to the Social Democratic leadership, still had a strong appeal. Lassalleanism died hard. Georg von Vollmar's speeches advocating a gradualist approach to Socialism found enthusiastic listeners; a large group of academicians, the so-called *Katheder-Sozialisten* ("Socialists of the chair,") loudly championed the cause of peaceful social reform. At the same time French Socialism, which had always prided itself upon its revolutionary tradition, was bringing forth a spate of reformists, with the great Jean Jaurès as their chief spokesman. Jaurès and his allies, the *possibilistes,* sharply disagreed with their revolutionary brethren and preached the feasibility of cooperation with the radical bourgeoisie, with a peaceful transition to Socialism as a consequence. Revisionism, when it came, then, was in tune with many live currents of thought.

Of even greater significance for Bernstein's intellectual development was the atmosphere in England which was, one might say, almost professionally reformist. Bernstein found almost daily evidence of the "free air of England." "Marx mellowed in London, why shouldn't I?"—so he seems to have reasoned. He was fond of regaling his friends with his amazing experiences in England. In a review of the third volume of Bebel's reminiscences, he told the following anecdote:

> Bebel and I got a good idea of the English way of doing things during our 1880 trip to London. We went to an evening's charity entertainment held in support of the widow of a Communard. The audience consisted almost exclusively of Socialists and revolutionaries. At the top of the subscription list, printed on the back of the program, we read these words: "Her Majesty the Queen has headed the list with £ 10." [14]

Another story, even more characteristic, involved a great London strike. London factory workers had gone out and the

[14] Newspaper clipping, Bernstein Archives.

employers were importing scabs from Germany. The trade unions asked Bernstein to address the strikebreakers, and he agreed to undertake the assignment. One afternoon, at closing time, he placed himself on a large rock outside the factory gates and began to harangue the German workers who were just leaving work for the day. He explained the issues to them and urged them not to scab, but to join their English brothers in the strike. All this while several policemen stood around calmly, eyeing the milling crowd and guarding against possible disorders. But the policemen did not interfere with Bernstein's speech, nor did they attack his listeners.[15] Occurrences like these made a profound impression upon German visitors, who were hardly used to such behavior from their Crown and their police. These events seemed to suggest that peaceful social change was, after all, a possibility.

The first signs of a change in Bernstein came in certain controversies which he conducted through the pages of the *Neue Zeit*. Naturally, he sought to refute his opponents, but these intellectual fencing contests left him with considerable doubts as to the correctness of his own Marxist orthodoxy. Albert Camus has said that a man whom you cannot persuade is a man who is afraid. Bernstein was not afraid; once in doubt, he worried sweeping theories as a terrier worries a promising but suspicious-looking bone. His honesty led to thoroughness and skepticism, qualities which are often fruitfully combined.

The two professors whose positions Bernstein attempted to undermine were both bourgeois liberals. The first, Gerhart von Schulze-Gaevernitz, had published a bulky two-volume study, *Zum sozialen Frieden*, which purported to be "a description of the sociopolitical education of the English people in the nineteenth century." [16] His conclusions: the class struggle has diminished in violence, the misery of the proletariat is disappearing, Great Britain is on the road to social peace. Schulze-Gaevernitz's second book, *Der Grossbetrieb*, continued this general line of argument: the very growth of large-scale industry insures increasing social accord since it

[15] Anecdote told the author by Otto Landsberg.
[16] Subtitle of *Zum sozialen Frieden*.

brings with it an improvement in the living standards of the British working class and makes the proletariat an accepted member of society.

Bernstein examined these contentions thoroughly.[17] He pointed out that Marxists had always acknowledged the progressive character of improvements in the means of production[18] and that Marx had fully recognized the function of the machine. But Marx had correctly insisted that "wage raises and shortening of hours are not equivalent to a decrease in surplus value." [19] While the growth of large-scale industry may have brought a "relative" improvement in the standard of living of the "labor aristocrats," the fact remained that "in capitalist society, big industry can create no lasting improvement of social conditions even under the most favorable circumstances. It can only develop the prerequisites for such improvement." [20]

Julius Wolf's *Sozialismus und kapitalistische Gesellschaft*, which had attracted general attention as a comprehensive onslaught on the whole Marxist system, was next on the carpet. Bernstein treated it with biting irony and a roughness unusual for a man of his generosity and fairness. The reviews sound as though Bernstein sought to convince himself and could do so only by shouting.[21] He called Wolf "the latest destroyer of Socialism," [22] and pictured him as only the most recent in a series of Saint Georges who had ventured forth to slay the Marxist dragon.[23] Wolf was shown to have misrepresented Marx's meaning. Yet Bernstein's performance remained unconvincing. He spent too much time criticizing Wolf's meth-

[17] Bernstein discussed *Zum sozialen Frieden* in "Carlyle und die sozialpolitische Entwicklung Englands," *Neue Zeit*, IX, 1 (1891), 665–73, 693–701, 729–36; and *Der Grossbetrieb* in "Technisch-ökonomischer und sozial-ökonomischer Fortschritt," *Neue Zeit*, XI, 1 (1893), 782–90, 819–29, 854–62.
[18] "Technisch-ökonomischer und sozial-ökonomischer Fortschritt," p. 782.
[19] *Ibid.*, p. 789.
[20] *Ibid.*, pp. 859, 861, 861–62.
[21] Cf. Bernstein, "Der neueste Vernichter des Sozialismus," *Neue Zeit*, XI, 1 (1893), 502–8, 534–39.
[22] *Ibid.*, p. 503.
[23] *Ibid.*, pp. 502–3.

odology and omitted any consideration of his specific claims, such as Wolf's attempted refutation of Marx's theory of the reserve army.[24]

Outwardly, little appeared to have happened. Schulze-Gaevernitz had been demolished; Wolf had been relegated to the ranks of the unsuccessful bourgeois knights-in-armor; Marxism had been saved once more. But Bernstein was uneasy—he had managed to show that both critics of Marx had committed important errors. Yet, as he admitted later,

I did not hide from myself the fact that the objections which they had raised had not been fully answered. . . . Much as I fought against it, I began to doubt doctrines which I had considered as incontrovertible until then. The next years brought events which further increased my uncertainty.[25]

The events to which he referred were the long period of European prosperity, the debate on the agrarian question in German Social Democracy in 1894, and the publication, in the same year, of Volume III of *Capital*,[26] with its famous "solution" to the puzzle of the profit rate.[27]

The transition to Revisionism was not easy for Bernstein. A man of strong loyalties, he was deeply pained to have to be the critic of a system to which he had held so faithfully. This is probably the chief reason for his unrealistic insistence that Revisionism was still Marxism.

His inner struggle affected his outward bearing. Usually affable, he became moody and inaccessible. In 1895 he even considered getting away from it all: he negotiated for a bank job in Transvaal. But nothing came of it—the battle must be

[24] Wolf recognized this well. Cf. his letter to the *Neue Zeit*, XI, 1 (1893), 760–68, and his autobiographical sketch in *Die Volkswirtschaftslehre der Gegenwart in Selbstdarstellungen*, I, 216–17.
[25] "Entwicklungsgang," p. 21.
[26] The bearing that these events had on Bernstein's thought is discussed below in pp. 121–30 (European prosperity), 198–204 (agrarian question), and 174–84 (*Capital*).
[27] We may add Bernstein's study of the Paris Revolution of 1848.

fought through. His friends were not blind to this conflict. The friendship between Kautsky and Bernstein grew distinctly cooler well before these two men engaged in any public controversy. In March 1898, shortly before her suicide, the perceptive Eleanor Marx complained to Kautsky that Bernstein was irritable and was making enemies everywhere. She expressed the fear that Bernstein was allowing himself to be used by the Fabians as a tool in their anti-Marxist campaign.[28]

In a letter which Bernstein sent to Bebel in October 1898, he described his transformation with a vividness that could not be improved upon:

This "moulting" of mine is the result of a very lengthy development or, rather, it took a long time before I was completely clear that this transformation did not confine itself to special questions but touched upon the very fundamentals of Marxism. Up to two years ago I tried, by stretching Marxist teachings, to bring them into accord with practical realities. Characteristically, or if you wish understandably, I fully realized the impossibility of such tactics when I gave a lecture at the Fabian Society on the subject, "What Marx really taught," about a year and a half ago. I still have the manuscript of that talk; it is a frightening example of a well-meaning rescue attempt. I wanted to save Marx; I wanted to show that he had predicted everything that had and had not happened. When I got through with my "artistic performance," when I read my lecture over, the thought flashed through my head: You are doing Marx an injustice, what you are spouting about is not Marx. And a few harmless questions which the acute Fabian Hubert Bland asked me after the talk and which I answered in the old manner really finished me off. I said to myself—this cannot go on. It is idle to try to reconcile the irreconcilable. What is necessary is to become clear just where Marx is right and where he is wrong.[29]

Bernstein's purge, the attempt to "become clear just where

[28] Eleanor Marx to Kautsky, March 15, 1889, Kautsky Archives.
[29] Bernstein to Bebel, October 20, 1898, Bernstein Archives.

Marx is right and where he is wrong," began to reach the public in a series of articles entitled Probleme des Sozialismus, which appeared in the *Neue Zeit* from 1896 to 1898.[30] They created a raging storm of discussion within Social Democracy. Not that Bernstein had been the first to warn his fellow So- cialists against expecting an impending collapse of capitalism —Vollmar, David, and others had been writing in a reformist vein for several years[31]—but his articles were the beginning of a *systematic* attempt to revise Marxism. The others had thrown doubt on specific parts of Marx's writings; Bernstein now went further. He questioned the relevance of Hegelian- ism to Socialist theory and advocated instead that ethics be reintroduced as an independently active social factor. He at- tempted to disprove such Marxist doctrines as the disappear- ance of the agrarian middle class and the withering away of the state. Most important, his articles threw doubt on the thesis of ever-growing crises and proletarian misery and sub- stituted for it the ideal of gradualist growth into Socialism. They contain, in germ, the basic tenets of Revisionism as later spelled out in his *Voraussetzungen.*

The first essays were still somewhat cautious. But in an article on "The Theory of Collapse and Colonial Policy" Bernstein undertook to reply to the strictures of Belfort-Bax, the British Socialist, who had charged him with ignoring the final goal of Socialism in his writings. "I confess openly," ran Bernstein's fateful rejoinder, "I have extraordinarily little interest or taste for what is generally called the 'final goal of Socialism.' This aim, whatever it be, is nothing to me, *the movement everything.*" "And by movement," it went on, "I understand not only the general movement of society, that is, social progress, but political and economic agitation and organization for effecting this progress." [32]

If ever a man got tired of having his own words quoted to him, Eduard Bernstein was that man. The party's reaction was sharp and instantaneous. Now Bernstein's colleagues reread his earlier articles and discovered his apostasy. Some, like the

[30] Reprinted, almost in full, in *Zur Geschichte und Theorie des Sozialismus,* pp. 167–286.
[31] Cf. Erika Rikli, *Der Revisionismus,* pp. 11–15.
[32] Bernstein, *Zur Geschichte und Theorie des Sozialismus,* p. 234.

publishers of the *Vorwärts,* criticized his phraseology; others, like Parvus, accused him of attempting to destroy Socialism. Before he could catch his breath he was involved in the controversy of his life. All other interests and activities were pushed aside, and for several years he did little else than to defend, elaborate, and clarify his views.

At the beginning he was anxious to explain his remark about the final aim of Socialism. The *Vorwärts* published a declaration by Bernstein:

Does it follow from my refusal to concern myself with the so-called "final aim of the Socialist movement" that I deny a definite goal to the movement altogether? I would regret it if my words would be taken in this way. A movement without aim would be a chaotic drifting, for it would also be a movement without direction. No aim, no direction—if the Socialist movement is not to pitch about without a compass, it must naturally have a goal at which it consciously aims. But this aim is not the realization of a plan for society, it is the carrying through of a *principle* of society. . . . The only thing of value is to be sure of the general course of the movement and to examine the relevant factors carefully. If we do this, we can be untroubled about the final aim.[33]

But this proved insufficient to calm the troubled spirits of German Social Democracy. The attacks on Bernstein continued. Aware that his views would be debated in the 1898 party congress at Stuttgart, he composed a letter which was to serve as a further explanation of his alleged deviationism. It was read to the convention delegates by Bebel "in the name of one who is absent." [34] In it, Bernstein stood firm:

The views I laid down in "Problems of Socialism" have lately been discussed in Socialist papers and meetings, and a request has been made that the party congress of the German Social Democrats should state its position regard-

[33] Reprinted *ibid.,* pp. 237–38.
[34] *Protokoll über die Verhandlungen des Parteitages der SPD,* 1898, p. 122.

ing them. . . . The vote of an assembly, however significant it may be, naturally cannot compel me to change
opinions which I formed after an examination of social
phenomena. What I wrote in the *Neue Zeit* is the expression of a conviction from which I do not find myself induced to depart in any particular.

He defended himself against the charge that the "practical
consequences of my articles would be the abandonment of
the conquest of political power by the proletariat organized
politically and economically," and he reiterated his primary
concern:

I set myself against the viewpoint that we have to expect
a collapse of the bourgeois economy in the near future, and
that Social Democracy should be induced by the prospect
of such an imminent catastrophe to adapt its tactics to that
assumption.

While the general theory of social evolution as set forth in
the *Communist Manifesto* was correct, several specific deduc-
tions had proved mistaken and should no longer serve as
guideposts to Socialist action. The concentration theory, he
wrote, was being disproved by actual developments, and the
prospect of catastrophes and revolutions was constantly diminishing. On the other hand, evidence was increasing that
exploitation of labor was lessening. "In all advanced countries we see the privileges of the capitalist bourgeoisie yielding
step by step to democratic organizations." He called Engels
to witness that changed circumstances required a corresponding adaptation of Socialist tactics.

No one has questioned the necessity for the working class
to gain control of the government. The point at issue is
between the theory of a social cataclysm and the question
whether with the given social development in Germany and
the present advanced state of its working class in town and
country, a sudden catastrophe would be in the interest of

Social Democracy. I have answered that question in the negative, and I do so still.[35]

The declaration was read to the assembled delegates, and a brief debate ensued—the first of the famous Bernstein debates, which were to occupy so much of the time and attention of succeeding party congresses. Bebel made it clear that he differed from Bernstein "in important points." [36] The skillful dialectician Kautsky spoke at length, setting the tone which the whole debate was to take in the next few years. He expressed his regret at having to speak against a man with whom he had been in closest alliance for eighteen years. He described Bernstein as a man who had "stood in the first rank of the party during its most difficult years" and who was now in exile because of his political activities.[37] That bit of politeness out of the way, he proceeded to deny Bernstein's basic contentions and to recall to the delegates the revolutionary truths of Marxist philosophy. He evoked lively applause with his rhetoric:

If Bernstein believes that we must have democracy first, so that we may then lead the proletariat to victory step by step, I say that the matter is just the other way around with us: the victory of the proletariat is the precondition of the victory of democracy.[38]

Again he was applauded when he exclaimed: "Does anyone believe that this victory is possible without catastrophe? I desire it, but I don't believe it." [39]

The one fruitful consequence of this debate, which was little more than a dress rehearsal for subsequent, more exhaustive clashes, was Kautsky's suggestion to Bernstein that he set down a comprehensive statement of his convictions.

[35] Bernstein's letter, which is here quoted and paraphrased, appeared *ibid.*, pp. 122–25.
[36] *Ibid.*, p. 125.
[37] *Ibid.*, p. 127.
[38] *Ibid.*, p. 129.
[39] *Loc. cit.*

Bebel was somewhat skeptical. "I don't think this is absolutely necessary," he wrote to Bernstein in October 1898, "since I am of the opinion that you have told us enough for us to know which way you are heading and where you want us to follow you. But if you accept the challenge, it might be all to the good." [40]

Bernstein set to work immediately, with Bebel's advice, "write clearly and definitely," fully in mind.[41] The book, rather clumsily titled *Die Voraussetzungen des Sozialismus und die Aufgaben der Sozialdemokratie*, was published in March 1899.[42] It became, and was to remain, the bible of Revisionism. Kautsky rightly called it "the first sensational book in the literature of German Social Democracy." [43] Almost overnight, it propelled Eduard Bernstein into the position of the leader of an important movement and made him famous throughout Europe. Its doctrines became the subject of violent verbal duels in the party press and in party congresses as well as in the non-Socialist world. Many opponents of Socialism greeted Bernstein as a convert with the same pious pleasure with which the Roman Catholic Church has welcomed ex-Communists to its bosom.

Bernstein was deeply shocked at the reception of his book, and the bitter "Bernstein debate" at the 1899 party congress did not serve to improve his state of mind. Always exceedingly sensitive to criticism, he tended to regard attacks on his theory as attacks on his person. In 1900 he determined to return to Germany to face his accusers even though the government had not yet dropped its charges against him. Through complicated negotiations, his friends in Berlin managed to persuade the government to let the warrant lapse in January

[40] October 16, 1898, Bernstein Archives.

[41] Bebel to Bernstein, October 22, 1898, Bernstein Archives.

[42] The edition used throughout this study is that of 1920. Literally the title means "The presuppositions of Socialism and the tasks of Social Democracy." Its title in the English translation is *Evolutionary Socialism*.

[43] Karl Kautsky, *Bernstein und das sozialdemokratische Programm*, p. 1.

1901, and Bernstein returned to Germany forthwith to conduct the great controversy in person.[44]

A study of Bernstein's correspondence with the party leadership during the years 1898 to 1900 reveals that Bernstein's
fears for his future within German Social Democracy were
far more than mere morbid imaginings. For a while, Bebel
was determined to have Bernstein expelled. His letters to
Bernstein were sharp and often unjust. In October 1898 he
accused Bernstein of being easily swayed by his environment
—first an Eisenacher, then a follower of Dühring, then a
disciple of Höchberg, then a revolutionary, and finally, "under
English influence," Revisionist.[45] Bernstein correctly replied
that Bebel had not only overstated Bernstein's volatility, but
that Bebel, too, had been a Dühring admirer at one time and
a most uncertain Marxist at others.[46]

But Bebel was undismayed by refutation. He told Bernstein that he no longer "stood on Social Democratic soil," [47]
and in April 1899 he wrote to the great Austrian Socialist
Viktor Adler, "in my opinion the situation with Ede has
reached the stage at which a break is inevitable." [48] He repeated this opinion, in strong terms, many times during these
years.

Kautsky's role in this whole correspondence was strange,
if not sinister. On the one hand he strenuously and repeatedly
denied any intentions of trying to push Bernstein out of the
party. "As you can see," he wrote to Viktor Adler in early
November 1898, "the point in question for me is not Ede's

[44] The exact sequence of events was as follows: Bernstein's friend
Auer consulted Heinrich Guttmann, a parliamentary journalist,
who in turn got in touch with the politically influential Paul
Nathan. Nathan directly went to Chancellor Bülow who saw to it
that the warrant was not renewed. Bülow's motives are far from
clear. It seems possible that he felt that the presence of Bernstein
might effectively split German Social Democracy. Of course, the
Stalinists are sure of this. Cf. V. Adoratsky, ed., *Selected Correspondence, Karl Marx and Frederick Engels*, p. 379.
[45] Bebel to Bernstein, October 16, 1898, Bernstein Archives.
[46] Bernstein letter to Bebel, in manuscript, "Ein Brief August
Bebels aus der Zeit unseres Streites," Bernstein Archives.
[47] Bebel to Bernstein, October 22, 1898, Bernstein Achives.
[48] Bebel to Viktor Adler, April 8, 1899, Bernstein Archives.

exclusion from the party, nor from the *Neue Zeit*. I just want him to give up his constant collaboration with the magazine." [49] On the other hand, Kautsky attempted several times to persuade Bernstein to leave German Social Democracy. Only a week before he wrote the words to Viktor Adler quoted above, he sent a long and dogmatic letter to Bernstein: "Your Marxism has collapsed. You have not further developed it to a higher form but have capitulated before its critics." Of course, it is painful for old friends to fall out, but it must be done for the sake of theory. And that is why he must ask Bernstein to give up his important post on the *Neue Zeit*, for Bernstein helps to determine the tone of the magazine and he is no longer a Marxist. But "I hope that our friendship will successfully overcome its trial by fire." Then came the clincher. What is Bernstein to do now? asked Kautsky. He had an answer ready:

> You have decided to be an Englishman—take the consequences and become an Englishman. You have a completely different position with the English press than with the German. . . . And do not deceive yourself, you have completely lost touch with Germany. . . . The development which you have undergone . . . heads away from German Social Democracy, although not from Socialism. Try to achieve a place in the English movement and to become a representative of English Socialism.[50]

And so on. Kautsky pursued this same theme in his letters to Adler: if Bernstein had only quit the party voluntarily (which, Kautsky felt, was his moral duty) all would have been so simple!

Why, then, if Bebel and Kautsky (to say nothing of Mehring) were so determined to be rid of Bernstein, did they not force through his expulsion? We can only speculate. Two reasons stand out. In the first place, Viktor Adler pleaded with Bebel to be moderate. Adler disagreed with Bernstein and criticized his *Voraussetzungen* severely in the press, but

[49] Kautsky to Viktor Adler, November 4, 1898, Bernstein Archives.

[50] Kautsky to Bernstein, end of October 1898, Bernstein Archives.

his frequently expressed maxim was: "Do not get yourselves into a position where you must take the definite stand that there is no room in our party for a man like Ede." [51] Bernstein, according to Adler, was one of the best of the party, a man who had brought into the open the doubts which all Socialists often felt.[52] Adler wrote to Bernstein: "I will tell you and everybody else frankly: in my opinion you have *not* put yourself *anywhere* outside Social Democracy, no matter how much I may dissent in some things. You represent, in brilliant fashion, a direction *within* the party." [53] Adler was sharply critical of Mehring's and Kautsky's role in this affair, and it is likely that Bebel (who, like everyone else, greatly respected Adler) finally listened to advice.[54]

Secondly, we know that, hotheaded though Bebel was, he was still an exceedingly shrewd politician. At first he was of the opinion that Bernstein's expulsion would not create a grave disturbance within the party. "I have no worry," he wrote to Adler, "that many will go along with the departing Bernstein." [55] But an informal survey he had taken within the party soon proved that he was badly mistaken. "The whole matter would be of little significance if there were only one Bernstein," he wrote in April 1899, "but we have a whole lot of them, and most in distinguished positions within the party." [56]

Be that as it may, Eduard Bernstein remained a member of German Social Democracy and returned to his homeland in January 1901, when the issue of Revisionism vs. orthodoxy was uppermost in the minds of German Socialists. This is the place, therefore, where we must turn from our consideration of Bernstein's life to the theory with which his name is enduringly linked.

[51] Adler to Bebel, November 1, 1898, Bernstein Archives.
[52] *Loc. cit.*
[53] Adler to Bernstein, March 17, 1899, Bernstein Archives.
[54] On Viktor Adler's articles on Revisionism, cf. Gustav Pollatschek, ed. *Viktor Adlers Aufsätze, Reden und Briefe,* VI, 222–54.
[55] Bebel to Adler, Nov. 4, 1898, Bernstein Archives.
[56] Bebel to Adler, April 8, 1899, Bernstein Archives.

BOOK TWO / THE THEORY

Chapter 4

The Pedigree

Marx and Engels: The Laws of Capitalist Evolution

> *Ce qu'il y a de certain, c'est que moi je ne suis pas Marxiste.*
>
> KARL MARX

POWERFUL POLITICAL THEORIES are never pure intellectual constructs. They emerge from a thinker's mind as the result of a fruitful combination of a number of things: the reading he has done, external events that tend to confirm his hunches, his sympathies, predilections, and interests. Disentangling all these strands is really an impossible task, but we may profitably guess at the answers to two questions: What were the chief influences that shaped the thinker's outlook? What environmental factors kept his theories alive by giving them plausibility?

There is not a single segment of Eduard Bernstein's Revisionism that can be grasped without reference to the work of Marx and Engels. Their theories were deeply ingrained in Bernstein's mind. When he followed their lead he acknowledged his indebtedness to them, when he dissented from them he was sure to explain why he could not accept a particular Marxist position. For that reason it will be necessary to refer to Marxism in detail when we analyze Revisionism. It will suffice here to cast a cursory glance at the Marxist scheme of thought.

The books of Marx and Engels, with their firm grounding in a philosophy of man and of history, were proof of the maturity of the Socialist movement. The foundation of Marxism is in the modern worker. He and the class to which he belongs, Marx holds, are subject to laws of development that can be discovered only if we study society as a whole and if we view it from the dynamic perspective of long-range social change. Marxism, then, is at once concerned with universality and history; it deals with the rules of the game and with the changes that this very game undergoes in the course of time.

We can readily see that Marxism differs qualitatively from previous Socialist systems of thought. While the great Utopians like Owen and Saint-Simon maintained an overriding dedication to ethics, Marx and Engels prided themselves on the "scientific" nature of their doctrine.[1] They tried to show that contemporary social and economic relations were *necessary*, and that the better life could not be achieved through the building of model communities and the condemnation of the rapacious capitalist, but through the mighty movements of history.

But to Marx and Engels man was more than a helpless piece of driftwood in the irresistible current of the stream of history; he was able, through united class action, to affect the course of events. In the past, Marx wrote, the bourgeoisie had acted as the great liberator: now it was up to the disinherited proletariat, the class whose cause was the cause of humanity, to help man to realize his full potentialities in a free society. Marxism thus was a system in which the organization of the proletariat into a revolutionary political party was of paramount importance. No longer was the worker the mere subject of reform, but he became at once instigator and beneficiary of the coming revolution.

The Marxist system makes the "assumption that the labor process determines the totality of human existence and thus gives to society its basic pattern."[2] In capitalism, Marx maintained, the relation of man to his work is unnatural, inhuman. Man works with tools that do not belong to him on products which someone else will sell and which he himself cannot afford. In precapitalist society human relations were undisguised throughout the whole process of production, exchange, and consumption. In capitalism the same

[1] This is not to argue, of course, that ethical involvement is absent in Marx. Indeed, moral indignation runs openly and strongly through Marx's writings. But Marx made a point of the *independent* validity of his system.

[2] Herbert Marcuse, *Reason and Revolution*, p. 295. This book approaches Marxism through its concern with man, an approach which has been adopted in these pages.

relations are veiled through such institutions as the "free" market and "private" property, and the relations between people are replaced by what appear to be relations between things. To this process Marx gave the awkward name *Verdinglichung*, which has been rendered, equally awkwardly, "reification."

These sociological concepts are most prevalent in Marx's early writings, the product of his stay in Paris. They are made more specific in *Capital*. There, in the famous chapter on the "Fetishism of Commodities," Marx tied them to his analysis of the economic processes of capitalism.[3] In this later period, other concepts took prominence: the class struggle and the revolution which is bound to be carried to its successful conclusion in the dialectical development of history; the labor theory of value and of surplus value, which are graphic descriptions to the worker of the manner in which he is being exploited; the abolition of class rule as well as the disappearance of the state and of labor itself. Underneath it all lies the conviction that labor under capitalism is, literally, inhuman, and that it can become human again only in a totally different system operating with totally different assumptions.[4]

Marx and Engels made no secret of their indebtedness to Hegel. Their dialectic method was a direct descendant of the Hegelian logic, and their emphasis on history as a grand evolutionary process was drawn from the same source.

The concern with evolution is manifest throughout the body of Marx's writings, and it is no accident that Marx originally wanted to dedicate *Capital* to Darwin. This evolutionary aspect of Marxism was of permanent importance to Eduard Bernstein. It is true that he gave the term "evolution" a rather different meaning from the one that Marx and Engels had appropriated for it, but he certainly owed his own conception to his study of Marx's and Engels's work on capitalist development. It remained the most significant contribution they made to his thought. When he had become a Revisionist it was his evolutionism that led him to maintain that he had

[3] *Ibid.*, pp. 295 ff. Cf. also Siegfried Marck, *Sozialdemokratie*, pp. 1–6.
[4] Cf. Marcuse, *Reason and Revolution*, pp. 287–95.

remained true to Marxism even in his reformism, while his opponents claimed it as evidence that he had really abandoned Marx.

Bernstein's debt to Marx and Engels, then, went far deeper than personal admiration and friendship. He recognized this clearly. In a pamphlet written by a number of outstanding Social Democrats on the occasion of the fortieth anniversary of Marx's death, Bernstein acknowledged how much he owed these two men:

> The great thing in Marx is not only that he recognized the close affiliation of the general development of society to the political destiny of classes (*Ausbildung der politischen Berufung ihrer Klassen*)—in bare outline others had done that too—but that he worked out, at the same time, a truly scientific theory concerning this connection which was based on an intensive study of economic development. . . . What is crucial in Socialism is its philosophy of history: the recognition of the close connection of the economy on the one hand (the development of productive forces, class structure, and class maturity) and politics on the other hand (organization, rights, power, and social activity of each class and its members). He who does not grasp this has not understood Marx, no matter how many Marxist formulae he may be able to declaim. . . . Marxism is an insight, not a recipe.[5]

This is how Bernstein evaluated the significance of Marxism to him. Marx, Bernstein believed, had seen the meaning of economics to society as well as the function of the class struggle, although he had overstated the importance of both. Further, Marx had established once and for all the historical character of seemingly "natural laws" and this insight had cleared the way for an evolutionary, dynamic theory of society. Such an estimate enabled Bernstein to declare himself a disciple of Marx and Engels and, at the same time, give up dialectical materialism and to deny the value of Marx's predictions as a recipe for political action.

[5] Untitled, undated pamphlet.

Ferdinand Lassalle: The Democratic State

> *Oh, not the first are you, nor yet will be*
> *The last of those men doomed to lose their*
> * heads*
> *By cunningness in great affairs. . . .*
> LASALLE *Franz von Sickingen*

The career of Ferdinand Lassalle is a biographer's dream. Other political philosophers led lives circumscribed by the bounds of their libraries; Lassalle alternated research with romance, and politics with passion. A Lassalle cult developed with astonishing rapidity in his last years and assumed considerable proportions after his untimely death. George Meredith even wrote a novel about the absurd love affair which precipitated the duel that was to be fatal to him; few thinkers have been thus immortalized.

Need we wonder that such a dramatic personality should have a lasting influence on a political labor party to which he devoted his many-faceted talents? Lassalleanism evoked enthusiastic response from German Socialism and never really disappeared from Social Democratic thought. While Lassallean Socialism was ostensibly erased from the Social Democratic program in Erfurt in 1891, Lassalle's powerful mind attracted the sympathetic attention of Social Democrats far beyond that date: the influence of a man cannot be wiped out by an arbitrary act such as the rewriting of a party platform.

Among those who went to school to Lassalle was Eduard Bernstein, but he did not join the Lassalle cult.[6] Indeed, he was fully aware of the profound contradictions that split Lassalle's political philosophy from his personality. Lassalle's Socialism rested firmly on the foundation of political democracy; he pressed for universal suffrage and independent action

[6] His first contact with the agitator's books was superficial, as has been pointed out earlier. But in 1891 he was commissioned by the party to edit Lassalle's complete works and was thus compelled to read all his writings. The charm of the persuasive pamphleteer soon worked its way into his consciousness.

by the "fourth estate" to bring about the classless state in which each worker was to receive the full product of his labor. But his aristocratic personality was deeply opposed to this emphasis on democratic processes. He was typical of so many intellectuals who are impatient with the slow progress of their cause and the stupidity of their supporters. Such men are often led into dangerous paths. Their lives are illumined by great ideals, but as man's shortsightedness and venality close one avenue after another, they cling to their goals ever more compulsively. It is the logical consequence of such an attitude that the achievement of the goal by *any* means will be ranked above the possible cost that the use of these means may impose upon society. Thus Lassalle, disillusioned at first with the liberals and then with his hopes for a spontaneous movement of the masses, began to make overtures to the government. If, he reasoned, Socialism could not be realized by independent action of the lower classes, it might be possible to conclude an alliance with reactionary Junkerdom as personified by Bismarck. The proponents of such an alliance justified it by pointing to the bourgeoisie as the common enemy of both workers and aristocracy. Critics of such opportunism could fairly say that while it faced one opponent squarely, it did so at the cost of alignment with an even greater enemy. What is more, it seemed likely that this enemy would succeed in garnering to himself alone the benefits resulting from a successful battle with the bourgeoisie.

Eduard Bernstein rejected this policy which Lassalle pursued with ever greater audacity during the last desperate year of his life. Bernstein was too close to liberalism to look with favor upon a procedure which was, fundamentally, absolutist. Clearly, he was under no illusions regarding Lassalle's character and fully realized its Caesarist traits.[7] Of greater impact on him was Lassalle's general system.

[7] Lassalle's personality led toward dictatorial methods not only in tactics but in his personal relations as well. He ruled the Verein with an iron hand. He could actually say in the Ronsdorfer speech: "Freedom and authority, the greatest contrasts, are most intimately united in our Verein. . . . This discipline rests on no other foundation than the spirit of our Verein, it rests upon the deep knowledge that the colossal labors of transforming society

Lassalle's economic theories have justly been described as one-sided and immature.[8] They are difficult to evaluate since they are scattered unsystematically through a collection of pamphlets, speeches, and works on legal or philosophical subjects and since his lack of candor on several points makes it impossible to determine just what he really believed.[9] Some generalizations may, however, be attempted.

In modern capitalism, Lassalle argued, the worker is exploited by the bourgeoisie. He expressed this relation formally in the Iron Law of Wages. This Lassallean law was closely akin to the wage-fund theory then widely held; it rested on the assumption that a rise in wages will automatically bring about an increase in the size of the family and the labor force as a whole.[10] This explains the opposition of the Lassalleans

---

(*die gewaltigen Übergangsarbeiten der Gesellschaft*) can be accomplished only with the Dictatorship of Insight, and not the diseases of individual opinions and grumbling. (Prolonged, thunderous applause.)" Eduard Bernstein, ed. *Ferdinand Lassalles Reden und Schriften,* II, 870–71. Cf. also Michels, *Political Parties,* pp. 41, 47. For his drastic separation of means from ends, cf. Gustav Mayer, *Bismarck und Lassalle, passim.*

[8] Gustav Mayer, *Lassalle als Nationalökonom,* p. 36.

[9] He always meant to write a comprehensive treatise, but never did, and his *Bastiat-Schulze von Delitzsch* is the best source for his economic thought. Rodbertus' characterization of Lassalle as "exoteric as well as esoteric" is disturbingly close to the truth. While he made production associations for workers a cornerstone of his program, he admitted privately to Rodbertus and Marx that he stood on far more radical grounds. Cf. Hermann Oncken, *Lassalle,* pp. 372–75, 272–74, and Bernstein, *Ferdinand Lassalle as a Social Reformer,* pp. 146–47.

[10] Cf. Lassalle, "Offenes Antwortschreiben," in Bernstein, *F. Lassalles Reden und Schriften,* II, 421: "The average wage is always reduced to that subsistence minimum which is customarily sufficient to keep body and soul together and for procreation. Around this point the daily wage oscillates without rising above it or falling below it for long." He did not claim to have discovered it, but prided himself on having derived it from the classical economists, such as Adam Smith, Ricardo, John Stuart Mill. Cf. "Arbeiterlesebuch," *ibid.,* pp. 511–23. On wage-fund theory, cf. Erich Roll, *A History of Economic Thought,* pp. 380–82, 401–2. It was successfully attacked in the last part of the nineteenth century by the marginalists. *Ibid.,* pp. 422–23, 462.

to unionism: the trade unions' struggle to increase real wages, they said, is Sisyphus labor.

We should note that Socialism does not necessarily follow from Lassalle's economic doctrines. It is true, of course, that he advocated Socialism, but his real aim—a fair share of the national product for the worker within the existing state system—could have been reached under capitalism.[11]

Bernstein, fully adopting Marx's analysis, criticized Lassalle's economics severely. He agreed with Marx that to complain merely of maldistribution of wealth is to accept the ground on which the capitalist system rests. For Marx, exploitation of labor was not a matter of disproportion, but a reality fundamental to capitalism which could disappear only with the complete abolition of the wage system.[12] "Lassalle," Bernstein wrote in 1891, "was much more indebted to Marx than he admitted in his writings; but he was a disciple of Marx in only a restricted sense."[13] Marx, as Bernstein correctly understood, had gone beyond Ricardo, Lassalle had not.[14] Lassallean economic theory, Bernstein concluded, was antiquated and applied only to early capitalism.[15]

While Bernstein criticized Lassalle's economics and rejected his tactics, he found his political philosophy somewhat more palatable.

In the first place, Bernstein was impressed with Lassalle's insistence on the importance of political democracy. Power and law are intertwined in the Lassallean system. Since a change in one will produce a change in the second, it becomes

[11] This analysis substantially follows that of Mayer, *Lassalle als Nationalökonom*, passim.

[12] Marx made his distaste for Lassallean economics bitingly clear, but his repeated denunciations did not prevent the Social Democrats from smuggling large segments of it into the Gotha Program. It stated, for example: "The proceeds of labor belong undiminished with equal right to all members of society," and it called for the "abolition of the wage system together with the 'iron law of wages.'" Cf. Marx, *Critique of the Gotha Programme*, pp. 3, 14.

[13] Bernstein, *Ferdinand Lassalle as a Social Reformer*, p. vii.

[14] *Ibid.*, p. xii.

[15] *Ibid.*, p. 134. He did not change his mind on this matter after becoming a Revisionist. Cf. a note he wrote in 1901, in *Zur Geschichte und Theorie des Sozialismus*, p. 91.

necessary for the working class to acquire a weapon with which it will achieve power so that it may change the laws. That weapon is universal, secret, equal suffrage. The laws of history, Lassalle maintained, operate dialectically in the direction of steadily growing limitations on private rights and their transfer to the public domain. The workers must, therefore, exert independent and united pressure to speed this historical process, and the best method is unquestionably the democratic suffrage. Economic reform, Lassalle argued, follows from political pressure: "Without universal suffrage, without a practical lever to realize our demands, we can be a philosophical school or a religious sect, but never a political party." [16]

Bernstein was deeply sympathetic to this primacy of political democracy. But he refused to accept Lassalle's theory of the state. Lassalle, a Prussian Nationalist, exalted the function of the state in lyrical fashion.[17] The state stands above the strife of civil society in its devotion to the absolutely general. The liberal "night-watchman state" is a sorry caricature and infinitely inferior to an energetic, socially conscious absolutism.[18] It stands to reason that the victorious working class will not scuttle the state but triumphantly dominate it.

Now Bernstein, too, did not trust liberalism and recognized that the so-called "weak state" was, in effect, an ideology which disguised the effective domination of property. Nor did his Revisionism advocate the withering away of the state. But he shared neither Lassalle's effusive nationalism, nor his vitriolic hatred of liberalism, nor his adulation of the state.[19]

[16] Letter to Rodbertus, quoted in Mayer, *Lassalle als Nationalökonom,* p. 73.
[17] A Hegelian heritage which Marxism had, of course, completely sloughed off. Cf. Lassalle, "Arbeiterprogramm," in Bernstein, *F. Lassalles Reden und Schriften,* II, 44–47. Cf. also pp. 16–18 above.
[18] Oncken, *Lassalle,* p. 402.
[19] Bernstein wrote in 1891: "The cult of the state as such means the cult of every state. . . . Lassalle's concept of the state is the bridge that was one day to bring together the republican Lassalle and the men fighting for absolute monarchy, the revolutionist Lassalle and the out and out reactionaries." *Ferdinand Lassalle as a Social Reformer,* p. 106. As is evident from the revised (1919) edition of this book, he did not change his opinion.

Another point of contact between Lassalle and Bernstein lay in their ethical theories. Lassalleanism postulated the independence of ethics: the state had a *moral* task, the fourth estate an *ethical* mission, the Iron Law of Wages was *unjust*. In his departure from dialectical materialism and return to ethical Socialism, Bernstein followed a similar path: Socialism is *desirable,* the cause of the proletariat is *just.* Revisionism, like Lassalleanism, took Socialism from the realm of historical necessity, into which Marx had placed it, and posted it as a goal to be striven for as an act of will.

It is, of course, possible that Bernstein derived his stress on radical political democracy and the vitality of ethics from sources other than Lassalle. But his careful, critical reading of Lassalle's impassioned works doubtless left a significant residue, and through Bernstein Revisionism was to remain deeply in debt to the fiery creator of the first German workers' party. As Kampffmeyer has said in a flowery but accurate passage: "The ethical soul which Lassalle breathed into Socialism lives and moves and has its being in the Social Democratic movement. In this respect, Social Democracy is Lassallean." [20]

Eugen Dühring: A Passing Fancy

> *The sole and proud origin of property is force.*
> *It is born and preserved by force. In that it*
> *is august and yields only to a greater force....*
>
> ANATOLE FRANCE

Some authors achieve immortality through the painful process of being demolished by men greater than themselves. Only a few specialists would know the name of Sir Robert Filmer today, were it not for John Locke's dissection of his ideas in the first treatise *On Civil Government.* Similarly, Eugen Dühring would be a name familiar to but a handful of economic historians had Friedrich Engels not launched his famous refutation of Dühring's system, the *Anti-Dühring.*

[20] Paul Kampffmeyer, ed., *Friedrich Ebert, Schriften, Aufzeichnungen, Reden,* I, 45.

If we peruse Dühring's books today, we wonder how such a shallow, bombastic, and confused writer should ever have enjoyed such a degree of popularity in German Social Democracy that he almost eclipsed Marx and Engels. The puzzle—for it is a puzzle—can best be solved through a review of Dühring's life and work.

Eugen Dühring had begun his career as a jurist, but when he became blind at the age of thirty, he turned to the free professions and devoted himself to writing and teaching. From his first days as a *Privatdozent* he was embroiled in controversies with his colleagues at the University of Berlin, and his notoriety won him a wide circle of admirers. In the late 1860s and early 1870s he published a number of books on political economy and philosophy which took a radically Socialist tone.

But Dühring's Socialism, a most peculiar brand, was derived chiefly from the optimistic positivism of the American economist Henry Carey, whom Engels had once pithily described as "amusing . . . stupid and ignorant." [21] These are strong words, but they pall beside the systematic insult that Engels later offered Carey's disciple in the *Anti-Dühring*.

Dühring claimed to have evolved a closely integrated philosophy. He called his system, which is a strange mixture of positivism and idealism, the "natural system or the philosophy of reality. . . . It dispenses with artificial and unnatural fantasies and makes, for the first time, the concept of reality the measure of all ideal conceptions." [22]

Ethics, Dühring begins, must avoid the corroding disease of skepticism which inevitably issues in "mere nihilism." [23] "Morality can be derived from the will, which may be defined

[21] *Karl Marx-Friedrich Engels Gesamtausgabe*, Third Division, IV, 236. Dühring published several studies in defense of Carey: *Die Verkleinerer Careys und die Krisis der Nationalökonomie* and *Careys Umwälzung der Volkswirtschaftslehre und Sozialwissenschaft*.

[22] *Cursus der Philosophie*, p. 13. Cf. Hanni Binder, *Das sozialitäre System Eugen Dührings*. I have followed the general outlines of her exposition but obviously do not share her enthusiastic and uncritical acceptance of Dühring.

[23] *Cursus der Philosophie*, p. 194.

as desire created by the connection of drives, passions, and rational insight with necessity." [24] Two human wills are exactly equal, and the fundamental law of ethics follows from this fact: "To abstain from hurting each other; that is, to value the desires of others as equal to one's own, is the first basic principle of intersubjective morality." [25]

We may note, in criticism, that this fundamental principle is but a clumsy restatement of the Golden Rule and of Kant's categorical imperatives. Further, Dühring's emphasis on the free individual is based on little more than the assertion of his importance, and it is questionable whether we can establish immutable moral laws on nothing but the "relation of will to will." It serves, however, as an excellent bridge to the doctrine that underlies Dühring's philosophy of history and of politics—the force theory. No matter to what part of Dühring's system we turn, we shall always come back to his contention that present-day social relations are the result of compulsion used by the stronger against the weaker. Dühring proposed to prove this principle historically. Any genuine science of history, he said, must begin with the origin of the state, for at this point human relations emerge honestly and free from legal cant. Here we will find the dominant role of force in all its nakedness:

> In history we find that suppression and coercion predominate. . . . As soon as a single person is stronger than any one who might challenge him to battle, he will oppress the whole group as long as he can manage to deal with individuals rather than with an organization of several opponents who act according to plan. If he can prevent the formation of such an organization (which is not easy) he will retain supremacy. Now, in place of such a strong individual imagine a despotic, well armed power, or a robbing and ruling group of any kind which is able to force smaller and perhaps peaceful groups of people under its yoke— here you have the historical picture of the fundamental scheme of all politics of oppression.[26]

[24] *Ibid.*, p. 197.
[25] *Ibid.*, p. 200.
[26] *Ibid.*, p. 269.

As history begins with force, Dühring continues, so it develops through the ages. History up to the present is a history of oppression and slavery. To look for explanation in economic relations is an error, for economics is dependent upon politics where the relationship of oppressor to oppressed is most blatant.[27]

Dühring's force theory stands in dialectical relation to his ethical postulates. The former sees oppression and inequality throughout history, the latter preaches freedom and equality. It remains, therefore, to resolve the contradiction between the two; to reshape history until it conforms with ethics. The victory of the second over the first will come in what Dühring called the "socialitary system."

It clearly follows that if we wish to achieve this system in which "equal reciprocity" will prevail, we must eliminate all those social institutions that rest on compulsion. Above all, the "force state" must go. But Dühring does not follow the lead of the anarchists all the way: he insists that a new kind of state will arise which will serve a free and individualistic society. The new state will not be based on the fear of violence, but on firmer soil: voluntary submission. The power of the governors is but a provisional grant which may be withdrawn as soon as "natural justice" is not observed.[28]

If the analyst searches for empirical or logical proofs for these contentions of Dühring he will be disappointed. Dühring claims that his "deeply rooted political economy" is the result of the "insight" that "the natural laws of politics and of right and wrong" are primary.[29] Apart from that we have his distinction of relations based on force (which are bad) and those based on "reciprocal equality" (which are good). And we must content ourselves with his assertion that he is really a most original thinker.

[27] Cf. *Cursus der National- und Sozialökonomie*, pp. 1–6. Dühring considered his force theory a vital step forward in social philosophy. For a criticism of it as a category of explanation, cf. Friedrich Engels, *Herr Eugen Dühring's Revolution in Science [Anti-Dühring]*, pp. 180–210, and R. M. MacIver, *The Web of Government*, pp. 12–16.

[28] *Cursus der Philosophie*, p. 265.

[29] *Cursus der National- und Sozialökonomie*, pp. 507–8.

Dühring's economics rests upon the force theory as well. He begins with an analysis of property which is almost identical with Proudhon's. Property may be acquired either through violence or through labor, but the former is far more frequent and far more significant. [30] While the propertied classes rationalize their wealth by claiming that it originated in labor, this is so rarely true that "possessions arising out of labor may be described as exceptional. Of course, accumulations of wealth do emerge from labor—not from the labor of the rich and their ancestors, but from the labor of the oppressed classes." [31] Such accumulations give power, and the poverty of the worker condemns him to dependence and political impotence.

On the other hand, Dühring continues, property based on labor, although rare enough in present-day society, will be the only justification for property in the socialitary system. [32] For Dühring, as earlier for Locke, private property based on work was essential to man's social realization. [33]

His other economic categories are equally dependent on the force theory: value is not equal to price in present-day society, for price is a social relation set on the basis of relative power of producer and consumer and not of worth of the product. Only in the socialitary system will value be the "cause" of price. [34] Again, ground rent depends largely on the social relations of domination of, say, the small farmer by the great landowner, and house rent may be regarded as

[30] *Ibid.*, p. 193: "Historically, property is for the most part derived from an earlier use of force."
[31] *Ibid.*, p. 195.
[32] *Ibid.*, pp. 257–58. This point of view gave Dühring a lever for criticism of Marxism which, he claimed at one point, converted one form of injustice into another by abolishing private property altogether. But elsewhere (*Kritische Geschichte der Nationalökonomie und des Sozialismus*, p. 515), he admitted that Marx did not want to destroy private property but to "expropriate the expropriators." He got out of this difficulty by ridiculing Marx's thesis as "stealing from other thieves."
[33] His distinction between "good" and "bad" property is, of course, analogous to his earlier distinction between the "good" and the "bad" state.
[34] *Cursus der National- und Sozialökonomie*, p. 21.

a form of "taxation upon the home-seeking public." [35] The same is true of wages: "Wage-labor is . . . a stage of . . . slavery and vassalage," [36] and as long as the wage system continues the size of wages will be inversely proportional to the workers' dependence on the capitalist.[37]

Dühring made it clear that the socialitary system would not tolerate such inequities. It would abolish wage labor, secure to the worker as large a share of value created as possible, and keep rents low, for, Dühring claimed, "the share that goes to ground rent is lost to wages and *vice versa.*" [38]

All this sounded radical enough. Dühring's proposed political tactics, although often contradictory and unclear, strengthened this impression of radicalism. Most important of his tactical suggestions was his advocacy of political trade unions. True, Dühring was an individualist: "Individuals are more than mere atoms in a social or political body; they are the sovereign representatives of all society. . . . Socialization does not exclude individualization but includes it." [39] But the single worker was weak and needed coalitions. Their chief weapon was the strike, their immediate objective, the negotiation of favorable contracts. But trade unions must become political: "One should note that these coalitions, formed to solve the question of wages, must do more than play a negative role. They must grow into a kind of parliamentary limitation on economic and social [exploitation]." [40]

This, in outline, is Dühring's system. Even this sketch reveals the disorder of his thought. It derived from the most disparate sources: he followed the bourgeois liberals with his

[35] *Ibid.,* p. 175.
[36] *Ibid.,* p. 196.
[37] *Loc. cit.* Binder, *Das sozialitäre System Eugen Dührings,* p. 31.
[38] *Cursus der National- und Sozialökonomie,* p. 199.
[39] *Ibid.,* p. 4.
[40] *Capital und Arbeit,* p. 223. This doctrine of direct working-class action came dangerously close to the theories of the men he called "the Jew Lassal," "the Jew Marx." It did not prevent him from being a strong proponent of free competition. In the socialitary system, *laissez faire* would contribute to the establishment of true equality. *Cursus der National- und Sozialökonomie,* pp. 354–56.

"natural laws" of political economy; he based his social contract and his views on property on early individualists such
as Locke; he derived his "socialitary system" largely from
the anarchists and his all-important force theory from such
Utopians as Saint-Simon. In economics he learned most from
Carey (who was not a Socialist) and from Rodbertus (who
was).

This is not to assert that original thought has no ancestry
and springs full-blown from the brow of the genius—that
would be to deny the very possibility of originality. But, for
the most part, originality consists of a fruitful synthesis of
older ideas; it provides a new focus through which familiar
facts appear in sharper, more significant outline. But that is
not what Dühring did with the writings from which he bor-
rowed so freely.

Combined with his mediocrity was the most inflated estimate of his own importance, which in his later years bordered
on megalomania. Dühring liberally despised his fellow economists and sprinkled his writings with an ugly anti-Semitism.
His Socialism, he said, was "German" and was designed to
counteract "Jewish Social Democracy." [41]

Still, Dühring was, for a while, a danger to the unity of
German Social Democracy, and we can now guess why. First
of all, German Social Democracy of the 1870s was intellec-
tually immature and poorly equipped to distinguish between
conflicting claims to greatness. None of the leaders of German Social Democracy was trained in political economy, and
Bernstein himself was just beginning his Socialist education
in these years. Secondly, it should be remembered that Düh-
ing was blind, and constantly involved in fights with his
superiors. The natural pity that the young Socialists felt for
his affliction was easily transformed into admiration for what
was regarded as his courage. Compared to most of the other
professors in Berlin, he was an extreme radical, with his
championing of labor organizations and his opposition to the

[41] Examples of his anti-Semitism and megalomania are abundant
in the works cited before, as well as in several specifically anti-
Semitic works. Engels has collected a whole bouquet of his in-
vective, *Anti-Dühring*, pp. 37–39.

wage system. As Marx once said about John Stuart Mill, Dühring's eminence was due to the flatness of the surrounding landscape. When, in June of 1877, Dühring was driven from the University of Berlin by the higher authorities, the Social Democrats came to his defense. While he was removed from his post as *Privatdozent* for his personal attacks on his colleagues, Berlin Socialists saw in the move an attack on Dühring's Socialist views and a curb on free teaching. Student demonstrations, instigated by the Socialists, clamored for his retention, but all in vain.[42]

But Dürhing would not have exerted such a strong influence on Social Democracy during the 1870s if it had not been for the assiduous discipleship of Eduard Bernstein and his friends. Bernstein had felt, as he was to admit freely in later years, that the death of Lassalle had left a theoretical vacuum which had to be filled. Lassalleanism seemed to be receding, Marxism was not yet understood. Therefore, when Dühring's *Cursus der National- und Sozialökonomie* appeared in 1872, Bernstein seized upon it eagerly.[43] He sent copies to his associates Bracke, Fritzsche, and Most, and when he visited Bebel in the Hubertusburg prison in the summer of 1873, he thoughtfully took the *Cursus* with him to present it to Bebel.[44]

In the light of later developments it is ironic to see how delighted Bebel was with the Dühring volume. He even published an extravagant review of it in the *Volksstaat*, hailing the author as a "New Communist" and calling the *Cursus* the best book on economics in recent times since *Capital*.[45] This general attitude pervaded German Social Democracy in spite of Dühring's unmeasured attacks on Marx and Engels. As late as 1876 Bracke could comment naively: "What I have found out about Dühring strengthens my opinion that he is a bit

[42] Dühring's autobiography shows how little he appreciated the intervention in his behalf of the "two-faced Jewish Social Democracy." *Sache, Leben und Feinde,* pp. 179–211.
[43] Gustav Mayer, *Friedrich Engels,* II, 281–82.
[44] Bernstein, "Entwicklungsgang eines Sozialisten," in *Die Volkswirtschaftslehre der Gegenwart in Selbstdarstellungen,* I, 10.
[45] Mayer, *Engels,* II, 283.

confused but thoroughly honest and definitely on our side." [46]

After some backing and filling, Liebknecht made up his mind that the Dühring vogue was a threat to German Social Democracy, and he urged Marx and Engels to start a counter-offensive. The Londoners had already had sufficient cause for alarm, but when in May 1876 Liebknecht sent them a manuscript glorifying Dühring which Most had submitted to the *Vorwärts*, they knew that further delay would be dangerous. Marx was busy on Volume II of *Capital*, Engels had turned to philosophical studies and was reluctant to enter a controversy with a blind man. But it must be done, and the resulting *Anti-Dühring* appeared in the *Vorwärts* from January 1877 to July 1878, and soon afterwards in book form.

There were difficulties. Most and other Dühring enthusiasts protested; Engels found himself maligned at the party congress of 1877; even Bebel thought the series too long for a newspaper. Only Liebknecht defended Engels without equivocation. Once the work had come off the press its true character emerged, and the book that Engels had written so unwillingly grew into a Socialist classic. It destroyed the Dühring boom forever.

During the period of his infatuation, Bernstein had gone to visit Dühring. The blind academician had been pleased with his young admirer and asked him to return frequently.

[46] Quoted in *loc. cit.* "The biting criticism," Bernstein wrote, "which Dühring practiced in his writings against the Socialism of Marx and Lassalle, did not detract from the admiration which we had for him. The theoretical differences between him and the author of *Capital* appeared to us as insignificant compared with the fact that a learned man (*Mann der Wissenschaft*) spoke in favor of Socialism with great decisiveness and fought for it in language and style which read considerably more easily than Marx's works." "Entwicklungsgang," p. 10. Bebel, in preparing his laudatory review of Dühring's *Cursus*, flamboyantly wrote to Bernstein: "I don't give a damn about the method (*ich pfeife auf die Methode*) if the cause is good." *Loc. cit.* Even Wilhelm Liebknecht, who was generally accepted at that time as the "official interpreter of Marx's theory, never really specified" the differences between Marx and Dühring. *Ibid.,* p. 11. The reason for Liebknecht's vagueness, we may suspect, was his uncertainty of the real meaning of Marxism. There seems to be less excuse for Bebel.

But Bernstein soon learned to distrust the combative *Privat-dozent*; he was shocked to discover in Dühring a contempt for all who disagreed with him which was unpleasantly combined with his anti-Semitism, and a fundamental viciousness which no bodily infirmity could excuse. Bernstein never paid a second visit.

This disturbing Dühring episode left practically no residue. It created Engel's *Anti-Dühring* which, as we have already noted, brought Bernstein into the Marxist fold. But that is all that remained; the "socialitary system" did not influence Revisionism to any noticeable extent.[47] Whatever parallels we can discover between Dühring and Bernstein are indications only of similarity; there is no evidence that Revisionism learned anything of importance from the self-styled "German Socialist." Dühring's impact on German Social Democracy was keen, but it was also short-lived; it had no more lasting effect than a passing fancy has on the personality of a young man.

[47] True, some phraseology of Dühring's is reproduced in Revisionism, but that is due not to any specific Dühring influence but to the general climate of opinion at the end of the nineteenth century. Writing of his pre-Marxist views, Bernstein said that he had not appreciated Dühring as a personality but as a "Socialist who had, in my opinion, supplemented (we might say, continued) Marx in more radical fashion than anyone else. Call it eclecticism or what you will, but I felt that the Socialist movement was comprehensive enough to contain a Marx and a Dühring at the same time. . . . What pleased me most about Dühring was his strong emphasis on the liberal element in Socialism. . . ." "Entwicklungsgang," p. 7. But Bernstein was to read many more convincing liberals before he turned Revisionist. Erika Rikli, who has studied Revisionism carefully, states that "Bernstein belongs to those German Socialists who stood under Dühring's influence in their youth." *Der Revisionismus*, p. 15. This is unquestionably correct, but her later statement that "Bernstein came to Socialism through Dühring" (*ibid., p.* 26) must be qualified. She is on safer ground when she includes Dühring among "social-reformist Socialists" who "wanted to achieve a fundamental transformation of property by step-by-step measures." *Ibid.*, p. 122. There are two reasons for the inclusion of the analysis of Dühring here: 1. He was a great, if evanescent, force in German Social Democracy in the 1870s. 2. It seemed essential to demonstrate that the theory of Bernstein's indebtedness to Dühring, although plausible, is false.

The Fabians: The Method of Gradualism

The workers of Germany have always looked to the English working class for example and inspiration, and we hope that our teachers are now satisfied with their pupils.

HERMANN MOLKENBUHR, SECRE-
TARY OF THE SPD, IN 1912

Even a superficial observer will recognize the fact that Fabianism and German Revisionism are brothers, if not twins. Since the two doctrines originated in the same country only a few years apart from each other, it has been taken as axiomatic that Eduard Bernstein got his fundamental ideas from the Fabians. The truth of this account needs to be further examined.

It is difficult to resist the temptation of describing the Fabian Society as typical of the British spirit of compromise and moderation. In the nineteenth century, freedom was "broadening down from precedent to precedent"; the victory of the upper middle class had been assured in the Glorious Revolution of 1688; the triumph of industrial wealth over landed property had climaxed in the repeal of the Corn Laws in 1846; the ruling oligarchy was widening its base with the Reform Acts of 1832 and 1867. Fabianism fits into this pleasant picture: almost from the very beginning, it espoused a moderate, nondoctrinaire kind of Socialism which sturdily rejected such Marxian blandishments as the inevitability of the class struggle and necessity for revolution.

While it is true that Fabianism represents this prominent aspect of British development, the England of the nineteenth century also experienced the stirrings of violence and deep undercurrents of discontent. These feelings first found expression in the physical-force Chartists, who came close to putting their theories to the test of action, and crystallized in the 1880s in Hyndman's revolutionary Social Democratic Federation, which derived its doctrines from Marx (although without acknowledgment).

The Fabian Society did not take the country by storm, no matter how much in line it might be with the "British way of doing things." Quite to the contrary, the Fabians gained adherents slowly and, in general, recruited members not from the proletariat but the radical, well-educated bourgeoisie. If, in the final outcome, it was the reformist Fabians rather than the revolutionary SDF that made policy for the British Labor Party, this was due as much to specific circumstances which stimulated Fabianism as to the British tradition. It should be stressed that the slow growth of Britain's political labor movement (as reflected in the small size of the Fabians and the SDF before the turn of the century) was primarily a consequence of the defeat of the Chartist movement. After 1848, the leaders of the working class turned to trade unionism and cooperation, and several decades elapsed before labor entered the political arena once more.[48]

The Society was born in 1884, an offshoot of the London branch of an ethical society called The Fellowship of the New Life. At first, its thinking was confused, and for a year or so well-meaning anarchists swamped the membership. Like Henry James's heroine in *The Princess Casamassima*, they hinted darkly at the coming smash-up. "In 1884," Shaw reminisced, "we were discussing whether money should be permitted under Socialism." [49]

But a severely practical and vigorously reformist Socialism soon replaced such Utopian speculations. It was introduced by a few outstanding intellectuals, the "Fabian Old Gang," who joined the Society within a few years of its founding— Bernard Shaw, Sidney Webb, Sidney Olivier, Graham Wallas, and others. These men, diverse as their interests were, soon evolved a united policy based on a multitude of intellectual sources. Chief among these was the utilitarian, liberal tradition of Bentham and John Stuart Mill.[50]

[48] Cf. Max Beer, *A History of British Socialism*, II, 172–74, 200–201.
[49] Bernard Shaw, *The Fabian Society, What it Has Done and How it Has Done it*, p. 3.
[50] Cf. Edward Pease, *The History of the Fabian Society*, Chapter I. He lists as the main influences: ethical and Christian Socialism, Darwin, Henry George, positivism, Jevons' neoclassical economics, and, of course, Bentham and J. S. Mill.

The similarity of Fabianism to the earlier Philosophical Radicals has often been remarked upon, and Fabians unhesitatingly admitted their deep indebtedness to Bentham. But this influence must not be overrated, and Sidney Webb's remark of 1894, "The Socialists are the Benthamites of this generation," has been taken far too literally.[51] The Benthamites believed in the malleability of man's nature and the betterment of his fate through the reform of social institutions. So did the Fabians. But the Benthamites wanted to leave the basis of property relations undisturbed: the enlightened self-interest of capitalists would necessarily result in social improvements. Here, the Fabians disagreed sharply: their chief aim was to recast property relations, and they grew more and more deeply distrustful of the possibilities of cooperating with the capitalists.

However, in the first decade of its activity (and this is, after all, the period crucial for our investigation) the Fabian Society was willing to make common cause with anyone, aristocrat or worker, capitalist or intellectual, who appeared willing to forward its aims. This policy rendered the Society suspect to many left-wingers who regarded Fabians as bourgeois opportunists. Fabian Socialism, wrote Engels scornfully, is

represented as an extreme but inevitable consequence of bourgeois liberalism, and hence follow [the Society's] tactics of not decisively opposing the Liberals as adversaries but of pushing them on towards Socialist conclusions and therefore of intriguing with them, permeating liberalism with Socialism. . . . As soon as they get on to their specific tactics of hushing up the class struggle it all turns putrid.[52]

Permeation, then, was a refined kind of lobbying, which might consist of a dinner given by the Webbs for several carefully selected non-Socialists. Once the guests were at the

[51] Webb's remark is in *Socialism, True and False*, p. 6. Max Beer seems to have exaggerated Bentham's influence. Cf. Beer, *History of British Socialism*, II, 276 ff.
[52] V. Adoratsky, ed., *Selected Correspondence, Karl Marx and Frederick Engels*, pp. 505–6.

table and thus defenseless, the formidable Webbs, "two type-writers that clicked as one," would begin to talk of whatever social reform they had in mind and keep up the good work of persuasion through the evening. This method which, as many Fabians admitted, had its flaws, was later replaced by advocacy of an independent labor party, but it was characteristic of the Fabian view of life. Socialists, the Fabians reasoned, were but the extreme of a continuum; they spoke the same language as the bourgeois reformists and there was no reason why Socialism could not be brought about by persuasion. It is in this relating of Socialism to reformism rather than in other matters that the influence of Fabianism on Bernstein must be sought.

At the beginning of his London years, Eduard Bernstein did not feel any sense of rapport with the Fabians. As he wrote in his reminiscences:

> The majority of the Fabians belonged, either by birth or by position, to the middle classes, and as they were accustomed to criticize the Socialist doctrines of Marx (as then preached by Hyndman, Aveling and others) in a somewhat condescending tone, they were in bad repute with many representatives of proletarian Socialism as parlor Socialists who thought of themselves as "superior persons." For a long time I had a prejudice against the Fabians, and therefore refrained from establishing personal relations with them.[53]

This prejudice gradually disappeared. Bernstein made friends with many of the leading Fabians and greatly enjoyed arguing tactics with them over dinner.[54]

It is this closeness to the Fabians that has led observers to attribute Bernstein's Revisionism to his Fabian contacts. Max Beer, Bernstein's successor as London correspondent of the *Vorwärts*, refers flatly to "writers like Eduard Bernstein, who during their sojourn in London imbibed Fabianism and

[53] Bernstein, *Aus den Jahren meines Exils*, pp. 244–45.
[54] He met Shaw, but their relationship was never more than a polite one. *Ibid.*, p. 245.

spread it in Germany." [55] Even more certain of his case is Edward Pease, the historian of the Fabian Society and a close friend of Bernstein's for many years:

> The revolt [against Marxism] came from England in the person of Eduard Bernstein, who, exiled by Bismarck, took refuge in London and was for years intimately acquainted with the Fabian Society and its leaders. . . .In England, and in Germany through Bernstein, I think the Fabian Society may claim to have led this revolt. [56]

This view, examples of which could easily be multiplied, was repeatedly disputed by Bernstein himself, and his disclaimer has a convincing sound: [57] he started from a tradition

[55] *Fifty Years of International Socialism*, p. 183.
[56] Pease, *History of the Fabian Society*, p. 239.
[57] He writes ("Entwicklungsgang," pp. 22–23): "My stay in England naturally gave me an opportunity to establish connections with English Socialists and to gain closer acquaintance with the English trade union movement. That was useful to me since it enabled me to examine my (so far second-hand) impressions of the English popular mind and of the spirit of its labor movement, and, if necessary, to correct my ideas. But [my acquaintances were] of small influence on my Socialist thought. . . . The opinion which has gained wide currency that I was converted to my Revisionism by the model of English Fabianism is wholly erroneous. Upon close acquaintance, I learned to value the Fabian Society and its outstanding leaders, but I was never ignorant of the fact that the special form of the agitation was so closely fitted to English conditions that any attempt to imitate it on the continent would necessarily be doomed to failure. That does not mean that I did not learn anything from the Fabians. The work of the Webbs on the cooperatives and the trade-union movement as well as the problem of the poor laws widened my horizon. Equally valuable were a number of anonymous tracts published by the Society on questions of economic and social conditions in their various ramifications. But these publications had little to do with the specific questions raised by Revisionism. Even the criticism of Marx's theory of value by leading Fabians impressed me only at a time when I had myself arrived at the opinion that it meant something different from what I had thought earlier. And this impression was not strong enough to induce me to abandon Marx's theory in its entirety and to replace it by the doctrine propagated by the Fabians."

different from that of the Fabians, he modified his Marxist opinions after he had fought specific controversies and lived through specific events.

On the other hand, his denial that he learned a great deal from the Fabians, and from the English in general, will not stand up. When, during the 1898 controversy, Bebel accused him of applying English conditions to Germany, Bernstein disagreed: "I haven't become *that* English. . . ." [58] But surely Bernstein underestimated the impact of his dozen years of residence in Britain. His English experience strengthened opinions at which he was arriving on his own, and the Fabian philosophy, a typical example of the reformist spirit, was a major influence that acted on him during his English years.

[58] Bernstein to Bebel, October 20, 1898, Bernstein Archives.

Chapter 5

If There Had Been
No Bernstein . . .

The Mass Party

> *The roster of members of the Italian Com-
> munist Party had reached 2,300,000, their
> leader, Palmiro Togliatti, recently reported.
> Irritable comment of a veteran party function-
> ary: "Too few to vote ourselves into power
> legally; too many to start a revolution."*
>
> NEW YORK TIMES
> FEBRUARY 5, 1950

IF THERE HAD BEEN no Bernstein, it would have been necessary to invent him. Political and economic conditions in Germany demanded a reformist doctrine around the turn of the
century. When Revisionism appeared upon the scene, it
represented no startling novelty but the rational recognition
of an already existing state of affairs. The immediate popularity of Revisionism, then, was due to the fact that it offered
German Socialists an alternative to Marxism, a rival concep-
tual scheme that, like Marxism, attempted to account for all
social facts with a coherent system.[1]

Conversely, the circumstances which called for a theory
such as Revisionism were the very factors that impelled Bernstein to modify his philosophy. He realized this well. "The
decisive influences on my Socialist thinking," he once observed, "were not doctrinal criticisms but facts which compelled me to correct my premises." [2]

The German Social Democratic Party, then, was already a
reformist organization at the time when Bernstein published
his *Voraussetzungen*.

[1] Cf. Carl Schorske, "German Social Democracy, 1905–1917,"
passim.
[2] "Entwicklungsgang eines Sozialisten," in *Die Volkswirtschaftslehre der Gegenwart in Selbstdarstellungen*, I, 23.

The year 1890 saw both the lapse of the anti-Socialist law and the end of Bismarck's chancellorship. The newly legalized Social Democratic Party responded to these favorable developments by multiplying its membership. When Bernstein flung down his challenge to orthodox Marxism less than a decade later, his party had become a democratic mass party and one of the leading political organizations in Germany.

A "democratic mass party" may be defined as an organization which accepts as members all those who subscribe to its program and which maintains the principle of responsibility of the leaders to the rank and file. Its opposite numbers are conspiratorial and Fascist parties; its structure entails some serious problems. A mass party may begin with a pure purpose (it need not, as the Nazis have shown); its theoretical conception may, as it were, be immaculate, but this purity must soon give way. In the political struggle the final aim is obscured, and compromises become more acceptable. The goal is still emblazoned upon the party standard, but what matters now is the growth of membership, victory at the polls, the "capture" of the state. That comes first, for once the state is in their hands, the leaders argue, party platform will become political reality.

This, as a general rule, is the fate of the democratic mass party. If it happens to be committed to a revolutionary doctrine, too bad for the doctrine. Once parliamentary activity becomes enjoyable and habitual, theoretical orthodoxy is subordinated to vote-getting: the road to opportunism is paved with parliamentary successes.

German Social Democracy had begun with dark suspicions of parliamentary participation. In 1870, Liebknecht had told the Eisenach party congress: "The Reichstag does not make history, it merely plays a comedy." [3] And he sponsored a resolution with Bebel which declared: "The Sozialdemokratische Arbeiterpartei participates in the Reichstag elections . . . purely for purposes of agitation. . . . It will enter into no alliances or compromises with other parties." [4]

[3] Wilhelm Schröder, ed., *Handbuch der sozialdemokratischen Parteitage*, p. 386.
[4] *Ibid.*, p. 387. Marx was willing to see a Socialist party operate legally to meet the bourgeoisie on its own ground, but he insisted

The end of the anti-Socialist law brought an impressive increase in the Socialist vote, and parliamentarism gained new support. While, in 1891, the party redrew its program along Marxist lines, it was by then firmly committed to parliamentary activity. Radicals such as Rosa Luxemburg deplored this growth into legalism and warned the party against sinking into the parliamentary swamp. They urged the expulsion of the Revisionists as "parliamentary opportunists." Revisionists, on the other hand, demanded that the party drop its revolutionary slogans and set up a program that would proclaim the truth: that the party had become a "democratic Socialist reform party." [5] The leadership, however, felt unable to follow either of these clear-cut policies. It was unwilling to lose the right wing, which was openly reformist, or to alienate the left, which was devoted to revolutionary incantations. It took all the diplomatic skill that Bebel possessed to keep all groups relatively satisfied. Eventually, this failure of the party leaders to be scrupulously honest had tragic consequences.[6]

There are two reasons why democratic mass parties tend to slough off any revolutionary vigor they may have possessed. Not that a large party necessarily loses "class purity." As the sequel will show, German Social Democracy remained surprisingly proletarian. But, in the first place, considerable segments of the proletarian party members are indifferent or even hostile to revolution. This hostility has a variety of

that it remain doctrinally pure. (Cf. Isaiah Berlin, *Karl Marx*, pp. 172–76.) During the lifespan of the anti-Socialist law, the attitude of the party towards parliamentarism began to change. Cf. the resolution passed at the 1887 St. Gall congress: "The party congress is of the opinion that the position of the party towards parliamentary activity of its members in the Reichstag and in the Landtagen must remain unchanged; as before, the main emphasis must be put on the side of criticism and agitation. Positive legislative activity must be cultivated only on the assumption that . . . it create no illusions." Schröder, *Handbuch*, p. 389.
[5] This is, of course, Bernstein's famous formulation. *Die Voraussetzungen des Sozialismus und die Aufgaben der Sozialdemokratie*, p. 230.
[6] Cf. Robert Michels, "Psychologie der anti-kapitalistichen Massenbewegungen," in *Grundriss der Sozialökonomik*, Vol. IX, Part I, pp. 241–359, esp. pp. 315–28.

causes: fear, complacency, devotion to authority and legality. And secondly, a mass party must think of more than its formal membership. It has followers who endorse its program and vote for its candidates but do not belong to it. This imposes upon the party the need for flexibility designed to attract ever larger numbers of votes. Once a Socialist party enters into the vote-catching game, that magic figure, 51 percent, tends to obscure other considerations.[7]

The organizational structure of German Social Democracy, although it was frequently altered, always tended to encourage the mass-party tendencies described above.

Lassalle's Allgemeiner Deutscher Arbeiterverein had been organized strictly autocratically. The president could, under many circumstances, act independently, handpick his subordinates to run branches of the party in various localities, and help to control the admission of new members. While Lassalle's immediate successors did not run the Verein on harshly authoritarian lines, this was due not to any disinclination on their part but to sheer incapacity. When von Schweitzer gathered the threads into his strong hands in 1867, the cry "dictator" was soon heard—and with much justice.[8]

On the other hand, the rival Eisenacher Sozialdemokratische Arbeiterpartei was organized in far more democratic fashion. The party *Ausschuss,* elected by the members at

[7] It will be obvious that Lenin's experience is no refutation. The Bolsheviks had no parliamentary institutions or traditions, and all mechanisms for the accomplishment of peaceful social change were absent. Lenin realized that a genuine mass party was not possible in autocratic Russia, and that is the justification he gave for his concept of the élite party. He knew, too, that Russia and Germany demanded different sorts of Socialist parties. Cf. *What Is To Be Done?* pp. 24, 113–14, 128. His one attempt to prove the close relation between the Russian Bolsheviks and German Social Democrats is strikingly unsuccessful. All Lenin managed to show was that German Social Democracy showed certain oligarchic tendencies. No top official of the Social Democratic Party ever dreamed of acting like Lenin's trained revolutionary!
[8] Cf. Wilhelm Schröder, *Geschichte der sozialdemokratischen Parteiorganisation in Deutschland,* pp. 10–13. For the basic administrative statute, *ibid.,* pp. 62–63.

large, was responsible for its actions to the party congress. In addition, the party selected a control commission which was to act as a watchdog committee to supervise financial disbursements and other activities of the *Ausschuss*.[9] Still another check on possible autocratic tendencies of the party leadership was the provision that important decisions of the party congress (altering the statute or the basic political line of the party) would have to be submitted to the membership at large for a referendum.[10]

When the two groups merged at Gotha in 1875, it was the spirit of the Eisenachers that prevailed in the organizational arrangements, although the democratic spirit was fortified with a strong dash of Lassallean discipline.[11] The party was to be run by a *Vorstand* elected by the party congress by simple majority. This *Vorstand* had considerable powers including the right of expulsion of those party members "acting against the interests of the party," but its freedom of action was strictly circumscribed by a control commission, which heard complaints, and by an eighteen-man body, called the *Ausschuss,* which adjusted serious differences between the *Vorstand* and the control commission.[12] It was this *Ausschuss* of which the young Bernstein became a member in 1875.

The merits of this scheme, which certainly discouraged arbitrary action by the party leadership, could not be tested. In the year following its establishment the party was "provisionally" outlawed in Prussia, and its members had to meet as like-minded individuals rather than as members of a political party. Two years later, when the Reichstag passed the anti-Socialist law, even this subterfuge could no longer be

[9] This control commission could also hear complaints from the membership and even suspend members of the *Ausschuss*.

[10] A simple majority of those voting was binding on the party. *Ibid.*, pp. 14–16. For the organization statute of 1869, see Schröder, *Geschichte,* pp. 66–69. "The whole organization of the party," says Schröder (*ibid.,* p. 18), "was not especially designed to further formal discipline."

[11] Schröder, *ibid.*, pp. 22–23, does not agree with this judgment. To him, the organization was largely Lassellean in nature.

[12] *Ibid.*, pp. 22–27. For the organization statute of 1875, see *ibid.*, pp. 69–73.

used. For twelve years, German Social Democracy had to resort to secret congresses and to organizational devices that were all but standard. Since official party activity was illegal, there was much decentralization of power, and the nature of local Social Democratic bodies depended solely on individual party leaders. While the rank and file had little formal control over its nine members representing German Social Democracy in the Reichstag, the party did manage to make its wishes known to them. Eduard Bernstein's *Sozialdemokrat,* which was regularly smuggled into Germany, played a major role in this connection and served as the unofficial conscience of the party.

But these were war conditions, and do not give a fair picture of the organizational intentions of German Social Democracy. That picture can be gleaned from an examination of the organization statute adopted by the party at their first legal congress in Halle in 1890.[13]

In that year, Germany was still plagued with statutory limitations on freedom of association, and the delegates assembled at Halle had to step warily. A draft statute submitted by the parliamentary delegation was rejected; it had proposed a concentration of power in the hands of the Reichstag members. In the draft which was finally accepted, central direction of party affairs was left to a twelve-man *Partei-Leitung,* chosen by the delegates at the annual party congress. These congresses were regarded as supreme in the sense that the House of Commons is supreme in the British constitution—hedged in by custom, self-interest, fear, and idealism, the congress made the final decisions. As representative of the whole party it elected the *Partei-Leitung,* received reports on the activities of the party leadership and parliamentary delegation, and decided on "party organization and all questions touching the life of the party." The congress, in other words,

[13] The party now changed its name to Sozialdemokratische Partei Deutschlands (SPD). The initials will be used interchangeably with this party name throughout the rest of the book.

There was a reorganization at Mainz in 1900, as well as several later changes made possible by greater freedom of association. They did not affect the basic character of the party. In any case, the changes made after 1900 do not concern us in this chapter.

made policy and supervised its execution.[14] While, in actuality, the party leadership had greater power than the statute would indicate, its democratic features were nevertheless significant. Up to 1905, the organization chart of the SPD gave a fairly accurate description of the actual functioning of the party.[15] The problem of the party bureaucracy as a conservative force—*Bonzentum*—did not arise to any serious degree until then.[16] After that, however, administrative and bureaucratic elements, which acted as a prop for Revisionism simply by their antirevolutionary bias, took the upper hand in party affairs. In other words, *Bonzentum* helped to keep Revisionism alive, but did not bring it into being. We may conclude, then, that the formal organization of the SPD was conducive to the formation and continuation of a mass party that needed something like the Revisionist philosophy as its raison d'être. Let us now turn to its social composition.

At the outset of our analysis we must make a careful distinction between two groups which, taken together, may be

[14] During the meetings, the *Partei-Leitung* as well as the Reichstag delegation had only an advisory voice. Of course, most of the policy speeches were given by members of the party leadership, but the rank and file delegations did have ample opportunity to be heard. The insistence of the statute on annual congresses recalls the English saying, "Where annual parliaments end, tyranny begins."

[15] The 1890 statute defined membership as follows: "Every person will be considered a member who embraces the basic principles of the party program and who supports the party to the best of his ability." In cases of doubt, the local party organizations had to make the decision. While this provision left much leeway to the local party, the provisions actually served to encourage persons of widely different persuasions to join the party. In other words, the phrase "who embraces the basic principles of the party program" was interpreted widely. Ten years later, the statute was rewritten, specifying obligations of membership more definitely. A member was now required to "embrace the basic principles of the party program" and "to support the party financially." See Schröder, *Geschichte*, pp. 76–80, for the 1900 statute. This insistence on financial aid was largely symbolic since many members could not pay anything, and since the party had outside income, such as the surplus from the *Vorwärts*.

[16] Cf. Schorske, "German Social Democracy."

called German Social Democracy: party members and non-members who, for one reason or another, vote the party ticket.[17] The relation between the two is difficult to assess, and often it depended entirely on local conditions.[18] A percentage of fifteen organized members for each hundred Social Democrats may be a roughly accurate estimate. Small though it may appear, it shows a higher degree of organization than German bourgeois parties could muster.[19]

Nonmember Socialist voters have been regarded as mere camp followers, but such a conception cannot hold true for long. Votes of nonmembers count as much as those of members and are indistinguishable from them. Their very uncertainty gives them a significance out of all proportion to their number.

While the composition of unorganized Social Democracy escapes exact appraisal, we may assume from all the evidence

[17] This distinction does not make the task of analysis any easier, but it must be maintained. Further, the party itself did not keep any exact membership statistics from 1875, when it had 25,659 members, to 1906, when it had grown to 384,327. Robert Michels, "Die deutsche Sozialdemokratie, Partei-Mitgliedschaft und soziale Zusammensetzung," *Archiv für Sozialwissenschaft und Sozialpolitik,* new ser., V (1906), 476. This article, a most careful analysis, has been heavily relied on in this section.

[18] Michels does point out, *ibid.,* p. 485: "The more rural the election district, the more unfavorable, as a rule, the relation." But in cities there was no uniform pattern. Take a few selected figures, based on the Reichstag elections of 1903:

	SPD Votes	SPD Members	Percentage of SPD Members to Voters
Fürth	6,500	3,200	49.1
Nürnberg	28,812	6,695	23.2
Breslau	32,348	3,998	12.4
Berlin and environs	330,456	36,513	11.0
Frankfurt (Main)	20,178	1,446	7.2

Taken from *ibid.,* p. 482.

[19] *Ibid.,* p. 486.

that it chiefly consisted of trade union members, elements in the petty bourgeoisie, and a few scattered intellectuals.[20]

The role of this unorganized group is difficult to assess. On the one hand, it strengthened the already pronounced anti-revolutionary sentiments of the party. Its members, on the whole, lacked political initiative, but it was more than a plastic mass that could be kneaded into any convenient shape. Its very weight of numbers, its inertia, and its instability directed the party toward parliamentarism and compromise. On the other hand, this very group played a strongly revolutionary part in the events of October and November 1918.

While this part of Social Democracy was of mixed social origin and generally antirevolutionary, the same was not true of party members. When we discuss the social composition of the party, we must distinguish between class origin and class position attained as a result of party activity.

The class origin of nearly all Social Democratic Party members was proletarian. All available evidence shows that the SPD membership remained surprisingly "pure" through the years. Figure after figure demonstrates this fact.[21]

Enemies of Social Democracy liked to picture it as "overrun" by "undesirable" Jews, *Lumpenproletariat*, *fils de fa-*

[20] Michels and Haenisch have shown that German trade unionists were, on the whole, reluctant to join Social Democratic clubs. Two statistics will illustrate this point: among the book printers in Frankfurt am Main, in 1905, there were 66 party members to 1,083 trade unionists. In the same city, the following figures obtained for the Reichstag elections of 1903:

Trade Union Members	SPD Members	SPD Vote
17,819	2,245	20,178

Michels, *ibid.*, p. 490, and p. 489, where he quotes a Haenisch survey from *Neue Zeit*. Michels estimates that of the 2,245 party members, a maximum of 2,050 could have belonged to trade unions.

[21] Take the political SPD club (*Wahlverein*) in Leipzig in 1904: 1,679 members, of which 1,541 (or 92 percent) were wage workers; 123 belonged to the petty bourgeoisie, and 15 were academicians or bourgeois. *Ibid.*, pp. 504–5. In Frankfurt am Main, a less highly industrialized town, the figures were surprisingly similar: 2,620 members, of which 2,464 (or 90 percent) were wage workers, 150 petty bourgeois, 3 academicians. *Ibid.*, pp. 499–500, 504.

mille. Nothing could have been further from the truth.[22] The members of the party belonged, on the whole, to the better-paid strata of the working class. Large numbers of unskilled laborers, while willing to vote the SPD ticket, were not ready to affiliate with the party.[23] Michels's conclusion is incontestable: "The social composition of the party has remained overwhelmingly proletarian." [24]

When we turn from the membership in general to the party leadership the picture changes only slightly: the editorial chairs of party newspapers and magazines were, not surprisingly, largely occupied by intellectuals. But an overwhelming majority of the SPD parliamentary delegation around the turn of the century was of proletarian origin.[25]

The party leaders, then, were chiefly recruited from the same strata of society as the ordinary party member, but their status had changed. The very fact of prominence in party councils raised the former proletarian to a higher economic and social bracket. While the effect of this separation from proletarian ties can easily be exaggerated, it was still a factor that affected in some measure the attitude of the party toward tactics.

What conclusions can we draw from this brief analysis? In what sense was the class structure of German Social Democracy favorable to Revisionism?

The issue is not clear-cut. Bernstein, who gave this matter some attention, was cautious. His contribution was confined to comment on a 1904 article which had claimed a serious impairment in "class purity" of German Social De-

[22] German Social Democracy contained few "poor little rich boys," and its membership was about as rational as could be found anywhere, as its annual conferences attest.
[23] As Michels wrote: the SPD has "up to now penetrated into the depth of single categories of workers, rather than spreading throughout labor generally." "Deutsche Sozialdemokratie," p. 518.
[24] *Ibid.,* p. 510.
[25] The 81-man delegation in the 1903 Reichstag, classified by Michels, showed 53 workers, 15 members of the proletarianized petty bourgeoisie, 13 bourgeois and academicians. *Ibid.,* p. 527. Among the last, Michels lists as the most prominent, "the most erudite of them all, the autodidact Eduard Bernstein, who stands out with his comprehensive knowledge in all fields." *Ibid.,* p. 528.

mocracy.[26] The author had calculated that of the 3,010,711 votes given the SPD in 1903 about one fourth had come from "bourgeois adherents." Bebel, in reply, would grant only one sixth. Bernstein rightly remarked that mere numbers were never decisive. The question to be answered, he said, was: What elements will assert their leadership and make policy for the party?

"Without ceasing to be primarily the party of the working class," he wrote,

> Social Democracy is ever more becoming a people's party. As once upon a time bourgeois democracy was a people's party from the point of view of the broad masses of the bourgeoisie, so Social Democracy is today a people's party from the point of view of the working class. Nonproletarian or not purely proletarian elements which join it accept the point of view of the workers and recognize them as the leading class.[27]

Beyond this Bernstein would not go. We may hazard several additional comments. Party organization definitely drove the party in a nonrevolutionary direction by making it a mass party. An examination of the class composition of the party does not weaken this conclusion: most of the proletarian members of the party were not favorably inclined towards revolutionary action—the tactics of violence were consistently championed by only a few intellectuals—and the bourgeois followers of the SPD further underlined the peaceful leanings of the party as a whole. Both organization and composition of the party made vote-getting rather than revolution the first item of business. Revisionism was strikingly well adapted to give rational expression to this view of the party's function in German politics.

[26] R. Blank, "Die soziale Zusammensetzung der Sozialdemokratischen Wählerschaft Deutschlands," *Archiv für Sozialwissenschaft und Sozialpolitik,* new ser., IV (1905), 541 ff.
[27] "Wird die Sozialdemokratie Volkspartei?" *Sozialistische Monatshefte,* IX, 2 (1905), 670.

The Riddle of Prosperity

For the proletariat and the disappearing middle class, the small businessman and farmers, [monopoly capitalism] means increasing uncertainty of subsistence; it means misery, oppression, servitude, degradation, and exploitation.

Forever greater grows the number of proletarians, more gigantic the reserve army of labor, and sharper the opposition between exploiters and exploited. . . .

The abyss between propertied and propertyless is further widened by industrial cris These have their causes in the capitalist system and, as the system develops, become ever more extensive and devastating. . . .

ERFURT PROGRAM, 1891

If German reformists of the 1890s wanted evidence that their tactics were superior to those of the revolutionists, all they needed to do was to look at their country's remarkable economic development since the founding of the Reich in 1871. Marxist philosophy, no matter how uncertain about the details concerning the birth of the new world, was clear enough in its conviction that capitalism would be increasingly unable to keep the economy going at high speed. When Germany did have long periods of good times, Marxism underwent a crisis. The effect of prosperity upon German Social Democracy was twofold: it sapped the proletariat's will to revolt by making nonsense of the revolutionary professions of the Erfurt Program, and it gave grounds for theoretical skepticism regarding several of Marx's basic tenets.

"A veritable spring storm broke over all civilized and commercial nations in the last years of the nineteenth century." With this rhapsody to German prosperity one Dr. Max Wittenberg began a public lecture in Berlin in the year 1900. "It filled the veins of national economy with invigorating magic, it awakened energy, made slumbering buds sprout and ripen. It seemed as if youthful energies had brought new life to this aging globe." [28]

Once we have struggled our way through the maze of extravagant explanations and voluminous statistics which, like the Sirens, beckon the eager student to his perdition with their persuasive song, we will find three important causes for German economic well-being of that time. First, Germany's prosperity was aided by the new state. The German government, immeasurably strengthened by unification, lent material assistance to expanding industry and commerce. Germany's stable bureaucracy facilitated economic activity,[29] and certain state projects, designed largely for military ends, also favorably affected the economy as a whole: the state subsidies for railroads, highways, and shipping are conspicuous examples.[30]

Bismarck's Reich had not been primarily created for the expansion of industrial and commercial capitalism. But the pressure of large industry brought with it a Bismarckian compromise: the Conservative Party, the mainstay of agrarian Junkerdom, accepted the National Liberal Party, the political voice of industrial capital, as an ally. The pact received preliminary confirmation by Bismarck's introduction of the protective tariff in 1879, a bill that had been urged by the agrarian interests frightened by overseas competition and was endorsed by industrial magnates who preferred protection-

[28] "Ein Blick auf den wirtschaftlichen Aufschwung am Ende des 19. Jahrhunderts," *Volkswirtschaftliche Zeitfragen,* XXII (1900), 3. Nor was this the only contribution to a lively topic: in 1905, in the United States, one Earl Dean Howard, Ph.D., won first prize in a Hart, Schaffner and Marx essay contest with a book on *The Cause and Extent of the Recent Industrial Progress in Germany.*

[29] On this whole matter, cf. Thorstein Veblen, *Imperial Germany,* a major contribution. "With unification," writes Veblen (pp. 174–75), "the economic situation entered on a new epoch in industy and trade, and the statesmen of the Fatherland entered on a campaign of economic policy directed to making the most of what the new system in trade and industry had to offer. In this new campaign, the ideals of statecraft remained the same as ever, but the new ways and means to be taken account of unavoidably altered the outline of the policy to be pursued, without deflecting it from the ancient cameralist aim of making the most of the nation's resources for the dynastic purposes of the state."

[30] Cf. *ibid.,* p. 214.

ist capitalism to Manchesterism.[31] While, at first, big industry and big agriculture had divergent interests, they came to share a common outlook. Such organizations as the Central Organization of German Industrialists and the Association of Agriculturalists developed similar programs. While the two major groups did not establish full accord until the inauguration of the large-scale naval building program in 1900, their interests were more often identical than opposed even before that date. Their unity was reflected in an increase in trade and industry as well as agriculture.[32]

However, this alliance, effective as it was for a while, was built on shifting sands. It could work permanently only if the liberal bourgeoisie willingly accepted its secondary role in German society and did not press strongly for representative government and free trade. This condition was substantially fulfilled. The bourgeoisie had long since capitulated to the industrial and agrarian aristocracies and seemed content to play an insignificant part in German political life. But to sustain the dynastic state, the alliance of Junkers and big industry also needed a politically impotent proletariat, and in this objective it failed in spite of all its efforts. Thus the Reich remained an unstable structure.[33]

[31] Cf. Sigmund Neumann, *Die deutschen Parteien*, pp. 18–19. When the tariff bill was presented to the Reichstag it obtained the support of the Center and of nearly all National Liberals and Conservatives.
[32] Cf. Eckart Kehr, *Schlachtflottenbau und Parteipolitik, 1894–1901, passim*, and Franz Neumann, *Behemoth*, p. 209. For an elaborate defense of the Bismarck policies, cf. Sartorius von Waltershausen, *Deutsche Wirtschaftsgeschichte, 1815–1914*, pp. 289–312. This brief account is, of course, oversimplified: in the 1890s the right-wing Conservatives opposed industrial expansion and a large navy; there was no real unity over aid to agriculture, since industry naturally wanted protection against foreign products but low wages (which meant low food prices). The agrarians naturally wanted the reverse. But the fact of the compromise between the two groups remains.
[33] A. Rosenberg, *The Birth of the German Republic*, pp. 2–5; Sigmund Neumann, *Die deutschen Parteien*, pp. 18–21. There is another reason why state policy was essentially of doubtful value to industry: in the long run, the policies of a dynastic state are bound to run counter to the real interests of large-scale industry. Modern capitalism has its own dynamics, and they best work

The second reason for Germany's impressive economic advance lay in its late start. The country swung into large-scale industrialization long after Britain was already supporting sizable fixed investments in the shape of factories and equipment, and at a time when British manufacturers were beginning to worry about obsolescence of their capital goods.

Coupled with this is the striking fact of German borrowing of English technology, which came to the Germans "ready made." While Germany thus lacked the advantage of gradually maturing along with the growth of technological advance, it gained by not having to commit the mistakes—social, economic, and technical—which an innovator is bound to make.[34]

The final cause for German prosperity can be found in the physical and cultural readiness of the country for rapid expansion. While the country did not possess raw material as abundantly as, say, the United States, its deposits of iron and coal were sizable, and other materials, such as timber, were available in generous quantities. Further, the available labor force was large and well qualified to support an unprecedented rate of growth. Germany was a highly educated country, and in consequence the needs for managerial personnel as well as for skilled labor could be met.[35]

---

themselves out in a state which subordinates its policies to the requirements of the industrial machine. The ideal political framework for capitalist enterprise varies with time; in its infancy it may need mercantilism, in its maturity it may demand what has been called, inaccurately, a "weak state." (On the so-called "weak state," cf. Franz Neumann, "Approaches to the Study of Political Power," *Political Science Quarterly*, LXV [1950], 167–68.) To quote Veblen once more: "The Imperial state . . . may be said to be unable to get along without the machine industry, and also, in the long run, unable to get along with it; since this industrial system in the long run undermines the foundations of the State." *Imperial Germany*, p. 271. The similarity of views on this matter of the German historian Rosenberg and the American economist Veblen are of great interest.

[34] *Ibid.*, pp. 85, 86, 88–89, 93.

[35] It may not be going too far afield to mention at this point what may be called the "spiritual" readiness of Germany. The Protestant ethic, which made a virtue of work and of accumulation, was strongly entrenched and had lost its religious content

Germany prosperity, which was built upon these miscellaneous factors, was by no means a continuous affair. Hard on the heels of victory in the Franco-Prussian war there followed a flood of speculative ventures. New companies sprang up in all fields; the stock exchange was the scene of the wildest manipulations. A crash was inevitable, and it came late in 1873. During the following six years, unsound enterprises were liquidated. Those that remained were to form the hard core of German economic expansion.[36]

With the introduction of the tariff of 1879 and returning world prosperity, Germany enjoyed prosperous times during the eighties which issued in the boom of 1888-90. A sudden short depression in 1890 was soon followed by moderately good times. But the boom that broke the Marxists' back began in 1895 and lasted, with brief interruptions, until the outbreak of the World War. With such a bright economic picture, who can wonder at the emergence of Revisionism?

Heavy industry spearheaded German expansion; German trade also increased impressively.[37] All figures add up to a

---

by that time. Cf. Max Weber, *The Protestant Ethic and the Spirit of Capitalism*. Bismarck's system of social legislation naturally further tied labor to the process of expansion.

[36] One of the uglier consequences was an anti-Semitic movement which attempted to explain the frauds of the founding years (*Gründungsschwindel*) by pointing to the influence of Jews in industry, trade, and finance. Prominent in that questionable group of anti-Semites were Eugen Dühring, Bernstein's old friend, and the reactionary court preacher Stöcker. Waltershausen approves of this moveemnt. He writes of Stöcker: "His starting point was religious. His highest goal was to bring new life to Christianity and fill it with social spirit. His practical demands were moderate: economic reforms directed against the degeneration of commercial life (*Entartung des Händlertums*), dismissal of Jewish teachers from the public schools, employment of Jewish judges in a percentage equal to that of the Jews in the population, reintroduction of religious population statistics." *Wirtschaftsgeschichte*, p. 277. This anti-Semitism was characterstic of many German intellectuals.

[37] Iron production increased from 2,700,000 tons in 1880 to 8,500,000 tons in 1900. Of other countries, only the United States kept pace with this growth. In steel, German output increased in the same period from 625,000 to 6,650,000 tons. In the same

126 / The Dilemma of Democratic Socialism

phenomenal growth of the German economy in the span of about thirty years. By the time of the Revisionist controversy, the outlines of modern German capitalism were clear.[38] German economic life was profoundly transformed during the time of Bismarck's rule; large-scale industry increasingly set the tone of German society.

There were three important techniques which the industrialists used to secure their domination over German society: cartelization, the concentration of production into large units, and the establishment of employers' associations.

The cartelization of German industry on a large scale began as early as 1871. By 1905, there were 366 industrial cartels in the country, concentrating power in many industries and totally eliminating competition in many others.

Furthermore, the concentration of economic enterprises into large units went on apace: from 1882 to 1907, the number of small-scale enterprises had risen 8 percent, medium enterprises 137 percent, and large ones, 221 percent. In total numbers of employees, the increase was: small industries, 24 percent; medium, 162 percent; large, 231 percent.[39] In 1907, 548 industrial giants, with more than 1,000 employees each, employed 1,277,788 persons. In other words, 0.03 percent of

years, U.S. production rose eight-fold, that of France and Britain only quadrupled. Werner Sombart, *Die deutsche Volkswirtschaft im 19ten Jahrhundert*, Appendix 31, p. 548. Railroad mileage rose from 18,549 km in 1870 to 50,900 km in 1900. *Ibid.*, Appendix 22, p. 541. From 1873 to 1900, the number of ships arriving in German ports doubled; total tonnage tripled. *Ibid.*, Appendix 28, p. 546. Many other figures could be given—they would only serve to strengthen the present impression.

[38] German economic historians, such as Sombart and Waltershausen, nostalgically recall the good old days and contrast them with the emphasis of quantity over quality, the predominance of slickness over creativity, of the new Reich. Waltershausen, *Wirtschaftsgeschichte*, pp. 365, 375. Sombart sadly ends his book on the German economy with gloomy remarks about the "desolation" (*Verödung*) of German political life. *Deutsche Volkswirtschaft*, p. 513. These authors leave the overwhelming impression that their nostalgia was nothing but contempt for modern mass society and possible mass democracy.

[39] Friedrich Zahn, *Deutschlands wirtschaftliche Entwicklung*, p. 165.

German industrial concerns employed 12 percent of the industrial labor force.[40]

Revealing as these figures are, they do not convey an adequate impression of the power of industry over German life. With the growth of cartelized large-scale industry and the rise of the trade unions, employers began to unify formally. Just as the National Association of Manufacturers was founded in the United States in 1895 in the belief that economic power could assert itself only if it was organized, so German industrialists began forming employers' associations for the same reason. The *Unternehmerverbände* began with an association of the metal industries in 1890. The date is significant: it marks the lapse of the anti-Socialist law and the revival of a powerful trade union movement.

The organization of industry was spurred on by strikes until, in 1913, 145,207 employers, employing 4,641,361 workers, were gathered in one association or another. The work of these associations is familiar—their chief function was to present a united front to the public, the government, and the unions. Such unity was of special importance during a lock-out, a favorite device of German employers. The associations aided the firm conducting the lock-out by keeping competitors from permanently depriving it of markets, or by enforcing a general lock-out throughout the industry if the issue was big enough. In other cases the associations provided "replacements" (read "scabs") for struck factories.

This is how German industry defended itself against the rising menace of Socialism.

The phenomenon of German prosperity could have been fitted into the Marxist system with some stretching, since Marx never denied that capitalism was capable of increasing the total national income. But it was necessary to show that, in the long run, this prosperity benefited only a small minority of the population. Unfortunately for orthodox Marxism, the very opposite could be demonstrated: the constantly rising national product was distributed over all segments of the population. It is true, of course, that the rate of increase was unequal, but it appears that *all* classes improved their

[40] *Ibid.*, p. 169.

position, and nothing could more effectively dampen any revolutionary class consciousness than this fact.

All departments of life showed improvements. People ate and dressed better.[41] The rich and poor no longer seemed to be living in two worlds. Many items, once considered luxuries, now were being mass-produced. Furniture, books, pictures, carpets, cigarets, pianos, watches, neckties, and roller skates entered general circulation. Similarly, entertainment became more universally accessible.

It is true, of course, that much poverty remained, that workers still lived, for the most part, in hideous slums, and that their health was unsatisfactory. It is equally true that the mass distribution of such luxury goods as pictures served to obscure the real abyss between the living standards of a parvenu manufacturer and the worker he employed. But if the former could proudly display, say, a genuine Watteau in his *Herrenzimmer,* the worker, if he was so inclined, might decorate his living room with an inexpensive reproduction of the same picture. Surely, the difference between the two pictures, if expressed in financial terms, was immense. But such trivial things as the availability of low-priced pictures helped to keep the proletariat from becoming revolutionary.

However, all generalizations about the improvements in the standard of living of German workers must remain tentative. There are no conclusive figures and many problems of German social history remain unexplored. We know that German workers benefited from Bismarck's social legislation: old age and sickness insurance increased the workers' sense of security and further committed them to the support of the state. We know, too, that the working day was generally shortened. The ten-hour day had long been a key demand of the trade unions, and, at the turn of the century, most industries had given in to it. While this is not extraordinary, it did represent an improvement over the twelve- to fourteen-hour day so common in 1870. Industry could afford

---

[41] Annual consumption of goods increased markedly: Consumption of sugar rose from 12 pounds per person in 1870 to 34 pounds in 1907; that of beer from 78 liters in 1872 to 123 liters in 1900. In 1873, average annual consumption of meat was about 59 pounds per person. That had gone up to 105 pounds in 1912. Waltershausen, *Wirtschaftsgeschichte,* pp. 364, 372, 373, 374.

to shorten the working day, since productivity per man had risen sharply.

But did real wages rise? Statistics point to a marked increase in money wages, but money wages alone do not tell the whole story, since prices also advanced. And did the rise in wages keep pace with the rise in productivity? In the absence of answers to these questions we must content ourselves with a strong impression of general improvement.[42]

This, in brief, was the economic picture in Germany when Revisionism came on the scene. What was said at the outset —that continuing prosperity brought both practical and theoretical problems—should now be confirmed. In practice, German labor grew ever more remote from revolution. The material gains which it had achieved were important not only for the feeling of contentment they gave in the present but also for the hope for further improvements they inspired for the future.

True, the gains were not spectacular enough to cause large-scale withdrawals from the SPD, but they were considerable enough to create a nonrevolutionary, not to say complacent,

[42] Social Democratic theorists did not often deal with these important issues. Such organs as the *Neue Zeit* published only a handful of articles on the wages problem. When the Bernstein debate broke out in full fury, the theoretical aspects of Marx's theory of growing misery were fully explored, but the practical relation of real wages to revolutionary consciousness was almost completely neglected. One exception was an article by the right winger R. Calwer in the *Sozialistische Monatshefte* in 1908. His findings for Berlin showed that industrial and commercial wages had increased about 35–38 percent in ten years, from 1895–1905. During the same time, commodity prices had risen an estimated 25 percent, which means that real wages rose about 1 percent a year. Gustav Brutzer's study of Berlin food costs, *Die Verteuerung der Lebensmittel in Berlin im Laufe der letzten dreissig Jahre*, is extremely cautious. He concludes that Berlin workers improved their living standards somewhat during the years 1880 to 1910. Jürgen Kuczynski has published several studies, but his conclusions are not above suspicion. He concludes, in *Löhne und Konjunktur in Deutschland, 1887–1932*, that the position both of the mass of workers and the "labor aristocracy" improved somewhat in the last decade of the nineteenth century, but has been deteriorating steadily since then, with the mass much worse off, of course, than the labor aristocracy.

mood. Among the factors contributing to prosperity, the German worker saw his party (which had carefully abstained from acts of violence), his trade union (which concentrated on the day-to-day economic struggle), and the state (which, after an experiment in suppression, now seemed to be willing to aid labor) The virtue of Bernstein's optimistic Revisionism, then, lay in the fact that it seemed to give a coherent theoretical explanation of the situation in which the German worker found himself around the year 1900.

Trade Union *vs.* Socialist Consciousness

> *Trade unions are the schools of Socialism. In the trade unions workers are educated to be Socialists because there they witness daily the struggle against capital.*
>
> KARL MARX

The relations of a labor party to the trade unions from which so much of its strength is necessarily drawn are of great practical import. The party may be imbued with revolutionary goals and great visions of a society free from economic exploitation. Trade unions, however, rarely harbor such ideas; they concentrate on the day-to-day contest with employers. A trade union leader, if he wishes to stay in power, must produce immediate and tangible results—higher wages, shorter hours, better working conditions. He knows that man cannot live on hope alone, nor can present hunger be satisfied by thoughts of the happiness of future generations. He knows, too, that short-run gains are best achieved by working within the existing social framework. It is obvious that the tactics he must employ are incompatible with revolutionary ideology.

All this is commonplace enough today, but at the turn of the century, when Revisionism first made its appearance, only a few writers had touched on the matter. Some of the Chartist leaders, particularly Ernest Jones, gave intimations that they were aware of the problem. Marx, who endorsed trade unions as the "schools of Socialism," was concerned over their political role. "The trade unions have hitherto paid too much attention to the immediate disputes with capital," he said in 1866. "They have not yet fully understood their mission against the existing system of production." [43] Finally, Lenin wrote in 1903:

> The history of all countries shows that the working class, exclusively by its own efforts, is able to develop only trade-union consciousness, i.e., it may itself realize the necessity for working in unions, to fight against the employers and to strive to compel the government to pass necessary labor legislation.[44]

Quite naturally, he continued, the unions perpetuate this consciousness by making the "fight against employers" their primary task. Yet " 'economic' concessions (or pseudo concessions) are, of course, the cheapest and most advantageous concessions to be made from the government's point of view, because by these means it hopes to win the confidence of the masses of the workers." [45] We must always remember, he warned, to keep trade union activities distinct from party activities: "Social Democrats lead the struggle of the working class not only for better terms for the sale of labor power, but also for the abolition of the social system which compels the propertyless class to sell itself to the rich." [46] To make the trade union struggle central, therefore, is to give in to the Bolshevik canonical sin of "Economism."

Nothing would be easier than to connect the "Economism" of trade unions to Revisionism, and to call it one of the major causes of the rise of Bernsteinism. But before we accept the conclusion that German trade unionism facilitated the rise of Revisionism we must prove three separate points: (1) that German trade unions followed the antirevolutionary pattern suggested by Lenin; (2) that they were closely tied to the

[43] From Marx's draft for a resolution for the Congress of the First International at Geneva in 1866. Quoted in Max Beer, *A History of British Socialism*, II, 219. For other relevant quotations, see A. Lozovsky, *Marx and the Trade Unions*, *passim*, especially Chapter I.
[44] Lenin, *What Is To Be Done?*, pp. 32–33.
[45] *Ibid.*, p. 62.
[46] *Ibid.*, p. 56.

party and exerted a decisive influence in it; (3) that they were influential at the time when the Revisionist controversy first arose.

A glance at the history of German trade unionism will show that its development followed the lines laid down as axiomatic by Lenin.[47] German labor was pacific from the outset and grew more conservative as it accumulated wealth and influence.

Its modest beginnings date from 1848.[48] That year saw the creation of a number of local organizations and two national unions, the printers and tobacco workers. But the years of reaction—the 1850s and early 1860s—stifled all union activities and it was not until the latter half of the 1860s that the movement really got under way. The English example was assiduously propagandized by Wilhelm Liebknecht, and his speeches coincided with a growing sense of independence on the part of the German working classes. The Liberal Max Hirsch attempted to make the German proletariat dependent upon the Progressive Party by founding the so-called Hirsch-Duncker trade unions. Somewhat later, a "social-Catholic" movement, originally inspired by Bishop Ketteler of Mainz, formed the "Christian Trade Unions." But neither of these organizations ever offered serious competition in number or activity to the "Free" (that is, Socialist) Unions.

The Free Unions began their revival with the formation of the printers' union in 1862 and of the cigar workers' union in 1865. Lassalle's successor, von Schweitzer, attempting to "rescue" the German worker from the blandishments of Marx on the one hand and the Liberals on the other, organized an *Arbeiterschaftsverband* which was to be a cartel of thirty-two trade unions securely fastened to the apron strings of the Lassalleans.

Meanwhile, the Marxists were not idle. Under the leader-

[47] The French *syndicats*, which were highly revolutionary, show that this is by no means the only direction in which trade unions can go.

[48] The best historical surveys of the Socialist trade unions are Adolf Braun, *Die Gewerkschaften vor dem Kriege;* Theodor Cassau, *Die Gewerkschaftsbewegung;* Otto Heilborn, *Die "Freien" Gewerkschaften seit 1890.*

ship of Bebel and Liebknecht they founded several "international" trade unions in 1869, the year in which the Eisenacher Social Democratic Labor Party was born. Marx had always favored trade unions (with the qualifications noted above); unlike Lassalle, whose rigid Iron Law of Wages denied any possibility of the improvement of the workers' lot, Marx saw in the trade unions a primary means of strengthening the working class, and the First International repeatedly gave expression to this belief.[49]

While the limited right to form coalitions existed in most German states prior to 1869, and was granted (with many restrictions) to Prussian citizens in that year, the federal government of the new Reich pursued a policy of judicial and police chicanery against the young trade unions. In 1878, the largest of them—the tobacco workers—had only about eight thousand members.[50] The anti-Socialist law, adopted in the same year, put an end to all national labor organizations for twelve years. With the fall of the law in 1890, trade unions, side by side with the Social Democratic Party, began the difficult task of reorganization.

For the next five years, the Free Trade Unions were unable to gather more than a quarter of a million members, and they were constantly faced with financial difficulties. It is during this period, however, that a most important step was taken: in 1891, a General Commission, comprising all Free Trade Unions, was created in Berlin. From now on, in spite of all disagreements and quarrels, German trade unions exerted a far stronger influence than before through an agency that spoke for them all. From 1895 onwards, the year in which high prosperity returned to Germany, the Free Trade Unions had both sufficient numbers and funds to make themselves heard in Social Democratic councils, and the party did not always like to hear what the unions had to say.

Karl Marx's characterization of the trade unions as the "schools of Socialism" was echoed by most Social Democrats.

[49] Adolf Braun, *Gewerkschaften*, p. 48.
[50] Cassau, *Gewerkschaftsbewegung*, p. 14. For the *Gewerbeordnung* of the North German Federation of 1869, see Franz Neumann, *Koalitionsfreiheit und Reichsverfassung*, p. 7.

After all, did not the trade union movement owe its ideological foundation and most of its organizations to Socialist theoreticians? And what was primary—the pedestrian struggle for minor improvements, or the great task of creating a better world? To a good party man the answer was too obvious to require argument.

As long as the unions were weak and dependent, they acquiesced in their secondary status. They remembered for a long time, that Lassalle had frowned upon them and that Marx, too, had put the political battles for the emancipation of the working class above the fight for the amelioration of its material state. But as soon as they gained in size and financial power, their self-confidence increased to the point where they were able to challenge the supremacy of the party.

The first flurry occurred at the 1893 party congress in Cologne. The outstanding leader of the Free Trade Unions was Carl Legien, chief of the cabinetmakers (*Drechsler*). A capable politician and organizer, he belonged to that group of Social Democrats whose practical ability was not informed by theoretical insight. The central organ of the trade unions, the *Korrespondenzblatt*, had maintained that leading Social Democrats were hostile to the trade union movement, and Legien sought to demonstrate the truth of this contention at the party congress of 1893. It was effectively refuted by Auer, and his resolution, accepted unanimously, smoothed over the ruffled feelings. "The party congress reiterates its expression of sympathy with the trade union movement and again impresses the duty on all party members to work unceasingly for the recognition of the significance of trade union organization." [51]

But while Legien had still followed the Marxist view in 1893 and called the unions the "recruiting school of the party," he soon preferred to emphasize the specific economic functions of the trade unions and evolved the thesis of "neutrality." This ominous word simply meant that trade unions ought to be regarded as equal to and separate from the Social Democrats, and that it was the aim of trade unions to emancipate themselves from the political guidance of any party. "Trade unions must seriously engage in social politics, but I

[51] Quoted in Theodor Leipart, *Carl Legien*, pp. 28–29.

am of the opinion that they should not engage in partisan politics." [52]

The consequences of this attitude were the recruitment of workers regardless of their political attitudes and the abandonment of the class struggle in favor of participation in the existing state. One state institution after another was recognized by the trade unionists; the state labor exchanges and the social insurance system acted as links that bound the organized worker firmly to the authoritarian Reich.[53]

It has been said [54] that the significance of the neutrality policy has been overrated. After all, were not most trade unionists also fervent Social Democrats? Had not Bömelburg, the influential chief of the bricklayers, told the fourth Trade Union Congress at Stuttgart, "The trade union movement and Social Democracy are one?" [55] Had not Legien himself said,

> The trade unions of Germany are not Social Democratic
> . . . because they do not make membership in the party
> a condition of membership in the trade union. But the
> members of the German trade union movement are, almost
> without exception, members of the SPD. That it could not
> be otherwise goes without saying.[56]

But all these statements do not change the basic fact that the policy of neutrality was a fundamental shift in trade union tactics which was to have far-reaching effects. By the turn of the century the union movement was evolving into a nonrevolutionary force which served as a counterweight to the revolutionary assertions of the Erfurt Program.[57]

[52] Schröder, *Handbuch*, p. 193.
[53] Cf. Schorske, who develops this in detail in "German Social Democracy."
[54] By Cassau, *Gewerkschaftsbewegung*, pp. 289–292.
[55] Heilborn, *Die "Freien" Gewerkschaften*, p. 161.
in 1899,
[56] Quoted in Siegfried Nestriepke, *Die Gewerkschaftsbewegung*, I, 431. Strictly speaking, Legien was wrong, for most trade unionists were *not* members of the party. However, most of them *voted* for the SPD.
[57] Legien, who tried to carry water on both shoulders, contributed to the confusion over trade union motives with his inconsistent

Around 1900 the more acute of the Social Democrats realized that the trade union movement had grown into a force to be reckoned with. The "party school" thesis had been supplanted by the "neutrality" program, but at the time that the antirevolutionary emphasis of the trade unions grew really marked, their indispensability to the party became equally obvious. Inevitably the Social Democratic Party was doomed to accept the trade unions into equal partnership and to abandon its prized freedom of action. Not that the party did not struggle hard. From 1900 to 1906, party theoreticians debated the issue in the *Neue Zeit,* the *Sozialistische Monatshefte,* and at party congresses.[58] The discussion took various forms, but for the most part it consisted of disputes over the political mass strike and work stoppages on the first of May—advocated by the party and rejected by the unions. The unionists' replies were usually short and blunt, for the trade unions were passing into the hands of bureaucrats whose favorite pastime was the vilification of party intellectuals. They were incapable of theoretical understanding of

---

pronouncements. As President Franklin Roosevelt once said about an opposing presidential candidate, Legien "talked out of both sides of his mouth at once." An example: "Trade union organization does not only enable the worker to carry on the class struggle, it represents that very class struggle in its most marked form. One cannot confine the concept 'class struggle' to its narrow limits of acts directed toward the abolition of the existing order of society. Every united activity of the laboring class which, consciously or unconsciously, has the aim of smoothing the road to a new social order must be taken to belong to the class struggle." *Sozialistische Monatshefte,* I (1897), 542. Cf. also his *Die deutsche Gewerkschaftsbewegung,* pp. 15–16: "The trade unions start with the conviction that there exists an unbridgeable abyss between capital and labor. . . . But in the first place trade unions attempt, through the power of their organization, to obtain favorable contracts from employers."

[58] A few selected examples of articles are: Carl Legien, "Ziele und Mittel der deutschen Gewerkschaftsbewegung," *Sozialistische Monatshefte,* IV (1900), 109–16; Legien, "Die Neutralisierung der Gewerkschaften," *ibid.,* IV (1900), 369–76; Eduard Bernstein, "Geschichtliches zur Gewerkschaftsfrage," *ibid.,* IV (1900), 376–88; Ignaz Auer, "Partei und Gewerkschaft," *ibid.,* VI (1902), 3–9; Adolph von Elm, "Sozialdemokratie und Arbeiterschaft," *ibid.,* VI (1902), 241–45.

the crucial relations between unions and political party and were thus reduced to denunciations of the "litterati." [59] Such anti-intellectualism presented great dangers to a party which prided itself on its theoretical heritage.

Bebel and the rising Friedrich Ebert recognized the storm signals. The trade unions insisted on being treated as partners, not as pupils, and they were growing powerful enough to put real weight behind their claims. The party, anxious to placate the unions, evolved a new policy. The outcome was the so-called Mannheim Agreement of 1906, which ratified the equal status of trade unions and party and prescribed full consultation between the General Commission and the party leadership. The General Commission was jubilant:

> It is to be hoped that the frequent ructions between the party and the trade unions between 1905 and 1906 will have a lasting good effect in that the complete cooperation which now exists, will never again be endangered by theorists and writers who attach a greater value to mere revolutionary slogans than to practical work inside the labor movement.[60]

The labor leaders had good cause for celebration; their great victory gave them far more than equality: in effect, it meant the surrender of the party to the unions.[61] It prepared the way for the ascendancy of party bureaucrats who were not "theorists" and who "could get along" with the union leaders. It resulted in the stifling of any vigorous activity such as the party youth movement. In short, it set the stage for the failure of the party in 1914 and for its breakup during the war.

The relation of Revisionism to trade unionism has never been fully explored. Contemporary evidence is far from complete, and Eduard Bernstein himself never carefully considered the matter. Still, we may be able to sum up the relationship briefly.

[59] Cassau, *Gewerkschaftsbewegung*, pp. 28–31, 153–54, 288–89.
[60] Quoted in Selig Perlman, *A Theory of the Labor Movement*, p. 100.
[61] Cf. Schorske, "German Social Democracy."

First of all, the trade unions never evinced the slightest interest in the theoretical side of Revisionism. Bernstein's rewriting of Marxism without dialectics, his demonstration that the middle class was not disappearing, his attempts to combine the Marxist theory of value with the new marginal utility approach, left the trade unions completely cold. These matters, to them, were intellectual pastimes of no value for practical affairs. They felt that they *knew*, empirically, that the lot of the working class could be bettered by reformist activity within the existing order. After all, were not their unions doing it every day? They were Social Democrats not for love of the Erfurt Program but because the SPD was the only party that consistently championed their cause.[62]

Secondly, the trade unions felt a deep affinity for the gradualist tactics of Revisionism.[63] They constantly practiced what was called *Gegenwartsarbeit* (that is, work for the present time), and they could subscribe fully to Bernstein's famous sentence, "The goal is nothing, the movement everything." Insofar as Revisionism was a practical reform movement it could count on the support of the trade unions. However, even here divergences became noticeable as soon as the Revisionists advocated truly radical procedure. Thus, Bömelburg had this to say about Bernstein's advocacy of the mass strike: "At one time, Eduard Bernstein does not know how far he ought to move to the right, another time he talks about the political mass strike. These *litterati* . . . are doing a disservice to the labor movement." [64] Even though the alliance was

---

[62] For this reason it seems questionable to me to include the top trade union leaders among the Revisionists, as is done by Rikli, *Der Revisionismus*, p. 25. Legien, the most important of them, did make occasional utterances that might seem to put him in the Revisionist camp. But the trade unions, in spite of his lip-service to the "class struggle," were to Legien engines of prosperity for the workers. His pro-government attitude during the war was characteristic. Cf. *Sozialistische Monatshefte*, XXI, I (1915), 165–67. There can be no questioning Legien's sincerity—he did yeoman service in leading the successful general strike against the Kapp Putsch in 1920. He was a good democrat who earnestly endeavored to improve the lot of the working man. But he was never a theoretical Socialist.
[63] Cf. Cassau, *Gewerkschaftsbewegung*, pp. 287-88.
[64] Quoted *ibid.*, p. 154.

uneasy, indeed never fully formulated, in tactical matters the trade unionists and the Revisionists were generally on the same side.

Thirdly, Bernstein's Revisionism gave the trade unions a leading role. He regarded them as the "indispensable organ of democracy and not merely as temporary coalitions." [65] whose tendency it was to "break the absolutism of capital." [66] However, he felt (against the syndicalists) that a country *run* by omnipotent trade unions would be neither Socialist nor democratic. But Eduard Bernstein never dealt thoroughly with the sociological question of what the trade unions would do—and were beginning to do—to that march into Socialism which he was so confidently expecting. It seems that he took at face value statements such as that by Legien:

> As little as it is possible in political life to leap from complete absolutism to democracy without the transitional stage of the constitutional state, so little (or even less) can production be radically transformed without the presence of the requisite preconditions. *The trade unions are striving to create these preconditions.*[67]

Nothing could be a better statement of Revisionist philosophy. Apparently, Bernstein never fully realized that the trade unions, far from smoothing the path of Socialism, might actually block it. Not that he ignored the transformation of the labor movement—his whole theory was built around just such a shift in outlook—but he estimated its effects incorrectly.[68]

In the fourth place, and this is of great significance, the trade unions remained silent during the great Revisionist con-

[65] *Voraussetzungen,* p. 175.

[66] *Ibid.,* p. 174.

[67] Quoted by Leipart, *Carl Legien,* pp. 35–36, from *Sozialistische Monatshefte,* 1900. Italics mine.

[68] Cf. Bernstein, *Die Arbeiterbewegung.* On p. 169 he admits that a powerful labor movement that has acquired political rights creates a feeling within the worker that is akin to citizenship responsibility. The worker no longer looks upon the state official as his enemy. "Of course," he writes, "meanwhile the state official has become quite another person."

troversy, and there is no evidence that they exerted their influence *sub rosa*. The unions maintained a discreet neutrality
during the decisive years of the Bernstein debate; both at
trade union and party congresses, the union leadership stayed
carefully on the sidelines. After the bitter Dresden party congress of 1903, the central organ of the trade unions went no
further than to regret the dissension and to hope for peace
within the party.[69] "At the time," writes Perlman,[70] "the trade
unions were too busy with the work of growing up, and were
as yet too humble in their own minds before the roaring lions
of the Social Democratic Party to risk taking a hand." [71]

On the basis of this evidence we may conclude: (1) From
about 1905 on, the trade unions were the key element in
Social Democracy which helped to keep the party on its reformist path. In this it was the ally of Revisionism and gave
that movement added strength. But the alliance was strictly
a *mariage de convenance* based on coincidence of interests. If
there had been no Revisionist movement, the trade unions
would have celebrated their 1906 Mannheim triumph without
it. (2) The unions did not *create* the Revisionist movement.
The leading Revisionists were intellectuals, not union leaders.
While it is true that Revisionism always held the trade unions
in high regard, the fact remains that they played a secondary
role in aiding its growth. In the climate of opinion in which
Revisionism was born, the general prosperity and the structure of the SPD were of far greater importance than the antirevolutionary "Economism" of the German labor movement.

[69] Cassau, *Gewerkschaftsbewegung*, p. 289.
[70] *Theory of Labor Movement*, p. 103.
[71] This is how Bernstein estimated the situation: "Many in our
party suspect our trade union leaders as Revisionists. I have the
strong impression that not many of them bother with theoretical
Revisionism, but one thing is true: No matter how radical the
trade union leader once was, no matter how radical he has remained in his heart, once he feels the load of responsibility in
a responsible position, he is forced to pay more attention to the
requirements of economic questions that the usual (*landläufige*)
radicalism can support." "Grundlinien des sozialdemokratischen
Radikalismus," *Sozialistische Monatshefte*, XII, 3 (1908), 1515.

Chapter 6

The Philosophy of Revisionism

Marxism Without Dialectics

> *The great things which Marx and Engels achieved they accomplished in spite of, not because of, Hegel's dialectic.*
>
> EDUARD BERNSTEIN

REVISIONISM was far more than a patchwork of "corrections" or "improvements" on orthodox Marxism. In the hands of its chief proponent it evolved into a full-scale attack on Marx's system. So far we have examined the background of the theory and its founder; in the succeeding three chapters we shall undertake an analysis of its content, beginning with the philosophical premises upon which it was based.

The dialectic is built into the very foundations of Marxism. It is true, of course, that Marxist dialectic differs markedly from the method of Hegel, yet the two systems are members of the same philosophical family. One might say that Hegelian and Marxian philosophy bear a dialectical relationship to each other. As Marx himself wrote: "My dialectic method is not only different from the Hegelian, but is its direct opposite." [1] "Old Hegel," as Marx and Engels affectionately called him, had the greatest value for the two materialists, and they never disavowed their profound debt to him. As Marx said:

> The mystification which dialectic suffers in Hegel's hands by no means prevents him from being the first to present its general form of working in a comprehensive and conscious manner. With him it is standing on its head. It must be turned right side up again, if you would discover the rational kernel within the mystical shell. [2]

[1] "Preface to the Second Edition," *Capital,* I, 25.
[2] *Loc. cit.*

It was this dialectical method that enabled Marx to look upon man as a totality, to see society as historically bound and deeply involved in contradictions; it gave Marxist evolutionism a unique philosophical flavor. "Hegel," writes Herbert Marcuse, broke "with the tendency of introversion" and proclaimed "the realization of reason in and through given social and political institutions." The dialectic "brought philosophy to grips with social reality," and this "resulted in the dissolution of the harmonious world of fixed objects posited by common sense and in the recognition that the truth philosophy sought was a totality of pervasive contradictions." In this manner,

> through the dialectic, history had been made part of the very content of reason. . . . Philosophy itself . . . made direct application to social theory and practice, not as to some external force but as to its legitimate heir. If there was to be any progress beyond this philosophy, it had to be an advance beyond philosophy itself and, at the same time, beyond the social and political order to which philosophy had tied its fate.[3]

This dialectical leap "beyond philosophy" into revolutionary social theory was made by Karl Marx in close collaboration with Friedrich Engels.[4]

[3] Marcuse, *Reason and Revolution*, pp. 256–57.
[4] In spite of overwhelming evidence, accepted by most close students of Marxism such as Cunow and Lukacz, and Marck in his *Hegelianismus und Marxismus*, a few writers have come to opposite, but unwarranted, conclusions. Thus Vorländer, misled by Marx's remark that he had "coquetted with the modes of expression peculiar to" Hegel in only one chapter of *Capital*, concludes that Marx really used Hegelian categories very rarely. Cf. Karl Vorländer, *Kant und Marx*, pp. 64–65. Vorländer, as Lukacz quite justly complains in *Geschichte und Klassenbewusstsein*, p. 9, thus wrongly regards the dialectic as a "superficial stylistic addition." Another example of an underestimation of the role of dialectics in Marx can be found in Paul Sweezy, *Socialism*, p. 116. "The term 'dialectical'," writes Sweezy, "as applied to Marxian philosophy has a broad and relatively simple meaning." After a broad and relatively simple explanation of what dialectics is he concludes: "As a rule, discussions of dialectical materialism make much of certain Hegelian formulas

Eduard Bernstein's attitude toward Marxian dialectics was, in many ways, peculiar. He moved the dialectical method from the center of the Marxist system to the periphery and substituted "evolutionism" as the core of Marxism. He insisted that the dialectic was a "survival" of Hegelianism, an excrescence which must be eliminated from Socialist theory. Once he had purged his own thinking of the dialectic, however, he indicated his conviction that he had not abandoned Marxism.[5] How can we explain this complex and apparently contradictory attitude?

Bernstein's refusal to admit that he had forsaken Marxism was due to the tremendous impact which that theory had had upon him. When he developed his Revisionism, he had stood in the forefront of the German labor movement for a quarter of a century. He had examined other forms of Socialist thought, particularly Lassalleanism and Anarchism, and found them wanting. The men whom he had most admired—Marx, Kautsky, and above all Engels—had for many years fixed his outlook in one direction. He had been steeped in Marxist literature for decades and had drawn far more from it than from any other intellectual source. It is small wonder, then, that he clung tenaciously to the label "Marxist," no matter what changes his thought was to undergo.

Bernstein came to technical philosophy late and without expert guidance. This is not to say, by any means, that anyone trained in philosophy would automatically become an addict of the Hegelian logic. Nor is it to accuse Bernstein of ignorance in philosophy. But his lack of a really thorough philosophical education drove him to rely on common sense and to give free play to his already powerful skeptical and

---

which Marx and Engels occasionally used for their own purposes. Most famous of these are the thesis–anti-thesis–synthesis triad, the 'transformation of quantity into quality,' and the 'negation of the negation.' *These are, however, minor aspects of Marxian philosophy and must be omitted from a brief review of fundamentals." Ibid.*, pp. 118–19. (Italics mine.) Mr. Seymour Harris has called the author of these words, "the leading Marxian in the United States"! *Ibid.*, Introduction, p. xii.

[5] We can understand this without having to impugn his honesty, as is done by Sweezy, *The Theory of Capitalist Development*, p. 159.

empiricist sympathies. As qualifications about the Marxist system began to plague him, these antimetaphysical tendencies became stronger.

He always maintained (and evidence confirms the accuracy of his statements) that he became skeptical of Marxism not because of doubts concerning the whole structure, but because events falsified some Marxist predictions. Had he been a metaphysician, he would probably have written off the errors in detail but retained the original method. This he refused to do, for he felt that it was the very method that would always lead to errors. It is instructive to contrast this attitude with a quotation from Georg Lukacz:

> Let us assume, for the sake of argument, that recent investigations had proved beyond doubt the factual incorrectness of every single assertion of Marx. In that case, every serious "orthodox" Marxist could unconditionally acknowledge all the new results, he could abandon all of Marx's single theses, without having to give up his Marxist orthodoxy for a minute. Orthodox Marxism is not an uncritical recognition of the results of Marxist investigations, it does not mean a "faith" in this or that thesis, nor is it the interpretation of a "sacred" text. Orthodoxy in questions of Marxism refers exclusively to method. It is the scientific conviction that dialectical Marxism is the correct method of investigation, that this method can be built up, continued, and deepened only in the sense of its founders. All attempts to overcome or "improve" it have led and will lead only to shallowness, triviality, and eclecticism.[6]

This passage well expresses the viewpoint of all those Marxists who are inclined to emphasize the philosophical heritage of Marxism. The only part of it which Bernstein could have accepted is the sentence that Marxism is not a sacred text. But he would have been appalled at the thought of retaining a method if all the predictions based upon it had proved false. Bernstein viewed philosophical method with the eyes of an empiricist: its acceptability was to be gauged by its effectiveness in explaining a given set of facts. If it was

[6] Lukacz, *Geschichte und Klassenbewusstsein,* p. 13.

contradicted by developments it must be abandoned in favor of another theory.

Bernstein analyzed the Erfurt Program, which foresaw the disappearance of the middle class, the increase of exploitation, and the growing bitterness of the class struggle. All these categorical claims, which Bernstein sought to disprove on empirical grounds, stemmed from a dialectical concern with "contradictions." That is why Bernstein characterized the "Hegelian-dialectical method" as a "snare." [7] The great danger of the dialectic, he thought, lay in the fact that it completely abandoned the empirical world for idle speculation.[8]

As an example of "historical self-deception" based on Hegel's logic he cited Marx's prediction in the *Communist Manifesto* that the coming German Revolution could "only be the prelude to a proletarian revolution." [9]

Another grave consequence of the Hegelian influence on Marx, according to Bernstein, had been Marx's heavy reliance on force to accomplish the Socialist revolution:

> Every time we see the theory of the economy as the basis of history capitulate before the theory which drives the cult of force to the limit, we will run into a Hegelian sentence. Possibly it will be used only as an analogy, but that makes it even worse.[10]

Such was Bernstein's view of the dialectical process. It ex-

---

[7] *Die Voraussetzungen des Sozialismus und die Aufgaben der Sozialdemokratie,* p. 51.

[8] "No matter how things may look in reality, as soon as we leave the soil of empirically ascertainable facts and think beyond them, we move into the world of derived concepts. If we then follow the laws of the dialectic as established by Hegel, we find ourselves, before we know it, again in the snare of the 'self-development of the idea.' Herein lies the great danger to science of Hegel's logic of contradiction. Under some circumstances, its sentences may very well serve to visualize relationships and developments of real objects. . . . But as soon as we anticipate developments deductively on the basis of these sentences, the danger of arbitrary construction begins." *Ibid.,* p. 53. It seems, however, that Bernstein here charged Marx with Hegel's sin, since Marx certainly never supported the "self-development of the idea."

[9] *Ibid.,* p. 54.

[10] *Ibid.,* p. 71.

plains why he sought to minimize its importance for the thought of Marx and Engels. As he said in a letter to Kautsky late in life:

> I had not turned from the fundamental concepts of the Marxian view of history, but had always merely opposed certain interpretations and applications. Further, I had sought to explain hasty conclusions of Marx and Engels as the consequence of their being seduced by the Hegelian dialectic, *which after all is not integrally connected with the theory*.[11]

But if the dialectic was not integral to the theory, what was? Bernstein believed he had found the center of Marxist thought in evolutionism.

It is beyond dispute that Marxism is deeply imbued with evolutionism, but it is evolutionism with a difference. First, it holds that history proceeds dialectically, through contradictions. Secondly, it makes the victory of the proletariat a necessary consequence of historical progress. The class struggle, the motor of history, may be speeded up or slowed down, but not turned around.

Eduard Bernstein accepted evolution as a principle, but he seriously modified these specific Marxian characteristics. With the elimination of the dialectic method, the dialectical conception of historical change naturally fell by the wayside. Bernstein substituted a unilinear concept of progress, which was closely akin to the view of the nineteenth-century Positivists. Bernstein described it as "organic evolutionism." His argument went somewhat as follows: Marx and Engels had demonstrated that Socialism was not a Utopian invention, but was already inherent in the economic processes of capitalism. By "drawing Socialism . . . out of the clouds of fantasy to the firm soil of the actualities of social existence," Marxism had given the labor movement its greatest impetus and its

[11] Bernstein to Kautsky, December 16, 1927, Bernstein Archives. (Italics mine.) It should be clear that I reject Bernstein's estimate of the significance of the dialectic to Marxism.

solid foundation.[12] This was Marx's and Engels's great contribution. Marx was writing as a true evolutionist when he said: "When a society has got upon the right track for the discovery of the natural laws of its movement . . . it can neither clear by bold leaps, nor remove by legal enactments, the obstacles offered by the successive phases of its normal development. But it can shorten and lessen the birthpangs." [13] Again, every Revisionist can subscribe to another of Marx's sentences: "The present society is no solid crystal, but an organism capable of change, and is constantly changing." [14] But to regard the struggle of opposites as the basis of *all* historical change is to go too far. It leads to an overvaluation of the "creative strength" of violence, an unwarranted stress on single, decisive acts. This Bernstein called "unorganic evolutionism." "I am not of the opinion," he wrote. "that the struggle of opposites is the basis of all development. The cooperation of related forces is of great significance as well." [15] It becomes necessary, therefore, to view social evolution as a gradual growth into Socialism. True, class antagonisms continue, but they diminish in force; immediate work *within* the state takes the place of intransigeant opposition to it.[16]

"The result," writes Marcuse of this line of reasoning, harshly but with some justice, "was that Revisionism replaced the critical dialectical conception with the conformist attitudes of naturalism." [17] Bernstein was no conformist, but the practical consequences which he drew from his version of evolution were a far cry from what he liked to call the "revolution-mongering" of the Left wingers in his own party.

Eduard Bernstein has given us a striking paragraph which outlines his divergence from Marxism on this vital point. It is worth quoting in full:

The old vision of the social collapse which rises before us as a result of Marx's arguments (after all, we Social Demo-

[12] Bernstein, *Der Revisionismus in der Sozialdemokratie,* p. 15.
[13] "Preface to the First Edition," *Capital,* I, 14–15.
[14] *Ibid.,* p. 16.
[15] Bernstein, *Zur Geschichte und Theorie des Sozialismus,* p. 347.
[16] *Ibid.,* p. 335.
[17] Marcuse, *Reason and Revolution,* p. 399.

crats are all pupils of Marx and Engels) is the picture of an army. It presses forward, through detours, over sticks and stones, but is constantly led downward in its march ahead. Finally it arrives at a great abyss. Beyond it there stands beckoning the desired goal—the state of the future, which can be reached only through a sea; a *red* sea, as some have said. Now, this vision changes, and another takes its place. The prospect we now see before us shows us the daily struggle of the workers, which proceeds and repeats itself in spite of all persecutions. Workers grow in number, in general social power, in political influence, and no party can evade it. *This* vision shows us the way of the working classes not only forward, but at the same time upward. Not only do the workers grow in numbers, but their economic, ethical, and political level rises as well, and thus grows their ability to be one of the governing factors in state and national economy. And that direction in Social Democracy whose adherents are called Revisionists works and agitates most effectively in the sense of *this* prospect.[18]

If Bernstein's substitution of unilinear progress for dialectical evolution was connected with some theoretical difficulties, his attempt to modify Marx's insistence on strict historical determinism and the necessity of the proletarian victory landed him in a philosophical morass from which he never fully extricated himself.

Marx, as we know, had said that the proletariat has no ideals to realize. Its historical mission was to recognize existing historical tendencies and to act accordingly. Marxism was anything but a quietist philosophy; it did not eliminate human volition, but gave greater weight to the impersonal forces of economic development.[19] Marx, we may say, unified theory and practice, for recognition and action could not be separated in his thought. The Socialist future was not to be discussed as something desirable, as an "ought." It *will* be. Marx's analysis of the nature of ideology was of immense

[18] Bernstein, *Der Revisionismus in der Sozialdemokratie*, p. 41.
[19] Cf. Siegfried Marck, "Die Philosophie des Revisionismus," in *Grundsätzliches zum Tageskampfe*, pp. 24 ff.

aid in this line of argument: ethical systems were not independent of the "social production which men carry on," but its reflection. They were not eternal truths to be critically determined but a part of the social superstructure which was transformed as the basic production relations themselves were altered.

Bernstein attacked this structure at two points. First he argued that these Marxist theses were too determinist. The materialist is a "Calvinist without God," he wrote[20]—a somewhat misleading description in view of Calvin's thoroughgoing irrationalism. As soon as materialism is introduced as a category of historical explanation, it means "from the outset the necessity of all historical events and developments." [21] But with growing human control of the social environment, "the iron laws of history" are limited in power, and "ethical factors" find greater room for "independent activity." [22]

Now, this was badly phrased, for it might be taken—and was—as an attempt to emancipate man's actions from history. Bernstein promptly conceded that he had expressed himself imprecisely, and soon abandoned this argument.[23]

The second point at which he sought to undermine Marx's determinism was on the notion of ideology. Bernstein argued that the Marxist view of the relation of the substructure of social production to production relations and "legal and political superstructures . . . to which correspond definite forms of social consciousness" was too stark and one-sided. Men have heads, and are guided, in part, by "ideal" motives. The proletarian's "interest" in the improvement of his life, first of all, has some ethical admixtures. Next, his "understanding" of certain basic ideas, such as his beliefs regarding the state, society, economy, history, and the attitudes he maintains concerning them may be called ethical in part.[24] What is more, these moral elements are frequent and in a wide area "of creative character." [25] Ethical elements are far more objective and independent than Marx would admit.

[20] *Voraussetzungen*, p. 33.
[21] *Loc. cit.*
[22] *Loc. cit.*
[23] Bernstein, *Zur Geschichte und Theorie des Sozialismus*, p. 323.
[24] *Ibid.*, pp. 262–85.
[25] *Ibid.*, p. 285.

Bernstein never doubted that economic factors had a powerful impact on all of society, and he never questioned the fruitfulness of the Marxist concept of ideology. But he was concerned with limiting its range and with claiming greater freedom for man's ethical thinking.[26] This is but one example of Bernstein's return to Lassalle.

The reintroduction of ethics as a causal factor into Socialist theory had several important consequences. Socialism, on this view, is no longer something that must be. Its arrival can no longer be scientifically predicted. Socialism now becomes ethically desirable, the proletariat ought to realize it, but whether or not it will become reality depends to a considerable degree on human will. This view relies on voluntarism as Marxism never did, and takes the ground from under Marx's definite predictions. The apodictic certainty of scientific Socialism is replaced with the hopefulness of ethical Socialism; Marx's monism of being and ought-to-be has been torn in two.

If this section has stressed Bernstein's divergences from Marx, we must always keep in mind the sizable area of agreement between the two men. But where Bernstein differed from his master, he made his apostasy clear to all. In order to show his rejection of the dialectic and his qualified adherence to the concept of ideology, he advocated that the term "dialectic materialist view of history" be replaced by "economic interpretation of history." [27] When Rosa Luxemburg charged that his theories surrendered the "immanent economic necessity" for the victory of Socialism and reduced that victory to mere desirability, Bernstein readily admitted the truth of this criticism. "I regard it neither as possible nor as desirable to give [the triumph of Socialism] a purely materialistic foundation." [28]

[26] It is characteristic that Bernstein quotes, with approval, Engels's celebrated letter to Conrad Schmidt, of October 27, 1890, in which Engels admitted limited autonomy to elements of the superstructure, such as the state. For the letter, see V. Adoratsky, ed., *Selected Correspondence, Karl Marx and Frederick Engels,* pp. 477–84.
[27] *Voraussetzungen,* pp. 42–44.
[28] *Ibid.,* p. 246.

As we noted before, in spite of these qualifications, Bernstein always sincerely considered himself a Marxist. We have shown, too, why we regard this belief to have been a mistaken one. But in spite of his abandonment of the fundamentals of Marxism, Bernstein remained a convinced and activist Socialist. It is worth keeping in mind, however, that he—and with him, Revisionism—gave up any trace of Hegelianism, and searched for another thinker who might furnish him with new philosophical foundations. Revisionism found that man in Immanuel Kant.

From Hegel to Kant

> *The ethics is the weakest part of the Kantian philosophy. . . . Its historical and social tendency. . . . has been that of toning down, of reconciling [social] antagonisms, not of overcoming them through struggle.*
>
> KARL KAUTSKY

During the 1870s there was a strong revival of interest in Kantian philosophy in Germany. For a number of years the success of Hegel and the vogue of Positivism had pushed the Critical Philosophy into the background. For a while (to paraphrase Marx on the fate of Hegel), Kant had been treated like a "dead dog." But the popularity of a rather crude materialism (shown, for example, in Büchner's *Kraft und Stoff*) impelled philosophers to return to epistemological questions. The materialism which was in fashion at the time assumed that knowledge presented no difficulties: we apprehend the world directly, as it really is. The problem of knowledge cannot be solved, however, by the simple statement that no problem exists, and thinkers became increasingly aware of the need for a reexamination of the rational foundations of knowledge. What was more natural, then, than to go back to one of the most profound epistemologists of them all, Immanuel Kant?

The neo-Kantian movement which sprang up in a number of German universities, with Marburg taking the lead, soon gathered to itself a number of leading professors. A mere list of their names—F. A. Lange, H. Vaihinger, Hermann Cohen, Paul Natorp, Rudolf Stammler, F. Staudinger, Ernst Cassirer —reveals the greatness of this Kantian revival.[29]

Social problems were close to the heart of nearly all of these men. While they rarely went beyond bourgeois reformism, their ethical philosophy made them sympathetic to the political Left. F. A. Lange, for example, wrote not only a highly regarded *History of Materialism,* but also a book on the labor question, *Die Arbeiterfrage,* which Engels read "with much interest," [30] and which went through many editions. Lange was never a Marxist, but his Socialist eclecticism stamps him as a forerunner of Revisionism. Even more remarkable was the work of Hermann Cohen, one of the keenest Kant students in the whole group. Cohen emphasized that Kant's philosophy, far from being confined to the theory of knowledge, had great political significance. Kant's ethical postulates, Cohen said, made him "the true and actual founder of German Socialism." [31] He did not want this statement to be taken literally; Kant himself had, of course, never been a Socialist. But Cohen regarded Kant as the father of German Socialism in a logical sense; he recalled the second formulation of the categorical imperative: "Act so as to treat man, in your own person as well as in that of anyone else, always as an end, never merely as a means." A century after Kant wrote these words, Cohen said, in a world that had changed greatly, this ethical maxim could only lead to Socialism.[32]

Such thoughts were echoed by most of Cohen's colleagues, and, interestingly enough, the social-philosophical emphasis of neo-Kantianism reached its peak in the decade in which Eduard Bernstein worked out, published, and defended his Revisionism.

---

[29] For this whole section, cf. Vorländer, *Kant und Marx.*
[30] Engels to Lange, March 29, 1865, in Adoratsky, *Selected Correspondence,* p. 198.
[31] Quoted in Vorländer, *Kant und Marx,* p. 124.
[32] Cf. *ibid.,* pp. 6–34, and Kautsky, *Ethics and the Materialist Conception of History,* pp. 39–69. I must confess that this argument does not make sense to me.

In spite of the overtures to Socialism made by the neo-Kantians, German Social Democracy evinced little interest in their efforts. The Marxists had read Kant, but, as convinced Hegelians, they rejected what they called his abstract idealism. It is true that some Socialists, such as Lassalle, Dietzgen, and Jaurès, had been deeply impressed by the Königsberg philosopher,[33] but the same cannot be said of Marx and Engels. These two men distrusted the Kantian philosophy. To them, Kant's insistence on the "good will" independent of results was an ideological screen for the bourgeoisie. Marx's famous eleventh thesis on Feuerbach, "The philosophers have only interpreted the world in various ways; the point however is to change it," is a direct challenge to Kant on this point. Marx and Engels felt that Kant's sharp bifurcation of knowable phenomena and unknowable noumena led to political impotence by limiting the range of human reason and by separating thought from action.[34]

This lead given by the masters of the movement was followed in German Social Democracy. Kant was not criticized; he was ignored.[35]

The first stirrings of Revisionism were accompanied by a sudden access of interest in Kant's Critical Philosophy. Conrad Schmidt and Ludwig Woltmann, two men whose special importance for Revisionism consists of their early questioning of Marx's philosophical foundations of Socialism, set the ball rolling in 1896 and 1897. Kant, wrote Schmidt,[36] was the most profound of German thinkers, and while Hegel was great, it was necessary to turn away from his metaphysical speculations to the true science of Kant's Critical Philosophy. To return to Kant in questions of epistemology did not mean

[33] Vorländer, *Kant und Marx*, pp. 75–115.
[34] Cf. Gustav Mayer, *Friedrich Engels*, II, 308, and Vorländer, *Kant und Marx, passim*. Adoratsky writes with charming naïveté: "This half-and-half character of Kant's philosophy makes it specially suitable and acceptable to the bourgeoisie and their agents in the camp of the working class, the Social Fascists." *Selected Correspondence*, p. 531.
[35] Vorländer patiently went through Volumes I to XX of *Neue Zeit* and found that Kant "was touched upon only superficially in a very few places." *Kant und Marx*, p. 155.
[36] *Ibid.*, pp. 156 f.

an unqualified acceptance of his whole system; indeed, Marx and Kant could be fruitfully combined.

Woltmann was far more critical of Hegel than Schmidt, and his acceptance of Kant was more throughgoing than Bernstein's. For our purposes, however, the connection of Bernstein to Kant's thought is of far greater importance, for neither Schmidt nor Woltmann was to play a leading role in German Social Democracy.

While he was still an orthodox Marxist, Bernstein shared Engels's feelings that Kantianism was essentially a debilitating, not to say destructive, force within Socialism. In an early article on the subject he reflected Engels's viewpoint closely, although he already admitted that the neo-Kantian movement had a "certain justification" in that it represented a "reaction against the shallow naturalistic materialism of the middle of this century on the one hand, and the excesses of speculative philosophy on the other." [37] His road to Kant was gradual and due to "a whole series of influences," [38] chief among which were his study of Friedrich Albert Lange and of Hermann Cohen's essay accompanying a reissue of Lange's *History of Materialism*.[39] The last in the series of articles which announced Bernstein's break with orthodox Marxism showed how deeply he had fallen under Kant's influence.[40] In this article, Bernstein made the suggestion that Kant was actually a far greater realist than "very many adherents of so-called Scientific Materialism." [41] He echoed Conrad Schmidt: "The phrase, 'Back to Kant,' is valid for the theory of Socialism up to a certain limit." [42]

This was startling, and puzzling as well, and Plekhanov attempted to refute Bernstein's position with Marx's and

[37] "Zur Würdigung Friedrich Albert Langes," *Neue Zeit*, X, 2 (1892), 102; the passage is quoted in Vorländer, *Kant und Marx*, p. 179.
[38] Bernstein letter to Vorländer, quoted by Vorländer, *loc. cit.*
[39] *Loc. cit.*
[40] The article, which appeared in *Neue Zeit*, XVI, 2 (1898), 225 ff., is reprinted in *Zur Geschichte und Theorie des Sozialismus*, p. 262 ff.
[41] *Ibid.*, p. 264.
[42] *Ibid.*, p. 263.

Engels's earlier arguments.[43] This controversy took place at the time at which Bebel asked Bernstein to clarify his general position in a book, and therefore Bernstein allotted some space to the probelm of Kantianism in the *Voraussetzungen*. Even a superficial consideration of what he has to say in that volume will show that he had not become a neo-Kantian.

The last chapter of the *Voraussetzungen*, entitled "Final Goal and Movement," bears a promising motto: "Kant against Cant." Bernstein begins by calling his readers' attention to the power of "tradition" which plays a vital role "even among Social Democrats." Socialist theory is full of cant; that is, talk which thoughtlessly or dishonestly parrots phrases which have no meaning.[44] The opposition to Bernstein's "the goal is nothing," is cant. To continue to hold the theory of the "hopelessness" of the workers' position in the light of changed conditions is cant. The remnants of Utopianism in Marxism (such as belief in the violent revolution and the dictatorship of the proletariat): cant. Without idealism and without criticism there can be no Socialism. What German Social Democracy needs to liberate itself from cant, therefore, is a "Kant who would keenly and critically examine our inherited dogma, and who would demonstrate that its supposed materialism is the purest (and therefore the most misleading) ideology." [45] He would warn that "contempt for the ideal and the magnification of material factors into omnipotent forces of evolution are both self-deceptions, which have been and will be exposed as such at every opportunity by the actions of the very men who proclaim them.[46] No literal return to Kant is needed, but a critical spirit can reform what must be reformed and retain those maxims that ought to be retained. Indeed, we might translate the phrase "Back to Kant" into "Back to Lange," because the latter not only "sincerely and courageously championed the working class in its struggle for emancipation" but also possessed a "great scientific objectivity which was ever ready to acknowledge errors and to accept new truths." [47]

---

[43] Plekhanov's articles in *Neue Zeit* are listed in the Bibliography.
[44] *Voraussetzungen*, pp. 234–35.
[45] *Ibid.*, pp. 256–57.
[46] *Ibid.*, p. 257.
[47] *Loc. cit.*

Is that all? These passages show us largely what Bernstein's "Back to Kant" was not—it did not mean an acceptance of Kant's theory of knowledge, nor a general reevaluation of Kant's ethical teachings. It did mean that German Socialism needed objective, keen criticism which rejected Hegelian dialectic dogmatism and accepted the validity of ethical judgments.

The question of Kant raged through the pages of the *Vorwärts*, the *Neue Zeit*, and the *Sozialistische Monatshefte* for several years. From being the most neglected, Kant had turned into the most discussed German philosopher in Socialist circles. The transformation, which had come nearly overnight, was largely due to Bernstein's few, and really inconclusive, sentences.

But Bernstein did not let the matter rest there. In May 1901 he made his last and by far most ambitious attempt to introduce Kantian concepts into German Social Democracy. The occasion was a lecture Bernstein delivered before a student club in Berlin, in the presence of some distinguished guests such as Adolph Wagner as well as a number of Revisionists who had never heard the man whose views they advocated so actively. Bernstein, be it recalled, had just returned from exile, and this was one of his first addresses on German soil.[48]

The title of the talk, "How Is Scientific Socialism Possible?" recalled Kant's *Prolegomena*. In the speech Bernstein reminded his listeners of Kant's great critical contribution and added: "Of course, we need not follow Kant slavishly in

---

[48] One of his most devoted followers, Lily Braun, has left us a vivid description of the occasion. Cf. *Memoiren einer Sozialistin: Kampfjahre,* pp. 385–90. She speaks of the high hopes with which she and her friends awaited the appearance of Bernstein, the man whom they trusted to lead their movement, and of her disappointment: "Then he spoke. With a voice that sounded brittle. In choppy sentences. A man who was used to the small study, not the public meeting. A shadow of disappointment flickered over the hopeful faces. Timidly and softly the questions arose: 'What does he offer? What does he want?' . . . We had expected a prophet of a new truth, and instead we saw before us a doubter. . . ." Pages 387–88.

putting our questions the same *way* that he did. . . . But we must put them in the same critical *spirit* as did Kant." [49]

Armed with this spirit, Bernstein plunged into his subject. Marxism, he began, is not the only brand of Socialism that has called itself "scientific": Proudhon, Saint-Simon, Owen, Fourier, and occasionally even Lassalle had clothed their systems in that cloak.[50] Engels, in advancing the claim, had based it on two Marxian "discoveries"—the materialist interpretation of history and surplus value. Marx, Engels had maintained, never based his doctrine on ethical demands, but on "the inevitable collapse of the capitalist mode of production, which is daily taking place before our very eyes." [51] Bernstein now argued that the discovery that in capitalism the worker produces more than he receives did not make Socialism a science. It can as little be used as scientific proof for the collapse of capitalism as the discovery that slaves produce more than they obtain can be employed to prove the necessary collapse of a slave society.[52] Again, even if we could prove scientifically the inevitability of the collapse of capitalism, can we deduce the necessary advent of Socialism? Bernstein denied this, and therewith returned to one of his favorite

[49] *Wie ist wissenschaftlicher Sozialismus möglich?* p. 18.
   In this discussion as to whether a "scientific" Socialism is possible, there arises a difficult linguistic problem. The German word *Wissenschaft* is far more comprehensive a term than the word "science" which is generally used as its English equivalent. The German term refers to any discipline which attempts to establish system, generality, on some definite method. "Science" on the other hand is largely limited to the natural sciences of physics, chemistry, etc., with their special methodology which stresses induction and empirical content. The difference between the two expressions is crucial. One might maintain that ethics is a *Wissenschaft* but at the same time not a "science." Kant's ethics, which is systematic and rigorous but uses methods and materials far removed from those of natural science, is precisely that: a *Wissenschaft* but not a "science." In what follows, the word "science" will be used to render *Wissenschaft,* but unless the reader keeps the distinction in mind, much of the subsequent discussion will be meaningless.
[50] *Wie ist wissenschaftlicher Sozialismus möglich?* pp. 7–8.
[51] Engels's preface to Marx, *Poverty of Philosophy,* quoted *ibid.,* p. 10.
[52] *Ibid.,* p. 13.

themes: Socialism is not inevitable, but it is supremely desirable. But before we examine his development of this point, let us see what Bernstein understands by "science." "Science, in its strict sense, is merely systematically ordered knowledge. Knowledge is perception of the true nature and relations of things, and . . . since there is only one truth, there can be only one science in each field of knowledge." [53] These definitions have justly been criticized as unclear (what is "systematic"? What is "true nature"?) and excessively empiricist.[54] Other definitions of science, scattered through the lecture, are more to the point. "Science is unbiased (*tendenzlos*)." [55] And earlier: "Scientific form does not make an intellectual structure scientific when its presuppositions and purposes contain elements that lie beyond unbiased perceptions (*tendenzfreie Erkenntnis*)." [56] Finally, and with categorical assurance: "No *ism* is a science." [57]

For Bernstein, then, science cannot serve as a guide to what is ethically desirable.

We can now understand Bernstein's conception of Socialism. According to Bernstein, Socialism may be defined either as creed or as movement. But no matter which approach is taken, both definitions contain idealist admixtures. Socialism is a "piece of the beyond (*ein Stück Jenseits*)," [58] that is, beyond positive experience. "It is something that *ought* to be, or a movement toward something that *ought* to be;" [59] it is a movement toward equal partnership. In other words, Socialism is a system of demands. Interest and desire play a vital role, for "without interest there is no social action." [60]

This analysis is developed more fully: Socialism demands a new social order. In describing this desired development, a certain Utopian element remains an integral part of the sys-

[53] *Ibid.*, p. 32.
[54] Vorländer, *Kant und Marx*, p. 184. His analysis of this lecture is careful and penetrating.
[55] *Wie ist wissenschaftlicher Sozialismus möglich?* p. 37.
[56] *Ibid.*, p. 33.
[57] *Ibid.*, p. 35.
[58] *Ibid.*, p. 19.
[59] *Loc. cit.*
[60] *Ibid.*, p. 20.

tem of thought. Socialism is "Utopian" not in the sense of building of castles in the air, but in being a movement toward something which is not now in existence. The difference between Marx and his forerunners is not that they were Utopians and he a scientist: they were all, to some extent, Utopians. The difference is one of degree, not kind.

When we confront Bernstein's definition of Socialism with those of science, the contrast will be obvious. *No ism is science*, for science is free from bias. But Socialism is the greatest of all *isms*, it is tendentious through and through. It makes claims upon the future, based on ethical considerations of social interest. Not that Socialism cannot learn from the sciences—it strengthens its foundations by relying upon insights into the structure of society. For tactical considerations science is invaluable; Socialism uses science, but it is not, in itself, a science.[61] Therefore, Bernstein proposed, let us rename our discipline "Critical Socialism."

Bernstein's approach is far removed from Kant's understanding of "Wissenschaft." Had Bernstein written in English and maintained that "ethics is not a science," it would have meant merely that ethics is not like physics or chemistry. This point of view Kant would have accepted fully. But Bernstein said, in German, that ethics is not a "Wissenschaft," and claimed to be following Kant. However, the whole point of Kant's ethical writings is that ethics is, indeed, a "Wissenschaft"; that is, subject to disciplined, rational understanding. While fundamentally different from the natural sciences, Kant held, ethics has its own laws and proofs and evidence. We must conclude, therefore, that Bernstein had, after all, misunderstood Kant.

---

[61] Bernstein emphasized in a later comment on his lecture that he had not suggested that Socialism could not rest on scientific foundations. The Socialism of Marx and Engels, as a theory of economic development, was scientific to the extent that it dealt with that development. But it was important to recall, Bernstein pointed out, that their doctrine contained imporant nonscientific elements. Too, we must remember that no doctrine is above criticism. "Entwicklungsgang eines Sozialisten," in *Die Volkswirtschaftslehre der Gegenwart in Selbstdarstellungen*, I, 38, 53.

Bernstein's excursions into Critical Philosophy brought forth a large number of objections from the party. Bebel sent Bernstein an angry letter, reminiscent of the 1898 correspondence between the two men:

I have seen a large number of reviews in the bourgeois press which prove once more with what greed these people have jumped on your latest talk. . . . After these discussions in the opposition press we shall not be able to avoid commenting in our party press on your lecture once it is available in print.

I doubt very much whether people in the party will be grateful to you. This continuous opening of new discussions creates bitterness in our ranks. . . .

But the worst thing is that we have to quarrel with each other once more, at a time when we should rally our forces against the enemy. . . .

You have done a disservice to the party with this talk. . . . I ask you: Why is *this* talk any business of students? If you have to deliver it at all, why not in a party meeting where it could have been answered immediately? [62]

In the ensuing debate, Bernstein did not materially alter his point of view. Its import is clear: in spite of some superficial resemblances to the Critical Philosophy, Bernstein was never a Kantian. True, he demanded a critical and searching examination of the presuppositions of Socialist theory, but he never followed through Kant's speculations in the realms of knowledge and ethics. His denial that ethics had the status of a rational discipline was a clear indication of the fact that he had never entered fully into Kant's thought, and therefore his slogan, "Under this banner—Kant, not Hegel—the working class fights for its emancipation today," [63] must be taken with a grain of salt. He called on Kant, but he remained a common-sense philosopher.

[62] Bebel to Bernstein, May 24, 1901, Bernstein Archives.
[63] Bernstein, ed., *Dokumente des Sozialismus,* V (1905), 421.

The Meaning of Revisionist Philosophy

> *Wer einmal an der Hegelei und Schleiermach-*
> *erei erkrankte, wird nie wieder ganz curiert.*

FRIEDRICH NIETZSCHE

Critics have succeeded in showing that Revisionism lacked profundity and originality—that, as a matter of fact, some of its assumptions rested on misunderstandings. Bernstein, as we noted, did not fully grasp the significance of the dialectic to Marxism, and he wrongly took Kant's separation of the natural sciences from the rational study of ethics for a denial that ethics could be a rational discipline. But it must be said that he had absorbed far more of the Marxist view of history than these criticisms would indicate. To Bernstein, Marx's interpretation was a living thing, not a stereotyped model. It was "above all a method of *understanding* history," as he once wrote to Kautsky,[64] and he objected, rightly, to a rigid application of Marxian terminology and categories. This procedure, he felt, put historical truth in a straitjacket in order to fit the infinite variety of life to a single scheme.[65] Bernstein's own use of Marx's historical materialism—in *Cromwell and Communism*—had resulted in a brilliant study which was free from the flaws of a narrow orthodoxy and which did not do violence to facts for the sake of a theory.

The core of Revisionist philosophy has now begun to emerge. We know that Bernstein abandoned dialectical materialism and approached, but did not adopt, neo-Kantianism. He stood between these two major schools and really belongs to a third: Naturalism.[66] Two elements gave Revisionism its

[64] Bernstein to Kautsky, May 11, 1928, Bernstein Archives.
[65] *Loc. cit.* He cites Mehring's *Lessing-Legende* as a bad example.
[66] Naturalism is difficult to define; it has been given widely differing interpretations. Many thinkers who sharply disagree with each other still classify themselves as "Naturalists." Fundamentally, they share a temper, a way of looking at the world. Cf. Yervant Krikorian, ed., *Naturalism and the Human Spirit* (New York: Columbia University Press, 1944).

particular form: one was its empiricism, the other its keen interest in naturalist ethics.

Bernstein's empiricism is apparent everywhere. His philosophical case against Marxism was really an afterthought; it was appended to his attempt to refute Marxist conclusions on empirical grounds. He distrusted metaphysical structures as Utopian constructions and suspected abstract thought of leading to unwarranted results. The world to him was "a complex of ready-made objects and processes." [67] True, his empiricism was not identical with the extreme antiphilosophical attitude of the Fabians, whom he condemned for reducing Socialism to "a series of sociopolitical measures, without any connecting element that could express the unity of their fundamental thought and action." [68] But his kinship to the Fabians was closer than he cared to admit.

Siegfried Marck has compared the period of Revisionism to a kind of Enlightenment epoch, that is, an era of doubt which usually follows on the heels of a time of dogmatic creativity. Revisionism, according to this theory, represents the application of the acid of skepticism to a theoretical structure; it is "the attempt to corrode dogmatic incrustations and to test the apparently eternal truths of orthodoxy in an empirical fashion." [69] Revisionism came, of course, at a time which was favorable to just such an enterprise. Further, Marck says that this empiricism is at once the strength and weakness of Revisionism. Strength, because the danger of drawing arbitrary conclusions from dialectical materialism was growing ever greater and needed the cool shower of empirical investigation supplied by the Revisionists. Weakness, because it gave up the very real advantages of the dialectical method and tended to pay too much attention to short-run developments. "Even the unjustified anticipations (*Vorwegnahme*), the false time estimates in the system of a genius have a peculiar endurance and force. Often, they are apparently contradicted by the happenings of the day, but they are then confirmed in the long run in the most striking fashion." [70]

[67] Bernstein, *Zur Geschichte und Theorie des Sozialismus*, p. 340.
[68] *Ibid.*, p. 177.
[69] Marck, "Die Philosophie des Revisionismus," p. 23.
[70] *Ibid.*, p. 30.

Bernstein's strong concern with ethical problems forced him to qualify his empiricism. His training—both the earlier influences of Marx and Engels and the later one of Kant—was far too strong to permit him to range himself along the side of the Positivists. The latter, in their infatuation with "facts" and with the methods of the natural sciences, reduced all investigations of human problems to ethically neutral pursuits.[71] In any event, Bernstein's "Positivism" must be sharply differentiated from twentieth-century Logical Positivism, for which ethical speculation is the remnant of outmoded metaphysical thinking and ethical issues are pseudo problems.

Marxist Socialism, following Hegel, had no distinct ethical theory. The work of Revisionism resulted in nothing less than the reintroduction of ethics into Socialism. Marxism, Bernstein argued, is partly an analysis of existing conditions and current developments. To that extent it is free from bias; that is, scientific. But Socialism is also a pattern of demands. True, in Marxism these demands are clothed in terms of predictions based upon the tendencies previously examined in scientific fashion, but this is merely a scientific cover disguising desires for a just society. These desires are not scientific, since they exhibit an orderly system of preferences—in other words, they are ethical judgments. A Socialist theory without these ethical elements would be sterile.

Equally sterile, Bernstein continues, would be a Socialist *movement* without ethics, and, in fact, the movement is shot through with moral preferences. The workers *want* a new world order. To the extent that this wish is more than self-interest grandiloquently expressed, it is a genuine ethical

[71] It is of importance to note that Bernstein himself held a different view. He said: "My way of thinking would make me a member of the school of Positivist philosophy and sociology. And I would like to have my lecture [How is Scientific Socialism Possible?] taken as proof of this attitude of mine. . . ." "Entwicklungsgang," p. 40. I cannot accept this. He shared an empiricist outlook with the Positivists, but it is possible to be an empiricist without being a Positivist (note our present-day Pragmatists). Bernstein was far too much interested in ethics ever to be a Positivist. Comte's ethics (and Comte was, after all, the father of nineteenth-century Positivism) is purely manipulative.

impulse. Thus the Socialist movement, side by side with the theory that animates it, is largely ethical in character.

Bernstein distinguishes two kinds of Utopianism. The first sort, championed by the great Utopian Socialists, set a goal apart from an investigation of the possibilities of its realization. The second, which Bernstein advocates, sets itself the task of studying present-day society without fear or favor. It then establishes its aims realistically; it goes beyond ascertained fact, making an imaginative leap into the future, but it is careful to curb its imagination. To Bernstein, the goal of Socialism appears as a never-ending task. The world is never finished, never perfect; the reformer's work, like the housewife's, is never done. This is one sense in which his remark, "The goal is nothing, the movement everything," may be understood. Bernstein's concept of never-ceasing effort was derived from Fichte, who had posited the Self (*Ich*) as incomplete, and as constantly striving to transcend its limitations. Fichte, like Bernstein after him, saw the eternal striving of the Self as the response to resistance and the overcoming of obstacles.[72]

This ethical theory of Revisionism, which allied Bernstein with Marx's predecessors, has been variously evaluated. Orthodox Marxists called it "a throwback to the most primitive level of the labor movement." [73] They regarded the revival of ethics as a paralyzing element which deprived the Socialist movement of its dialectical certainty of victory and of its "scientific" character.[74] The unity of thought and action, of dynamic interpenetration of tactics and final goal, so highly prized by the orthodoxy, was destroyed by Revisionism.

More friendly critics, on the other hand, pointed out that the separation of theory from practice was necessary for the clarification of either. If we pretend to see the final goal in every move of the working class, if we put the proletariat in place of the Hegelian Absolute Spirit, these critics reasoned, the dialectic finally becomes the snare that Bernstein had thought it to be; anything and everything can be deduced

[72] Cf. Richard Kroner, *Von Kant bis Hegel*, I, 513–18.
[73] Lukacz, *Geschichte und Klassenbewusstsein*, p. 36.
[74] *Ibid.*, pp. 36–37, 50; hints of it are in Marcuse, *Reason and Revolution*, pp. 399–400.

from such speculative constructions.[75] What is more, it is not true to say that the positing of ethical goals weakens the proletariat. Quite on the contrary, this would strengthen it by placing a value on the moral will of the participant in the struggle. Marxist neutral determinism had acted to cripple just that moral will. The loss of the certainty of victory is small compared to the gain that lies in the recognition of the ethical worth of the struggle and the moral character of the hoped-for goal.[76]

Philosophical questions were not as significant for Revisionism as the analysis of economic and political developments. But whatever the impact of philosophy on the movement, its stress was on ethics and the striving for limited, attainable goals. It strongly supported the other Revisionist arguments against revolution and in favor of parliamentary gradualism.

[75] Marck, "Die Philosophie des Revisionismus," pp. 27–30.
[76] Cf. Robert Michels, "Psychologie der antikapitalistischen Massenbewegungen," in *Grundriss der Sozialökonomik*, Vol. IX, Part 1, pp. 301–11.

Chapter 7

The Economics of Revisionism

Capitalism: From Competition to Monopoly

> *I was led by my studies to the conclusion that legal relations as well as forms of state could neither be understood by themselves, nor explained by the so-called general processes of the human mind, but that they are rooted in the material conditions of life which are summed up by Hegel . . . under the name "civil society"; the anatomy of that civil society is to be sought in political economy.*
>
> KARL MARX

JUST AS REVISIONISM attacked the philosophical foundations of Marxism, so did it lead a determined assault on Marxist economics. As the divergences between Revisionist and orthodox Marxist economics are analyzed in this chapter, the reader should bear in mind the vital difference between the attitudes fundamental to the two schools of thought: the former believed in a peaceful but not inevitable growth into Socialism, the latter held that the transition from capitalism to Socialism was dialectically necessary and would probably come through revolution.

To Marx and Engels, capitalism was a historical phenomenon that had begun its career as a profoundly liberalizing drive. It had spread civilization, built cities, and deeply altered the relations of man to man. Capitalism was a social system primarily devoted to the production of goods designed for sale in the market. Capitalist societies, Marx says at the beginning of *Capital*, present the picture of "an immense accumulation of commodities." [1] These products are created

[1] I, 41. Marx here quotes himself, from *Critique of Political Economy,* p. 19.

by "free" wage labor, by men and women who are not legally bound to work (as serfs or slaves would be) and who are "free" also in the ironic sense that they have no property other than their labor power which they are compelled to sell.

Capitalism can develop only if capital is accumulated. Factories must be built, old processes and machinery must be replaced by new, additional labor power must be hired for expanded operations—all this calls for tremendous sums of capital. In other words, capitalist societies produce far more wealth than is immediately consumed.

As capitalism achieves maturity, Marx believed, its economic contribution to human civilization diminishes. Contradictions become apparent within the system, the solid structure starts to crack: "From forms of development of the forces of production, these [social] relations turn into their fetters." Capitalism fundamentally changes its character; free competition gives way to monopolies. It is in the analysis of the nature of this transformation that we can find the first serious conflict between orthodox Marxists and Revisionists.

The growth of capitalism, Marx held, is fueled by ever-increasing sums of capital. These accumulations find their way into the hands of fewer and fewer capitalists. This process may be observed to take two distinct forms: the increase in the size of corporations (as well as production units such as individual factories within a corporate structure) and the concentration of wealth into fewer hands.[2]

The centralization of economic power through enlargement of production units results in the elimination of independent producers and in the transfer of their holdings to big business or industry.[3] As Marx put it, the "development of the productiveness of social labor presupposes cooperation on a large

[2] I have used, for this chapter as a whole, Paul Sweezy's interesting *The Theory of Capitalist Development,* which I found most useful in spite of many disagreements. For this section, pp. 254–69 were most relevant. Cf. also Karl Renner, *Die Wirtschaft als Gesamtprozess,* and Erika Rikli, *Der Revisionismus,* pp. 44–56.

[3] Cf. Marx, *Capital,* I, 681–89: Chapter xxv, Section 12. The social consequences of this process, the gradual disappearance of the middle class and the impoverishment of the proletariat, will be analyzed later in this chapter.

scale." [4] Capitalist production feeds on money freed for investment, and capital enters into the productive stream in an ever-increasing magnitude:

> Every accumulation becomes the means of new accumulation. With the increasing mass of wealth which functions as capital, accumulation increases the concentration of that wealth in the hands of individual capitalists and thereby widens the basis of production on a large scale. [5]

But as capital accumulations increase, so does the number of capitalists, so that we have two counteracting tendencies operative at the same time. As social wealth grows, more men become capitalists, but, on the other hand, there constantly occurs an "expropriation of capitalist by capitalist" [6] which results in centralization: "Capital grows in one place to a huge mass in a single hand, because it has in another place been lost by many." [7]

Marx does not develop this centralization process in detail, but hints at a number of social forces that bring it about. He cites, first of all, the function of the competitive market, which tends to favor the large producers over the smaller since the former can undersell the latter. Next, as modern industry takes sophisticated shape, the amount of capital required to carry on business becomes greater. The credit system enters the game at this point. It begins

> as a modest helper of accumulation and draws by invisible threads the money resources scattered all over the surface of society into the hands of individuals or associated capitalists. But soon it becomes a new and formidable weapon in the competitive struggle, and finally it transforms itself into an immense social mechanism for the centralization of capitals. [8]

[4] *Ibid.*, p. 684.
[5] *Ibid.*, p. 685.
[6] *Ibid.*, p. 686.
[7] *Loc. cit.*
[8] *Ibid.*, p. 687.

On these twin foundations of competition and credit is built the structure of monopoly capitalism. The growth of cartels and trusts, which came after Marx's death—but in time to be noted by Engels—added considerable weight to this analysis.[9]

Marx's chapter on centralization is important to his system, because it leads him directly to the causes of the inevitable demise of capitalism. The accumulation of capital, speeded up and extended by concentration and centralization, leads to a change in what Marx called the organic composition of capital. The proportion of constant capital (plant, equipment, raw materials) increases in relation to variable capital (that is, the wages bill). Since surplus value is drawn only from the latter, Marx saw capitalism faced with an ever-falling rate of profit. This process leads to a "surplus laboring population," [10] the "industrial reserve army of the unemployed." It is accelerated by the advances of accumulation.[11] Crises become the outward symptom of the contradictions of capitalism, the industrial reserve army the very symbol of the failure of the system to organize the economic potential of society—capitalism must inevitably be replaced by Socialism.

How did the Revisionists feel about this account of capitalist development?

Eduard Bernstein accepted the theory of the growth of competitive into monopolist capitalism "as a tendency." "The forces described," he proceeded, "are present and work in the direction" indicated by Marx.[12] Indeed, the Marxist thesis has a solid empirical basis:

> The falling rate of profit is a fact; the advent of overproduction and crisis is a fact; the periodic destruction of capital is a fact; concentration and centralization of industrial capital is a fact; the increase in the rate of surplus value is a fact.[13]

[9] Cf. Sweezy, *Theory of Capitalist Development*, pp. 262–65.
[10] *Capital*, I, 693.
[11] *Ibid.*, p. 697. In these pages Marx drops all pretense of scientific neutrality and writes with fiery irony.
[12] *Die Voraussetzungen des Sozialismus und die Aufgaben der Sozialdemokratie*, p. 83.
[13] *Ibid.*, p. 84.

But Marx's picture—and this is where the objection enters —leads to false conclusions because it is overdrawn. While Marx qualified his categorical statements at the outset, he concluded with a dogmatic assertion: "One capitalist always kills many." [14] The Marxist view of capitalist society as two hostile classes facing each other in bitter battle—a small wealthy class of bourgeois against a large, poor, but mature proletariat—is incorrect. Strongly centrifugal economic forces counteract the trends which Marx described.

The psychological importance of the two varying theories is obvious. The Revisionists were anxious to agree with Marx that capitalism was undergoing a fundamental shift, for that shift would help to explain their theory of transition from capitalism to Socialism. Centralized giant industries could be more easily socialized than scattered holdings, and give capitalism the kind of ripeness one expects of a ripe apple: it is ready to fall. At the same time, it was imperative to show that the centralization process was not as thoroughgoing or comprehensive as Marx made it out to be. A peaceful transformation of capitalism into Socialism required both a gradual and incomplete movement toward monopoly capitalism.

Bernstein argued, then, that concentration and centralization were indeed taking place, but that the continued existence of independent small enterprises and the infinite variety of industrial establishments should not be forgotten. Modern capitalism does not simplify its class relations but differentiates them to an ever greater degree.[15] Small and medium-sized enterprises are not growing at the rate of the giant industrial combines, but they have shown themselves viable, and that is, after all, the crucial issue.[16] To prove this point, he cited statistics from both England and Germany.[17] See Table page 171n.

In many cases the very existence of giant enterprises calls forth new small and medium-sized businesses; through division of labor the former deliver semi-finished goods to the

[14] *Capital*, I, 836.
[15] *Voraussetzungen*, p. 89.
[16] *Ibid.*, p. 98.
[17] Cf. *ibid.*, pp. 94–108. One example (p. 100) must suffice here:

latter, which prepare the product for the market. What is more, small businesses have more direct access to consumers and are thus in a position to offer successful battle to large industry—take bakeries as an example.[18] Commerce, transportation, and agriculture are three lines of endeavor in which the process of centralization will not succeed in wiping out the small entrepreneur.

When Kautsky came to reply to Bernstein's arguments, he found that he and his opponent really disagreed about very little. This did not prevent "Pope" Kautsky from presenting a very detailed refutation. Actually, Kautsky admitted, Marx's strikingly "concise" description of the process of capitalist development had to be taken "cum grano salis"; [19] we cannot tell exactly *when* all the small businesses will have disappeared. In any case, the chief question is whether the tendency noted by Marx exists or not.

Of course, Both Kautsky and Bernstein agreed that it did, and one cannot help but feel that this argument—like so many others between the two men during these years—was

WORKERS EMPLOYED IN TRADES

	1882	1895	Increase in Percent
Small enterprises (1–5 persons)	2,457,950	3,056,318	24.3
Medium-size enterprises (6–10 persons)	500,097	833,409	66.6
Larger enterprises (11–50 persons)	891,623	1,620,848	81.8

Bernstein comments: "In the same period of time, the population increased by only 13.5 percent. Although large enterprises increased their legions even more—by 88.7 percent—this meant the absorption of small businesses in only a few cases. . . . The figures show that the extension and expansion of large industries by leaps and bounds represents only one side of economic development."

18 *Ibid.*, pp. 98–99.
19 *Bernstein und das sozialdemokratische Programm*, p. 50.

largely a matter of words.[20] The difference of opinion was, after all, only one of emphasis.

About twenty years later, Bernstein took up the same problem once more, and it is interesting to note that he had not changed his point of view, although he was now inclined to give the process of concentration somewhat more weight. "If a significant measure of concentration of factories has taken place," he said in 1921,

> it did not occur to the degree to which it had been assumed and as the Erfurt Program had proclaimed when it said, "The medium-sized industries are disappearing." They are not disappearing. But let us not mix up a factory (*Betrieb*) with an enterprise (*Unternehmung*). An enterprise often comprises several factories. . . . If we had a statistical compilation of factories, we could observe a far greater degree of concentration than now appears in the figures.[21]

However, countervailing tendencies were still powerful.

It is regrettable that Bernstein was too old to take up the problem once more after 1924, when German industry centralized and cartelized on a scale never before known in German history. The new facts would have compelled him to revise his concentration theory drastically. What effect this would have had upon the rest of his thought is, of course, impossible to say.

The second result of capitalist accumulation in Marxist thought—the concentration of wealth into fewer hands—found Bernstein presenting objections far stronger than those offered against the concentration-of-industry theory. While he never claimed that social differences were disappearing, he dissented from the categorical view of Marx that the middle class was vanishing and that the number of property holders was diminishing. The contrary was true, he maintained: the propertied were actually growing in number.

In attempting to buttress his theory, Bernstein did not dis-

[20] Bernstein recognized this well. Cf. "Abwehr wider Kautskys Schrift," in *Zur Geschichte und Theorie des Sozialismus*, pp. 406–16.
[21] *Der Sozialismus einst und jetzt*, p. 41.

tinguish between those who owned capital and those who controlled it. What mattered to him was not how many—or rather, how few—people controlled the destiny of the economy; he wanted to show that the owning classes were not shrinking in size and that the process of the bifurcation of society into two hostile groups which Marx had predicted was not taking place. He made wide use of contemporary statistics and cited the rise of widespread shareholding in corporations as a proof of his argument.[22]

Another source on which Bernstein relied was income statistics. A study of tax returns in the industrialized countries of Europe showed sizable proportions of the populations to be enjoying respectable incomes,[23] and there were no indications of a deterioration anywhere. "The number of propertied is growing absolutely and relatively," was Bernstein's conclusion.[24] Given his definition of "propertied," his conclusion seems valid enough.

In his letter to the Stuttgart Party Congress, which preceded the writing of the *Voraussetzungen*, Bernstein had said:

Social conditions have not reached that acute tension which the *Communist Manifesto* had predicted. Not only would it be useless, it would be the height of folly to conceal this from ourselves. The number of propertied persons has not diminished but become larger. The enormous increase in social wealth is accompanied not by a shrinking number of capitalist magnates but by a growing number of capitalists of all ranges of wealth. The middle classes change their character, but they do not disappear from the social scale.[25]

[22] Share-selling corporations in most countries were "anonymous societies," but at the turn of the century many English corporations listed the shareholders by name and by stake in the company. In taking these figures, Bernstein found the number of propertied persons to be extraordinarily large. Lipton's Tea Co. had 74,262 shareholders, the Manchester Canal Corporation about 40,000 shareholders, etc. Cf. *Voraussetzungen*, pp. 85–86.
[23] *Ibid.*, pp. 86–88.
[24] *Ibid.*, p. 88.
[25] Quoted *ibid.*, Preface, pp. 6–7. On the fate of the middle class, see also below, pp. 204–219.

To this view Bernstein held fast in spite of Kautsky's strenuous attempts at a refutation, and he said in 1902:

> The assumption that the development of enterprises would parallel the development of income distribution is fundamentally false. . . . Property in great enterprises is becoming more collective in character or is being spread more and more widely through society by the growth of corporations, limited liability companies, and similar partnerships.[26]

Bernstein's qualifications of the Marxist concentration-of-industry and rejection of the concentration-of-wealth theories had widespread ramifications in the field of Socialist tactics. These tactics, of course, also rested on the Revisionist modification of the Marxist impoverishment and crisis theories. But before we turn to these subjects, let us cast a glance at the Marxist-Revisionist dispute over value theory.

Value

> *Accumulate, accumulate! That is Moses and the prophets!*
>
> KARL MARX

Marx believed that he had found the secret of capitalist accumulation. In the first volume of *Capital* he elaborated this discovery in an exhaustive exposition of his laws of value and surplus value. It is not the object of these pages to offer a full outline of his reasoning, but to discuss it as it bears on the Revisionist controversy.

It must be said at the outset that Marx did not make matters easy for himself. The terms in which he saw the problem eliminated a number of solutions that would have given a plausible explanation of how the money that is injected into the capitalist system is obtained. Marx denied that it originated in circulation or in the fact that the capitalist buys

[26] Bernstein, *Die heutige Einkommensbewegung und die Aufgaben der Volkswirtschaft*, p. 13.

commodities below, or sells them above, their value. This common-sense approach was rejected. The capitalist "must buy his commodities at their value, must sell them at their value, and yet at the end of the process must withdraw more value from circulation than he threw into it at starting. . . . These are the conditions of the problem." [27]

The solution of the riddle must be sought in the process of production itself. Marx started from the classical labor theory of value, as perfected by Ricardo. But he gave that theory a special twist. Briefly, it is this: Commodities of all sorts are exchanged on the market. The very fact that they can be exchanged for one another must mean that they possess a common element. But what do, say, twenty yards of linen have in common with ten pounds of tea? "If," Marx says, "we leave out of consideration the use-value of commodities, they have only one common property left, that of being products of labor." [28] Again, if we bring all labor on a common denominator, we are "reduced to one and the same sort of labor, human labor in the abstract." [29]

The magnitude of the value of a commodity, then, is to be measured in the amount of labor power embodied in it; that is, "the labor time socially necessary" for the production of the commodity in question.[30] It follows that commodities with an equal amount of such labor time contained in them must be of equal value. This law of value, according to Marx, governs exchange relations. Barring accidental fluctuations, commodities ultimately are exchanged according to their values.[31] This is important, and Marx emphatically maintains this thesis throughout Volume I of *Capital*.

But the laborer is the source not only of value but also of something called "surplus value." These are not two activities but one: "If we . . . compare the two processes of produc-

[27] *Capital*, I, 185.
[28] *Ibid.*, p. 44.
[29] *Ibid.*, p. 45.
[30] *Ibid.*, p. 46.
[31] *Ibid.*, p. 184n. Also: "It is true, commodities may be sold at prices deviating from their values, but these deviations are to be considered as infractions of the laws of the exchange of commodities. . . . In its normal form, the circulation of commodities demands the exchange of equivalents." *Ibid.*, pp. 176–77, 178.

ing value and of creating surplus value, we see that the latter is nothing but the continuation of the former beyond a certain point." [32] The capitalist, Marx explains, treats the worker as a commodity. The wage he pays is for purchase of the worker's labor power. Now the value of the laborer is like the value of any other commodity: it depends on the working time required to replace him. It if takes a worker, let us say, five hours of labor to earn his bare subsistence (which we shall set, for the sake of simplicity, at $5) then no surplus value would arise if the worker were paid that $5 and worked the necessary five hours. But the capitalist, in control of the labor market owing to the existence of a reserve army of unemployed, buys the laborer at his value ($5 a day) and then compels him to work, say, ten hours. In this case, the worker, who has been purchased at his full value as a commodity, produces twice as much. For five hours a day he literally works for nothing. The work done during that time (five dollars' worth) is surplus value and accrues to the capitalist.[33] This explains, then, how a capitalist can buy and sell commodities at their values and still obtain funds for investment. He literally steals them from the worker, although the theft is disguised. The mystery is solved.

Other Socialists before him had made a moral issue of the fact that the capitalist robbed the workers, but it was left to Marx to put the problem into cold, scientific terminology. But this did not mean that all difficulties had been overcome: there is a corollary which follows from the above theories that got Marx into serious trouble.

Marx assumed that surplus value arises out of labor, and out of nothing else. In other words, only those elements of a commodity which are traceable to variable capital (the wages bill) could be the source of surplus value, but not those derived from constant capital (plant, equipment, raw mate-

[32] *Ibid.*, p. 218.
[33] For a very clear exposition, cf. *Capital,* I, 239–40. The part of the day during which the laborer earns his subsistence is "necessary" working time—"necessary," for he would have to work that long even if he were self-employed. The other part, during which he creates no value for himself, may be called "surplus labor-time." *Ibid.*, pp. 240–41.

rials). It follows that the larger the proportion of variable to constant capital (or, as he put it, the lower the organic composition of capital), the greater the profit—if (as Marx had categorically maintained) commodities are exchanged according to their values.

The only trouble is that this assumption can be demonstrated to be false: rates of profit tend toward equality and have little to do with the labor power embodied in the products.

Theoretical economists have fought over this question of the "contradiction" in Marx's economic system for well over half of a century. It would be absurd to assume that a political scientist could provide the answer; these are deep waters, even for the economist. Let us content ourselves with a look at the various approaches that have been made.

Marx himself was aware that a difficulty existed. He had written the relevant chapters of Volume III at about the time he was working on the same problem in Volume I. In Volume I he assumed that values are expressed in actual prices. In Volume III he abandoned this assumption and began to worry the problem of *transformation* of values into prices. Marx proposed this solution: Competition among capitalists tends to bring the rate of profit into equilibrium. New capitalists enter highly profitable fields of endeavor and leave low-profit lines. Thus demand plays a major role in price determination. Prices no longer correspond to value, but the *total sum* of values in a given society is equal to the total sum of prices; the exclusive reliance on labor power is relinquished.

This solution was generally regarded as unsatisfactory. Everyone, critic and apologist alike, agreed that Marx had changed his position as he moved "from the simple dogmatism of the first volume of *Capital* to the intricate formulations of Volume III." [34] Among the earliest and most distinguished critics was the Austrian economist Eugen von Böhm-Bawerk, who had maintained in 1884, before the long-awaited appearance of Volume III, that Marx was caught in an insoluble contradiction:

[34] Joan Robinson, *An Essay on Marxian Economics,* p. 10. Her essay is a brilliant analysis of Marxian economics from a Keynesian point of view.

Either products do actually exchange in the long run in proportion to the labor attaching to them—in which case an equalization of the gains of capital is impossible; or there is an equalization of the gains of capital—in which case it is impossible that products should continue to exchange in proportion to the labor attaching to them.[35]

He buttressed his position in 1896 with a brilliant and influential essay, *Zum Abschluss des Marxschen Systems.*

Of more recent critics the most notable is the British economist Joan Robinson who has argued that Marx would have built a more solid theoretical structure if he had not used his theory of value. "No point of substance in Marx's argument depends upon the labor theory of value." Indeed, "none of the important ideas which he expresses in terms of the concept of value cannot be better expressed without it." [36]

The defenders of Marx, not unexpectedly, took an opposite position. They argued that the first volume of *Capital* dissected capitalism at a high level of abstraction, which could make the assumption that exchange values and prices tended to be identical, and that nothing was lost by giving up this point once capitalism was analyzed in more concrete fashion.[37] Hilferding, in a direct reply to Böhm-Bawerk, complained that his opponent looked upon economics from the viewpoint of the individual, and not of society, as Marx had done. "It is . . . because labor is the social bond uniting an atomized society, and not because labor is the matter most

[35] *Karl Marx and the Close of his System,* p. 28 (translation of *Zum Abschluss des Marxschen Systems;* the quotation is taken from his own earlier book, *Kapital und Kapitalzins* [2 vols.; Innsbruck: Wagnersche Universitäts-Buchhandlung, 1884–89]).

[36] *Essay on Marxian Economics,* p. 20. Harold Laski felt that Marx's explanation of the "seeming disharmony" was "hardly satisfactory," and that the Marxian theory of value was not defensible as an economic analysis. But, Laski concluded, "at the root of Marx's view there lies an ethical test of value," and its appeal to the workers, as well as its partial truth as a description, is unquestioned. *Communism,* pp. 100–101, 116, 120. Similar positions are held by Joseph A. Schumpeter, *Capitalism, Socialism, and Democracy,* 2d ed., pp. 27, 29, and by A. D. Lindsay, *Karl Marx's Capital,* pp. 53–108.

[37] Sweezy, *Theory of Capitalist Development,* pp. 69–70.

technically relevant, that labor is the principle of value and that the law of value is endowed with reality." [38] If we look upon economic categories such as commodity or price or value "in isolation," we shall never be able to understand modern society in its totality—a favorite charge leveled by Marxists against "bourgeois economists." Von Bortkiewicz, a skillful German statistician, claimed that Marx had made no more than a logical error in his solution of the transformation problem, and he set out to correct this error in a highly mathematical paper.[39] This last approach to the problem has been adopted by Paul Sweezy in what is probably the most accessible book on Marxist economics in English.[40]

These are minor variations on the same theme. One thing they have in common—a sturdy defense of Marx's theory of value. Why not start with price calculation and abandon the Marxist value theory? Sweezy asks rhetorically. The answer is significant, because it directly contradicts the opinion of such critics as Joan Robinson, as well as the Revisionists:

> One might be tempted to go farther and concede that from the formal point of view it is possible to dispense with value calculation even in the analysis of the behavior of the system as a whole. . . . Price calculation [however] mystifies the underlying social relations of capitalist production. Since profit is calculated as a return on total capital, the idea inevitably arises that capital as such is in some way "productive." Things appear to be endowed with an independent power of their own. From the point of view of value calculation it is easy to recognize this as a flagrant form of commodity fetishism. From the point of view of price calculation it appears to be natural and inevitable. . . . If we believe, with Marx and the great classical economists, that profit can be understood only as a deduction from the combined product of social labor, there

[38] Rudolf Hilferding, *Böhm-Bawerk's Criticism of Marx,* p. 134.
[39] Ladislaus von Bortkiewicz, "On the Correction of Marx's Fundamental Theoretical Construction in the Third Volume of *Capital,*" translated by Paul Sweezy, reprinted in Böhm-Bawerk, *Karl Marx and the Close of his System,* as an appendix.
[40] *The Theory of Capitalist Development,* referred to earlier.

is no way of dispensing with value calculation and the labor theory of value on which it is based.[41]

Orthodox Marxists have clung to the labor theory of value as one of the pillars of their social theory. Their devotion is easy to understand. The theory is objective and ostensibly removed from variations of taste as exemplified in demand or mere subjective preferences which are beyond the reach of quantitative verification. Its objectivity helps to sustain the claim that it is scientific. And this claim to science does more than merely enhance its propaganda value: it seems to demonstrate that exploitation is not an accident but of the very essence of capitalism.

But the Revisionists did not quite see it that way.

Along with most other Socialists, Bernstein was greatly disappointed in Volume III of *Capital,* which he read immediately upon its appearance in 1894. He felt that it expressed the deep inner struggles of Marx, who had been compelled to acknowledge that capitalism could not be grasped as simply as he had indicated in Volume I. Bernstein admitted later that he had found Marx's solution of the value-price relation "sobering," and that it led him to doubt the validity of the whole Marxist theory of value.

The two decades preceding the publication of Volume III had witnessed the creation and elaboration of a new value theory. Several remarkable Austrian scholars—Menger, Wieser, Böhm-Bawerk—introduced marginal analysis into economics, and an English economist, William Stanley Jevons, worked out the same approach independently. The value theory of the Austrian school was the reverse of the Ricardian-Marxian theory. Value, according to this group of thinkers, cannot be calculated on the basis of cost of production or labor embodied in the product. It is, on the contrary, a function of utility; that is, it is derived from the cumulative desires (backed by ability to pay) of individual purchasers. Utility—or value—may be determined at the margin. This formidable statement merely means that value

[41] *Ibid.,* pp. 129–30.

depends on the relation of wants and available supplies. Only if wants are greater than supplies does the problem of allocation arise. Menger takes as his example a farmer who has x sacks of grain on hand. With his supply he feeds his family and his livestock, he keeps a supply for seed and for the brewing of beer. If all these wants can be adequately satisfied, no problem arises. But assume that the last sack of grain is destroyed or stolen. (Since all sacks have the same value, any one of them could be that last sack.) Then which one of the wants for which the grain has been allocated will remain unmet? The least important one, of course. Which one that will be depends on the subjective make-up of our farmer. In our example he is most likely to give up brewing beer for a year, but, if he is a confirmed toper, he might just as well decide to let his family starve.[42] In short, "the value of any portion of goods, when a supply exists, is represented by the least important use to which such a portion is applied." [43]

This theory was further refined over the next few years, but we do not need to go into its intricacies here. It is sufficient to note the contrast with the Marxist view of value. The marginal theory is subjective; prices are determined on the basis of inner preferences and of bargaining between buyer and seller. Value is not an intrinsic characteristic of a commodity. It can change in many ways: growth of demand, new discoveries of supply, different methods of manufacture, better advertising—all play a part in the determination of value. The individual making a choice with his money is once again in the center of economics.

The Austrians gained great influence over economic thought. In England, Jevons' parallel theories were used by the Fabian Socialists, whose leading economists—Bernard Shaw and Sidney Webb—were confirmed marginalists.

Eduard Bernstein was fully acquainted with the literature on value.[44] He occupied himself with the problem in the

[42] Menger's example is from *Grundsätze der Volkswirtschaftslehre,* as summarized by Alexander Gray, *The Development of Economic Doctrine,* pp. 345–48.
[43] *Ibid.,* p. 348.
[44] The only other Revisionist who was well informed on this subject was Conrad Schmidt. Cf. Rikli, *Der Revisionismus,* pp. 68–74.

period of his renunciation of Marxism, and his suggestions are most interesting:

> Peter and Paul stand before a box filled with mineral. "These are parallel-planed hemihedral crystals," says Peter. "They are pyrites," says Paul.
>   Which of the two is right?
>   "Both are right," says the mineralogist. "Peter's statement refers to form, Paul's to substance." . . . The same is true in the quarrel over value theory.[45]

Both concepts of value, the Marxist and the marginalist, Bernstein believed, contain part of the whole truth. "Economic value is androgynous: it contains the element of utility (use value, demand) and cost of production (labor power)." [46] Since the two theories represent, as it were, different sectors of the same problem, it is not possible to choose between them. In this point Bernstein once more showed his indebtedness to the Fabians by following the lead of Graham Wallas, and Bernard Shaw.[47] Bernstein further maintained that the two theories were not as far apart as commonly assumed: he defended Marx against the charge of having omitted considerations of demand from his value theory. Marx's concept of "socially necessary labor time," which plays such a vital part in his work on value, relies in the final analysis on the function of demand, for how else can we determine whether the labor time employed to produce a commodity has been "socially necessary" or not? [48]

But beyond these hints at a synthesis between Marxism and marginalism Bernstein did not go. His few excursions into value theory betrayed, to Kautsky's despair, a thoroughgoing skepticism. His agnosticism fits in well with the rest of Revisionist thought with its bias against metaphysics and abstraction. A synthesis of the two theories would not produce anything useful: "We search for the laws of price formation

[45] Bernstein, "Arbeitswert oder Nutzwert?" *Neue Zeit*, XVII, 2 (1899), 548–49. On the whole subject cf. Rikli, *loc. cit.*
[46] "Arbeitswert oder Nutzwert?" p. 549.
[47] Cf. *Dokumente des Sozialismus*, II (1903), 78 ff., and V (1905), 555–56.
[48] Cf. *Voraussetzungen*, pp. 76–78.

more directly today, and avoid the detour of the convolutions of that metaphysical thing, 'value.' " [49]

Bernstein's discussion of this problem is not free from difficulties; they stem mainly from his failure to distinguish consistently between "value" and "price." [50] His own interests, in any event, lay in the direction of "real price" rather than "abstract value." [51] In the *Voraussetzungen,* Bernstein submitted Marxist value theory to a close analysis and called it a "purely abstract concept." [52] And this abstraction, along with that of the Austrian school, is "admissible as proof for certain purposes only and can claim validity only within definite limits." [53] Value theory, in short, is useful but not universal.

Once Marxist value theory has been limited in this fashion, it follows that the theory of surplus value, too, must be reduced to a mere formula. [54] This does not mean, Bernstein emphatically declared, that exploitation does not take place under capitalism. It most certainly does. But

> the existence of surplus value is an empirical fact which can be demonstrated in experience and needs no deductive proof. Whether Marx's value theory is correct or not is of no significance whatever for the proof of the reality of surplus value. It serves, in this respect, not as a proof but as an aid to analysis, and as an illustration. [55]

Once more, Revisionism approximated English Fabianism by attempting to establish a theory of Socialism without an abstract, universal theory of value or surplus value. Once

[49] *Dokumente des Sozialismus,* V (1905), 559.

[50] Cf. Rikli, *Der Revisionismus,* p. 73.

[51] Bernstein, *Zur Geschichte und Theorie des Sozialismus,* p. 380.

[52] *Voraussetzungen,* p. 73.

[53] *Ibid.,* p. 78.

[54] *Ibid.,* p. 73.

[55] *Ibid.,* p. 78. Cf. also Bernstein, *Die heutige Sozialdemokratie in Theorie und Praxis.* Of course, this Revisionist view also qualifies the Marxist theory of capitalist accumulation, which is based on surplus value, and approaches the liberal economic concept of "waiting," although the idea of accumulation based on exploitation is most certainly not given up.

again, Revisionism called in the aid of ethics and of empiricism to replace one of the cherished "scientific" tenets of Marxism.

Must Capitalism Collapse?

> *"You are wrong; capitalist economy is far more viable than you think."*
>
> KARL HÖCHBERG TO BERNSTEIN

Disagreements between orthodox Marxists and Revisionists regarding such matters as accumulation and value theory were keen enough, but they sank into insignificance when compared to the acrimonious contest over the true nature of capitalist collapse. Here the stakes were much higher, for Socialist tactics depended directly, rather than remotely, on the form which the solution to this theoretical problem would take. The quarrel was all the more bitter in that the two sides were never quite sure what the other was talking about.

Karl Marx held that constantly recurring depressions were an outward sign of the insoluble contradictions of capitalism. His crisis theory (closely connected with other parts of his system, such as the falling rate of profit, underconsumption, the industrial reserve army), represented a revolutionary break with the sunny optimism of Say's Law. The latter had blithely demonstrated the logical impossibility of depressions by explaining that supply creates its own demand, so that overproduction can never occur. "Nothing can be more childish than the dogma," Marx wrote in an acute passage,

> that because every sale is a purchase and every purchase a sale, therefore the circulation of commodities necessarily implies an equilibrium of sales and purchases. . . . Its real purport is to prove that every seller brings the buyer to market with him. Nothing of the kind. . . . No one can sell unless someone else purchases. But no one is forthwith bound to purchase, because he has just sold. . . . If the split between the sale and the purchase becomes too

pronounced, the intimate connection between them, their oneness, asserts itself by producing—a crisis.[56]

Marx's analysis of depressions was subtle, and its elaboration cannot concern us here. Its import, however, is obvious: crises are a constituent factor in capitalism; they cannot be cured by meliorative measures since they are a public expression of the anarchy of the market. Here, as everywhere else in his work, Marx points up the inevitable failure of capitalism and the equally fated advent of Socialism.

But Marx never presented a coherent picture of just how capitalism would come to an end. Would it suddenly fall apart and refuse to function altogether, like the one-hoss shay? Would capitalism gradually sink to a level of chronic crisis, as Kautsky believed for many years? Or would the revolution break out well before that low point had been reached, as Rosa Luxemburg taught?

We cannot obtain a conclusive answer from Marx's own works, although a number of hints are scattered throughout his writings. Crises are an ever-repeated feature of capitalism, and the working class must always expect them: "Capitalist production comprises certain conditions which are independent of good or bad will and permit the working class to enjoy . . . relative prosperity only momentarily, and at that always as a harbinger of a coming crisis." [57] There are many causes for these crises, and we must not oversimplify, but "the last cause of all real crises remains the poverty and restricted consumption of the masses." [58] In any event, "the contradictions inherent in the movement of capitalist society impress themselves upon the practical bourgeois most strikingly in the changes of the periodic cycle, through which modern industry runs, and whose crowning point is the universal crisis." [59]

What is more, Marx asserts that these crises become ever more severe. Again we must rely on indications, but they are

[56] *Capital*, I, 127–28.
[57] *Capital*, II, 476. This and the following citation from Marx appear in Sweezy, *Theory of Capitalist Development*, pp. 151, 177.
[58] *Capital*, III, 568.
[59] *Capital*, I, 26: Preface to 2d ed.

strong enough. Marx and Engels put it quite plainly in the *Communist Manifesto:*

> Modern bourgeois society with its relations of production, of exchange and of property, a society that has conjured up such gigantic means of production and exchange, is like the sorcerer who is no longer able to control the powers of the nether world whom he has called up by his spells. For many a decade past the history of industry and commerce is but the history of the revolt of modern productive forces against modern conditions of production, against the property relations that are the conditions for the existence of the bourgeoisie and of its rule. It is enough to mention the commercial crises that by their periodical return put the existence of the entire bourgeois society on trial, *each time more threateningly.*[60]

And, Marx and Engels ask,

> How does the bourgeoisie get over these crises? On the one hand by enforced destruction of a mass of productive forces; on the other, by the conquest of new markets, and by the more thorough exploitation of the old ones. That is to say, by paving the way for *more extensive and more destructive crises,* and by diminishing the means whereby crises are prevented.[61]

Elsewhere, Marx was scarcely less emphatic. "We start from the premise," he wrote to F. A. Lange in 1865, "that the same forces which have created modern bourgeois society— the steam engine, modern machinery, mass colonization, railways, steamships, world trade— . . . are now already, through the *permanent trade crises, working toward its ruin and ultimate destruction."* [62]

---

[60] *Communist Manifesto,* pp. 14–15. (Italics mine.)
[61] *Ibid.,* p. 15. (Italics mine.)
[62] March 29, 1865, in V. Adoratsky, ed., *Selected Correspondence, Karl Marx and Frederick Engels,* p. 199. (Italics mine.) The sentence quoted in the text is incomplete, but not out of context. By the way, it should be said that it is easy to overuse quotations

The Marx-Engels correspondence reveals the firm conviction of both men that crises were growing in size and intensity, and the great hopes which they placed on the revolutionary possibilities of these low points in the capitalist trade cycle. The 1891 Erfurt Program fully endorsed this view.

Alongside of this grim picture of capitalist economy stood the equally drastic theory of the impoverishment of the proletariat. Two celebrated passages in Volume I of *Capital* express this idea succinctly:

The greater the social wealth, the functioning capital, the extent and energy of its growth, and, therefore, also the absolute mass of the proletariat and the productiveness of its labor, the greater is the industrial reserve-army. The same causes which develop the expansive power of capital, develop also the labor-power at its disposal. The relative mass of the industrial reserve-army increases therefore with the potential energy of wealth. But the greater this reserve-army in proportion to the active labor-army, the greater is the mass of a consolidated surplus-population, whose misery is in inverse ratio to its torment of labor. The more extensive, finally, the lazarus-layers of the working-class, and the industrial reserve-army, the greater is official pauperism. *This is the absolute general law of capitalist accumulation.*[63]

---

from letters. Nineteenth-century intellectuals wrote letters with an imaginative abandon of which we have no conception in this age of the telephone and memorandum pad. Many times, suggestions or *aperçus* are thrown out which would today receive no more permanent form than would, say, a brilliant remark at a university lunch table. Nineteenth-century letters are often forms of thinking aloud and should be used only if they accord with the general trend of the writer's thought.

[63] *Capital*, I, 707. The sentence immediately following this statement qualifies it somewhat: "Like all other laws it is modified in its working by many circumstances, the analysis of which does not concern us here."

In a later paragraph, Marx describes the expropriation of one capitalist by another and then continues:

> Along with the constantly diminishing number of the magnates of capital, who usurp and monopolize all advantages of this process of transformation, grows the mass of misery, oppression, slavery, degradation, exploitation; but with this too grows the revolt of the working-class, a class always increasing in numbers, and disciplined, united, organized by the very mechanism of the process of capitalist production itself.[64]

It has been noted before that Marx never gave details of the nature of the capitalist breakdown. But details really do not matter. What is of importance is the existence of a *tendency* which will result in a breakdown. The evidence is overwhelming that Marx believed in such a tendency in a capitalist system which "created its own negation." [65] Marx's failure to predict either the date or the exact character of the negation is not a valid argument against this evidence. It is for this reason, as we shall see, that Kautsky's attempted refutation of Bernstein's crisis theory really rests on an irrelevancy.

On the other hand, Bernstein's attack on this sector of Marxist theory, whether correct or not, went straight to the point. Before we discuss it, however, it is necessary that we dispose of an important logical problem. Bernstein opposed Marx's crisis theory because he felt that there was empirical evidence which refuted the predictions that must be drawn from the theory. Several authors, including A. D. Lindsay and Paul Sweezy, have held that Marx's method was abstract and did not take the form of concrete predictions. Lindsay takes the problem now under discussion as an example:

[64] *Ibid.,* pp. 836–37. The famous paragraph concludes: "The monopoly of capital becomes a fetter upon the mode of production, which has sprung up and flourished along with, and under it. Centralization of the means of production and socialization of labor at last reach a point where they become incompatible with their capitalist integument. This integument is burst asunder. The knell of capitalist private property sounds. The expropriators are expropriated."
[65] Cf. Henryk Grossmann, *Das Akkumulations- und Zusammenbruchsgesetz des kapitalistischen Systems,* pp. 78–79.

There has been a great deal of discussion in Marxian circles in Germany over the Marxian prediction of "growing misery." . . . It is often pointed out as if it were a refutation of this doctrine of Marx, that the misery of the undeveloped capitalism of the early part of the nineteenth century was much greater than the misery of the developed capitalism of the end of the century, that, as capitalism developed, the average of real wages on the whole has gone steadily up; the misery, in short, has decreased, rather than increased. Defenders of Marx often feel themselves bound to contend that the misery has increased, as if they would be denying Marx if they admitted that any improvement in conditions had taken place. *Really the whole controversy is beside the point.* The period under review saw the development of capitalism . . . but it also saw the rise and development of quite another system, that of social control as exercised through trade unions and social legislation. What has actually happened is not the outcome of capitalism but the outcome of social control and capitalism acting on one another. But when Marx talked of increasing misery, he was talking of what would be the outcome of unmodified capitalism.[66]

Sweezy follows a similar line of reasoning. He says that the "specific task of abstraction" is "to bring the essential into relief and to make possible its analysis." Marx, Sweezy contends, did just that by concentrating on the bare essentials of the anatomy of political economy. For the sake of simplicity, Marx assumed away most of the complicating factors:

The results achieved in Volume I have a provisional character. In many cases, though not necessarily in all, they undergo a more or less extensive modification on a lower level of abstraction, that is to say, when more aspects of reality are taken into account. It follows that *the tendencies or laws enunciated in Volume I are not to be interpreted as direct predictions about the future. . . .* Recognition of this fact would have saved a great deal of sterile controversy,

[66] *Marx's Capital,* pp. 24–25. (Italics mine.)

such as the controversy over Marx's theory of growing misery.[67]

Now, no one would dispute the abstract character of Marx's analysis. But if Lindsay and Sweezy are right, Bernstein's Revisionism is one vast irrelevancy; it attacks nonexisting predictions. This viewpoint seems to me mistaken, for the following reasons: 1. Abstract theories can be modified by concrete evidence, but the former are hardly correct if they are refuted by the latter. The problem is one of tendency, of direction. If Marx held, abstractly, that growing misery was the lot of the workingman, then his concrete remarks can only serve to lengthen the process or to make it more complex. Contingent developments, in other words, cannot do more than modify the total system. They cannot at once destroy the theory and still keep it valid. 2. If Marx's statements in Volume I of *Capital* were "in no sense a concrete prediction about the future," Bernstein's criticism of them would indeed be an irrelevancy. But so would Marx's theory be useless, for if the theory cannot be submitted to the empirical test of events, it violates the first tenet of what a hypothesis should be—namely a statement capable of verification or refutation. 3. If we were to admit, for the sake of argument, that Marx's statements regarding the development of capitalism are *not* predictions, it would clearly be the job of his successors, like Bernstein, to make such predictions, so that political action may be based upon them. But Marxist parties all over the world have always acted in the belief that these statements were to be taken as predictions. 4. The quotation from Lindsay implies that the abstract statements of Marx are modified as they are applied to real capitalism, which is far from the pure being that Volume I of *Capital* makes it out to be. If this is true, then Bernstein's work is doubly valuable. For could it not be argued, on Lindsay's terms, that the more capitalism is modified in actuality, the more must we qualify Marx's stark laws? But that is precisely what Bernstein was doing when he presented his milder version of Marxism.

While there is no intention of arguing that Bernstein was

[67] *Theory of Capitalist Development,* pp. 12, 18. (Italics mine.)

right throughout, the point remains that his work, whether right or wrong, does not merely rest on a logical misunderstanding.

In the 1880s, the belief in the impending doom of the capitalist order had been widespread in German Social Democratic circles. Bebel, and indeed Bernstein, were two of the leading "pessimists"—they greeted every minor market fluctuation, every bank scandal, as a harbinger of the great and glorious collapse. But, to paraphrase the proverb, "One depression does not make a breakdown," and capitalism continued to show surprising resiliency for a system which the Socialist doctors had gleefully given up as a hopeless case.

When Bernstein worked out his Revisionism in the mid-nineties, Germany and the industrial world as a whole were in the grip of a particularly stubborn siege of prosperity. Now Bernstein recalled the warnings of his early mentor, Karl Höchberg, concerning the vitality of capitalism, and he developed a crisis theory which would take the new facts into account.[68]

The contrast between Marx's and Bernstein's views can be most graphically illustrated by means of two curves which Bernstein drew on a blackboard for the benefit of his hearers in a lecture he delivered in 1909. The loyally Marxist Erfurt Program demanded a trade cycle line that would look somewhat as follows:

[68] "Entwicklungsgang eines Sozialisten," in *Die Volkswirtschaftslehre der Gegenwart in Selbstdarstellungen,* I, 23.

But, Bernstein asserted, the true development had been very different.[69]

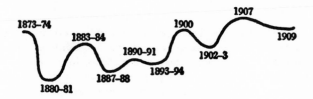

As he summarized it elsewhere: "The intervals separating periods of prosperity from periods of prosperity have narrowed; the intervals separating periods of depression from periods of depression have widened." [70] Bernstein distinguished between two elements in his crisis theory: the general direction of capitalism is upward, and the disturbances interfering with this development have become rarer and milder.[71] Bernstein repeatedly affirmed, however, that "general insecurity" had not diminished and that "the working classes in the various countries are still the victims of the trade cycle." Further,

> This insecurity hits not only the working class, but also the majority of the other elements of the employed classes, and even the businessman. . . . The fact that the old crisis scheme has become untenable should not seduce us into a false optimism.[72]

He repeated this point emphatically many times. "The references to the tendency toward milder depressions are under no circumstances to be taken as a defense of the capitalist economy." [73] In spite of these assertions this sector of Revi-

[69] Bernstein, *Der Revisionismus in der Sozialdemokratie*, pp. 35–36.

[70] "Revisionismus und Programmrevision," *Sozialistische Monatshefte*, XIII, 1 (1909), 407.

[71] Rikli, *Der Revisionismus*, pp. 76 ff.

[72] *Der Revisionismus in der Sozialdemokratie*, p. 37.

[73] *Der Sozialismus einst und jetzt*, p. 56.

sionist theory is far from satisfactory; granted that cycles are
not the only undesirable feature of capitalism to Bernstein,
the fact remains that Revisionist crisis theory leaves at least a
theoretical possibility that capitalism may cure its own evils.[74]

It has been charged that the Revisionists established the
meliorative trends in capitalism in a "purely descriptive
fashion." [75] It is true that the origins of Bernstein's crisis
theory can be found in an empirical account of the depressions which Germany had undergone since the founding of
the Reich. But once the data had been gathered, Bernstein
undertook to bolster them with theoretical considerations.

Bernstein did not deny the efficacy of the factors which
Marx listed as crisis-creating. The falling rate of profit, underconsumption associated with large-scale unemployment,
and disproportionality in the employment of the means of
production (economic anarchy)—these three were never
openly discredited. When Tugan-Baranowsky sought to disprove Marx's underconsumption theory, the Revisionist
Schmidt vigorously defended it.[76]

But Bernstein claimed that capitalism created certain
countertrends which vitiated most of the disturbing influences
associated with falling profits, disproportion, and underconsumption.[77] May not some other factors, Bernstein asked, act
to establish a favorable equilibrium rather than chronic disturbances? His suggestion that modern capitalism was slowly
but surely overcoming the anarchy of the market was first
thrown out in his series of articles, Probleme des Sozial-

[74] "According to this view the program of the reformist Socialists
was calculated to keep capitalism going indefinitely." Sweezy,
Theory of Capitalist Development, p. 197.
[75] Ibid., 193.
[76] Cf. ibid., pp. 169–70. It should be noted that there is some
doubt whether Marx had an underconsumption crisis theory at all.
Grossmann and Renner say no, Sweezy yes. The latter cites as
proof Marx's own statement: "The last cause of all real crises remains the poverty and restricted consumption of the masses."
Capital, III, 568. Marx's chapter, "Die Krisen," in Theorien über
den Mehrwert, Vol. II, Part 2, pp. 262–318, seems to bear Sweezy
out.
[77] Marx, of course, admitted these countertrends, too. But they
could not, in his view, stop the eventual breakup of capitalism.

ismus.[78] It was given its definitive form in a chapter of his *Voraussetzungen*. Here, Bernstein detailed the social forces calculated to serve as counterweights to trade fluctuations. They were: the growth of the world market, coupled with the extraordinary improvements in communication and transportation; the increased wealth of European industrial states; the flexibility of the modern credit system; and the rise of industrial cartels.[79] All these have increased the adaptability of modern capitalism, Bernstein argued; they make it unlikely that, "at least for a long time, general crises similar to the earlier ones" will occur.[80]

He admitted that Rosa Luxemburg's criticism, that the credit system leads to speculation and thus to insecurity, had some validity, but pointed out that speculation was rife largely in new industries, and diminished as an enterprise became more settled.[81] He conceded, too, that under capitalism production was never truly proportionate to demand. "To a certain degree overproduction is inevitable. . . . But," he warned, "overproduction in several industries cannot be equated with a general depression." [82] And the richer a country, the less chance was there of a depression induced by speculation or disproportionality, for in such a country "the opportunities for adjustment are even greater." [83]

Eduard Bernstein denied Rosa Luxemburg's claim that capitalism had not yet reached maturity, and that this was the *only* reason why the crises were not more severe. He pointed out that Marx's scheme was not a Utopia, but a "picture of the present," so that we should be experiencing graver crises now, after Marx, than before.[84] The fact that these depressions were not, in fact, occurring, proved Marx mistaken, and his error could not be remedied by any talk of the immaturity of capitalism.

Finally, Bernstein conceded that the "organization of the

[78] Especially in "Zusammenbruchstheorie und Colonialpolitik," in *Zur Geschichte und Theorie des Sozialismus*, pp. 218–36.
[79] *Voraussetzungen*, pp. 113–14.
[80] *Ibid.*, p. 114.
[81] *Ibid.*, p. 117.
[82] *Loc. cit.*
[83] *Ibid.*, p. 118.
[84] *Ibid.*, p. 119.

market" through cartels was, at best, a mixed blessing. It was true, of course, that they imposed order on chaos by eliminating waste and cutthroat competition.[85] It was equally correct, however, that the cartels enforced monopoly prices and artificial customs barriers. In this fashion they increased market anarchy and created crises:

> I have no intention of denying the harmful effects of present-day . . . protectionism. Nor do I present an apologia for manufacturers' associations. It has not occurred to me to claim that cartels are the last word in economic development and could ever permanently eliminate the contradictions of modern economic life.[86]

This ambivalent attitude toward the concentration of economic power through trusts foreshadows a similar but much more fateful indecision of German Social Democracy in the 1920s. Bernstein never doubted that the large clusters of economic power represented by the trusts and cartels would have to be socialized. But it apparently never occurred to him that the concentrated power of organized, mature, private industry might make the task of socializing it without the use of violence a very difficult one.

When we examine Bernstein's crisis theory after fifty years, we find it at best indifferently successful. Certainly he always left himself a backdoor through which he could retreat if the facts became too uncomfortable. Many elements in the theory are vague, but it did state clearly that social wealth was growing generally, so that the workers, too, were getting their share. Further, Bernstein definitely maintained that capitalism, no matter how resilient, could never solve its own problems. But as to the exact point at which a country would step legally into Socialism, Bernstein left some confusion—confusion, be it noted, which bears a striking resemblance to the vagueness of Marx's controversial breakdown theory.

But beyond the ambiguity which surrounds some of Bernstein's discussion of modern economic institutions, such as

[85] *Ibid.*, pp. 121–22.
[86] *Ibid.*, p. 124.

cartels, the most unsatisfactory aspect lies in his neglect of the *political* impact of economic disturbances. He notes, in a footnote in the *Voraussetzungen,* that he considers only "the economic reasons for crises. Crises as the effects of political events (such as wars or serious threats of war) . . . are, of course, always possible." [87] But, one is entitled to ask, may not wars be at least partially caused by threatening crises? Not that a political theorist is obliged to seek the explanation of politics in economics, but one may expect a Socialist theorist at least to deal with the problem.

In spite of these qualifications, however, the Bernsteinian crisis theory [88] was a strong link in the chain of proof in favor of gradualist, parliamentary Socialism.

Of all the Kautsky-Bernstein controversies of 1899–1900, the one about the Marxist collapse theory was most barren. In his anticritique, Kautsky expressed his conviction that crises will continue under capitalism.[89] But in the question of capitalist collapse Kautsky descended to a purely semantic argument, one that (as even anti-Revisionists have admitted) missed the point at issue altogether.[90]

Kautsky did nothing less than deny that Marxism contained a collapse theory: "A distinct collapse theory was never established by Marx and Engels." [91] Indeed, the very word was "invented" by Bernstein. Nor did the Erfurt Program speak of collapse.[92] Bernstein, so Kautsky concluded, had attributed a theory to Marx and Engels which was "ridiculous." [93]

Now this whole argument nowhere rests on factual untruths, but its import is to throw the discussion off on a tangent. It is true, as Kautsky claimed, that Marx envisaged an active role for the proletariat in its class struggle against

[87] *Ibid.,* p. 125n.
[88] Which was adopted, with few qualifications, by Schmidt and Kampffmeyer.
[89] *Bernstein und das sozialdemokratische Programm,* pp. 135–52.
[90] Cf. Sweezy, *Theory of Capitalist Development,* p. 194; Grossmann, *Akkumulations- und Zusammenbruchsgesetz,* pp. 16–20.
[91] *Bernstein und das sozialdemokratische Programm,* p. 42.
[92] *Ibid.,* p. 43.
[93] *Ibid.,* p. 49.

the capitalist, and that Marx had spoken of the growing "revolt of the working class, a class always increasing in numbers and disciplined, united, organized by the very mechanism of the process of capitalist production itself." But Marx had never deviated from his idea that capitalism would grow ever more cumbersome and self-defeating and that the final stages of the system would witness a growing "mass of misery, slavery, degradation, exploitation." [94]

It was most unfortunate that Kautsky should pitch the discussion at this level, although it becomes understandable when we recall that he was trying, at this time, to persuade Bernstein to leave German Social Democracy entirely. The matter that needed discussion was, of course, which of the two contrasting pictures—Marx's ever deteriorating, or Bernstein's ever consolidating, capitalism—was closer to reality.

Three years later, however, Kautsky came out into the open. Reviewing a book by Tugan-Baranowsky in *Neue Zeit*, he committed himself to the conception of growing crises. "One can say in general," he wrote, "that crises are becoming ever more severe and extensive in scope." The economic situation was tending to degenerate into a "period of chronic depressions." It seemed likely that the masses of the people, laden with misery, would seek to escape their bitter lot by turning to Socialism before capitalism had reached its lowest point. But this last was of little significance for the analysis of capitalist development—what mattered was the steady deterioration of the system.[95]

In the late 1920s, Kautsky relinquished this "growing crisis" theory in favor of one that was barely distinguishable from that of the Revisionists. But then much had happened, both to the world and to Kautsky. It was the Kautsky of

[94] Joan Robinson concludes: "In one passage Marx admits that a rise in productivity may raise real wages so that the workers obtain some share in the achievements of technical progress, but it seems clear that the argument of *Capital* did not lead him to expect any appreciable upward trend in the level of real wages under capitalism, while the *Communist Manifesto* predicts an actual decline in wages. . . ." *Essay on Marxian Economics*, p. 32.
[95] This article is well summarized in Sweezy, *Theory of Capitalist Development*, pp. 197–200. The passages quoted here occur on p. 198.

1902, the man who predicted "crises, conflicts, catastrophes," who was Lenin's hero. In these years, he embodied the radical Marxist view of capitalism most clearly, and his distance from Bernstein and Revisionism had never been, and would never be, more pronounced.

The Agrarian Sector

> *The bourgeoisie has subjected the country to the rule of the towns. It has created enormous cities, has greatly increased the urban population as compared with the rural, and has thus rescued a considerable part of the population from the idiocy of rural life.*
>
> MARX AND ENGELS

Western Socialism is predominantly an urban theory, applied to urban situations. The worker, not the farmer, is in the center of Socialist thought, and it is only in Eastern Europe that rural problems achieved primacy. But this concentration on industry rather than agriculture did not prevent German Socialists from dealing, at least sporadically, with the state of agriculture, and this subject, too, was contested by orthodox Marxists and Revisionists.

The Erfurt Program of 1891 associated the farmer with the worker in its categorical prediction of the "sinking middle strata." It proclaimed that private property in the means of production had become an instrument of expropriation wielded by capitalists and large landowners against small businessmen and farmers.

Starting at the party congress at Frankfurt in 1894, the agrarian question was made subject of a debate which later merged into the whole question of Revisionism. A commission was formed to draw up an agrarian program for the party. Its proposals were rejected at the congress of Breslau in the following year. The reasons for this move become apparent once we read the draft prepared by the commission. It saw the task of the party in agrarian matters to be the "lifting of the condition of the agrarian laborers and small farmers," and it proposed measures that looked toward the securing of private property in land, with socialization only of forests, sources of water power, land insurance, and mortgages.[96] Opposition speakers, such as Schippel and Kautsky, pointed out that such an addition to the Erfurt Program would amount to "political charlatanry" designed to capture rural votes. Kautsky recognized that "agriculture has its own laws of development which differ from those of industry." But no program designed to strengthen private property—and thus present-day capitalism and the exploiters—could find the approval of German Social Democracy.[97] The Schippel-Kautsky view prevailed.

But the debate did not cease, and the demand for a Social Democratic agrarian policy was not silenced. In 1898 the ubiquitous Kautsky rose to the challenge with an ambitious volume on the agrarian question.[98] Kautsky's professed aim in writing his book was to inquire if Social Democracy could realize its aim of socializing property in agriculture as well as industry. His conclusion: agrarian developments, while following a path peculiar to them, were hurrying towards the same goal as industry; both farms and factories could be considered as "linked together in a total process." [99] Present-day agriculture, employing the insights of soil science and the aid of mechanized implements, needed more and more capital to operate profitably. "The modern agricultural enterprise is therefore a capitalist enterprise." [100] While certain variations exist and while there are limits as to how capitalistic farms can become, agricultural production may be studied with the same analytical tools as industry. Private property and the commodity nature of goods are characteristic of the products of town and country alike. In agriculture, as in industry, the large enterprise is technically superior to the small. Big farms

[96] Wilhelm Schröder, ed., *Handbuch der sozialdemokratischen Parteitage,* pp. 12–13.
[97] *Ibid.,* pp. 15–16. Bernstein lists this debate as one of the factors leading him toward Revisionism. "Entwicklungsgang," pp. 21–22.
[98] *Die Agrarfrage.*
[99] *Ibid.,* p. 6.
[100] *Ibid.,* p. 132.

can rationalize production through better utilization of manpower, implements, transportation, sale, credit, etc. It is true, however, that small farms have not yet disappeared; indeed, statistics show that they were even on the increase in the 1890s.[101] But statistics do not always tell the whole truth: while small farms are showing surprising tenacity, much of this is due to government subsidization of economically unproductive small farms. The latter stay alive, not because they can compete with large farms, but precisely because they have ceased to compete with them.[102]

One important consequence of the impact of modern capitalism on agriculture, Kautsky argued further, is the proletarization of the peasant. More and more the farmer, whether self-employed on rented land or dependent laborer, assumes the face of the urban proletarian. His relations to the means of agricultural production closely resemble those of the worker to the machinery in his factory. Small farmers, particularly, turn into proletarians whose only saleable commodity is their labor power.

On this analysis Kautsky based a Social Democratic agrarian policy. He warned that neglect of the agrarian population would be a grave mistake.[103] What happens to the farm population is of deep interest to the urban proletariat: economically, the proletariat needs a sound peasantry without which the society of the future could hardly function; politically, the proletariat must become solidary with the farmers or, at least, transform their hostility to Social Democracy into neutrality. The best step to be taken is an agrarian plank in the Social Democratic program which would distinguish a short-range and a long-range goal. The first is the strengthening of the rural proletariat in its struggle with overwhelming economic forces. This can be accomplished by legal safeguards in behalf of agrarian associations, protection of women and child laborers, provision for education, shortening of the work week, improved housing, lower ground rent. The second goal would be achieved through the socialization of agricultural production. This would take place not through

[101] *Ibid.*, p. 132.
[102] *Ibid.*, p. 163.
[103] *Ibid.*, pp 3–5, 305.

forcible expropriation but persuasion and gradual rationalization. The parasitic tenant farmer will gladly give up his dubious independence, the useful small peasant will retain his land but become a vital member in the new partnership of agriculture and industry. In any event, a Socialist regime, anxious to make the financial lot and social position of the farmer a favorable one, will not use violence to achieve these goals.

This, in bare outline, was the agrarian program advocated by the orthodox German Marxists. It was soon challenged by the Revisionists.

As usual, it was Eduard Bernstein who sounded the "A" in the Revisionist orchestra. In his brief section on the agrarian question in the *Voraussetzungen* he gave his assent to most of Kautsky's proposals but pointed out that they were really "applications of the demands of bourgeois democrats to agriculture." [104] His own program did not differ sharply from Kautsky's. It suggested "the struggle against all remnants and supports of agrarian feudalism, and the fight for democracy in commune and district; protection for and relief of the laboring classes in agriculture; the struggle against the absolutism of property, and the encouragement of cooperatives." [105] Bernstein emphasized that he had arrived at this program by studying statistics which ran counter to the Marxist concentration theory. "There can be no doubt," he said, "that in all of Western Europe and, by the way, in the eastern section of the United States, the small and medium-sized agricultural enterprises are growing in numbers, while larger or giant enterprises are declining." [106] Here, if anywhere, the difference between orthodox and Revisionist agrarian theory must be sought.

This viewpoint was further developed in a book by the Austrian specialist Friedrich Otto Hertz, an avowed Bernsteinian and a decided opponent of Kautsky. His book appeared in Vienna in 1899, with a short preface by Bernstein.[107]

[104] *Voraussetzungen*, p. 217.
[105] *Ibid.*, 218–19.
[106] *Ibid.*, p. 107.
[107] *Die agrarischen Fragen im Verhältnis zum Sozialismus.*

Hertz acknowledged the high quality of Kautsky's researches and found much with which he could agree. But, he said, large parts of Kautsky's work on agriculture were simply wrong. Basically, Hertz wrote,

> The number of independent farmers and especially of owners is constantly on the increase. . . . Therefore Bernstein is completely correct in the agrarian sector when he maintains that the number of the propertied is growing. In view of these facts Kautsky's claims for growing concentration are downright ridiculous.[108]

Furthermore, Kautsky's statement that large agricultural enterprises are superior to small ones is contrary to fact.[109]

Basing himself on these assumptions, Hertz outlined his agricultural program, which foresaw the continuation of private property (limited by society), the organization of farmers on a local level for purposes of joint utilization of labor and machinery, the institution of popularly elected agricultural boards that would determine the allocation of resources among different products.[110] The local cooperative which directs production and distribution democratically is the basis of Hertz's system.

A similar approach was taken at greater length by Eduard David in a bulky and thorough book which appeared in 1903 and which firmly fixed the Revisionist position on agriculture.[111] David, one of Bernstein's staunchest supporters in the Great Debate,[112] had become a Revisionist on the basis of his studies in agriculture, in which he had found statistics that appeared to disprove Marx and Kautsky.

There is no need to give a full review of his 700-page volume here, but the salient points may be summarized. David called Kautsky's *Agrarfrage* "a desperate attempt" to save the concentration theory.[113] He cited, with full approval, state-

[108] *Ibid.*, p. 28.
[109] *Ibid.*, p. 40.
[110] *Ibid.*, pp. 131–32.
[111] *Sozialismus und Landwirtschaft.*
[112] He had called himself a "Bernsteinian" in a letter to Bernstein, November 9, 1900. Bernstein Archives.
[113] *Sozialismus und Landwirtschaft*, p. 52.

ments by Bernstein and Hertz which attacked it. David's view of Socialism was rather a mild one: "General well-being and spiritual culture (*Geisteskultur*)." [114] On the agrarian front this could be achieved through protection of the farmer and through aid measures which would increase productivity. "But the small farm offers the most favorable conditions for rational production with intensive cultivation of the soil." [115] With such farms as the nucleus of all-embracing producers' cooperatives, we have the basis for a sound farm policy. The government should cease its artificial protection of large farms through agricultural tariffs and other measures.[116] As to private property, we can find a middle way between absolute license and complete expropriation. "Practical experience will soon teach us to balance the final property right of the community as a whole against the right of the individual to dispose over what is his own (*Nutzniessungsrecht des einzelnen*)." [117] Finally, we must do more than merely neutralize the farmers and farm laborers politically:

It is a fatal error to believe that the champions of social justice and cultural progress will gain power . . . merely through the growth of the urban proletariat. . . . The winning of the laboring agricultural population to our party is indispensable for the conquest of political power.[118]

These were the lines on which Marxists and Revisionists took their stand.[119] The agricultural program was never a de-

[114] *Ibid.*, p. 684.
[115] *Ibid.*, pp. 698–99.
[116] *Ibid.*, p. 699.
[117] *Ibid.*, p. 701.
[118] *Ibid.*, p. 703. The orthodox reply to David was given by Ludwig Quessel, "Landwirtschaft und Industrie," *Neue Zeit,* XXI, 2 (1903), 450–56, 481–90, 513–19. He maintained, in direct opposition to David, that the Socialists would come to power solely through industrial developments. The agrarian statistics had brilliantly vindicated Marx's law of development; as farms become industrialized they become capitalist. David's *Sammlungspolitik* (coalition politics), trying to unite workers with small-scale farm entrepreneurs who are really capitalists, would be fatal to Social Democracy.
[119] Bernstein accepted David's conclusions. He praised his book

cisive issue, since the Social Democratic Party never gained large support from the rural areas of Germany. We have discussed it here because it reflects, and can serve as an introduction to, a far more tricky problem—the "disappearance of the small farmer" is, in miniature, the question of the "disappearance of the middle class." It is to the latter that we can now turn.

Found: The Disappearing Middle Class

> *White-collar people carry less rationality than illusion and less desire for freedom than the misery of modern anxieties.*
>
> C. WRIGHT MILLS

All recorded history, runs the bold assertion of Marx and Engels, is the history of class struggles. With the advent of modern capitalism the struggle is simplified: marginal groupings disappear, ranging themselves on the side of one or the other of the remaining two adversaries in the historic battle. The most spectacular victims of this process of elimination are the noncapitalist middle groups: "The lower strata of the middle class—the small tradespeople, shopkeepers, and retired tradesmen generally, the handicraftsmen and peasants— all these sink gradually into the proletariat. . . . Thus the proletariat is recruited from all classes of the population." [120] "Of all classes that stand face to face with the bourgeoisie today, the proletariat alone is a really revolutionary class. The other classes decay and finally disappear in the face of modern industry." [121]

---

highly: "David's book marks an epoch in the Socialist discussion of the problem of agriculture. . . . It is a scientific accomplishment of which its author and his party may both be equally proud." "Die Bedeutung von Eduard Davids Agrarwerk," *Sozialistische Monatshefte*, VII, 1 (1903), 115.

[120] *Communist Manifesto*, p. 17.

[121] *Ibid.*, p. 19. The relevance of these sociological generalizations to economics becomes evident once we realize that they have been touched upon throughout this chapter: centralization and

Bernstein disputed the validity of the theory of growing misery and the disappearing middle class and substituted his own sociological scheme of class relations. While the dialectical Marxist theory saw a society growing ever more unstable, the Revisionists envisioned a development of increasing stability, a society in which nonviolent solutions to social conflicts were becoming ever more possible.[122]

"Class," thus runs Bernstein's definition, "is a social stratum which is largely formed by similarity of living conditions." [123] Class, then, was more than a mere intellectual construct imposed upon society by the observer. But the Revisionists objected to what they considered a *simpliste* interpretation of class by the orthodox Marxists. For Bernstein,

---

concentration implied the disappearance of small entrepreneurs. The section on value and surplus value was based on the assumption of a struggle between two classes with fundamentally opposed relations to the means of production. The class struggle came to the surface in the analysis of the crisis and collapse theories: ever-growing depressions were acting as recruiting agents for the industrial reserve army and consequently the militant proletariat. They also served to eliminate the small entrepreneur, just as did the process of concentration ("one capitalist always kills many"). Finally, the section concerning the agrarian program dealt with the class struggle directly with its contention that the small farmer was becoming proletarized.

[122] References to "class" can be found scattered throughout Bernstein's writings. Ironically enough, he regretted Marx's failure to treat the subject of class systematically. We can charge Bernstein with the same failure.

[123] *Der Sozialismus einst und jetzt,* p. 62. It is "fundamentally to be distinguished from estate (*Stand*)," and is "subject to the general development of society." *Loc. cit.* Elsewhere he repeats his definition in very similar language: "A class in modern society contains elements of that society which, in the main, exist under similar living conditions." *Was ist Sozialismus?* as quoted by Theodor Geiger, *Die soziale Schichtung des deutschen Volkes,* p. 9. It differs from Marx's definition, of course, which defined class as "relation to the means of production." It is similar to Marx's in using objective rather than subjective criteria (class-consciousness). Bernstein liked to point out that Marx himself never oversimplified the nature of modern society, and cited Marx's cautious formulations in Volume III of *Capital* where he spoke of "infinite splits of interests and position which subdivide all classes."

modern capitalist society was a highly articulated organism, and classes themselves were complex. "The structure of society has not become simplified. Far from it. Rather, both as far as income and economic activity are concerned, it has been further graduated and differentiated." [124] The best example of this may be found in an examination of one class, the proletariat.

What is the modern proletariat? Bernstein asks. If we count all the propertyless as its members, the absolute majority of the populations of advanced countries would belong to it. But then "this 'proletariat' would be a mixture of extraordinarily divergent elements, a mixture of groups that show greater differences than the 'people' of 1789." [125] Even the relatively restricted group of wageworkers has a hierarchy and is far from homogeneous.[126] This may be observed not only in England but in Germany as well. Nor is it surprising: "Considerable differences in kinds of employment and income levels create, in the last analysis, different behavior and demands from life." [127] True, these divergent groups feel deep sympathy with each other; they recognize the others as fellow wage earners engaged in the same struggle with the employer that they themselves are carrying on. "But there is still a great difference between such political or social sympathy and true economic solidarity." [128] Classes are rent by subgroups; special cases abound (what of salaried white collar workers? what of independent small farmers? what of anti-Socialist workers?) and the picture of a multimillion proletarian army is simply a gross deception.[129]

By thus treating the concept of *the* proletariat as a "purely mental construct" which falsified reality, Bernstein came close to abandoning the whole notion of class altogether.[130] When Kautsky charged that Bernstein was trying to make "the class solidarity of the proletarians, and the class conflict between

[124] *Voraussetzungen*, p. 89.
[125] *Ibid.*, p. 135.
[126] *Loc. cit.*
[127] *Ibid.*, p. 137. Bernstein here uses the economic interpretation against the Marxists.
[128] *Loc. cit.*
[129] *Ibid.*, pp. 139–42.
[130] Cf. *Zur Geschichte und Theorie des Sozialismus*, pp. 382–83.

them and the capitalists, appear quite small" Bernstein denied it. But Kautsky's criticism was substantially valid: the Revisionists did emphasize collaboration between classes and played down solidarity within each class.

However, Bernstein was strongly enough imbued with Marxism not to give up the class concept entirely in favor of a view which saw society as an ultimately harmonious congeries of competing interest groups. Indeed, he held that probably the chief function of the Social Democratic Party consisted of the pulling together of divergent group interests *within* the proletariat: economic developments prove to us the

> necessity of an organ of the class struggle which holds the entire class together in spite of its fragmentation through different employment (*Berufstrennung*), and that is the Social Democracy as a political party. In it, the special interest of the economic group is submerged in favor of the great general interest of all those who depend on income from their labor, of all underprivileged.[131]

The temptation is great to describe this as similar to the American theory of party as an alliance of interest groups. But Bernstein interpreted his theory in Marxist fashion. The proletariat is the only class whose class interest is identical with the general good: "The activity of the workers as class coincides with their activity as political party, as Social Democracy." [132] Workers acting as a class thus act as a people's party in the genuine sense of that phrase.

This is how Bernstein retained the idea of class. The concept of the class struggle underwent a similar metamorphosis at the hands of the Revisionists; it was watered down but not given up.

"In no way do I deny," Bernstein wrote, "that a class struggle is going on in modern society. But I wish to argue against the stereotyped conception of this struggle as well as against the claim that it must necessarily assume ever

---

[131] *Die heutige Sozialdemokratie in Theorie und Praxis*, p. 33.
[132] *Von der Sekte zur Partei*, p. 45.

208 / The Dilemma of Democratic Socialism

harsher forms." [133] The class struggle continues, but it now has a milder character. The major social groupings in modern society confront each other with more or less pronounced conflicts of interests. Large agrarian rentiers struggle against peasants; consumers fight producers; artisans combat mass industry; and so on. "Here we see a class struggle which is not fought in the streets but in parliament and press. But struggle remains struggle." [134] And the greatest of them all is still the struggle between the workers and the capitalists.[135] The political side of this contest more and more takes the form of the quest for influence in legislatures and over public opinion. Its economic aspect is represented by the work of trade unions and cooperatives:

> All these activities are forms of the class struggle conducted by the worker in capitalist society. Taken together they add up to an organized fight which generally appears quite non-revolutionary and which is not always conducted through traditional economic and political battles. But this fight embodies the possibility of a true social liberation of the working class.[136]

So far we have treated the Revisionist theory of class from the vantage point of the proletariat. What about the middle class?

On this point Bernstein was categorical. "The middle classes change their character, but they do not disappear from the social scale." [137]

We have already seen how he buttressed this contention from the empirical, descriptive angle: income statistics, lists of shareholders, and similar data were used to advantage to prove that the number of propertied was increasing. But Bernstein also tried to bolster his position by theoretical means: the idea of growing misery was, to put it plainly,

[133] *Zur Geschichte und Theorie des Sozialismus,* p. 398.
[134] *Der Sozialismus einst und jetzt,* p. 66.
[135] *Ibid.,* p. 67.
[136] *Ibid.,* p. 74.
[137] *Voraussetzungen,* p. 7; this is from his letter to the Stuttgart party congress.

completely incorrect. Modern methods of production are characterized primarily by the tremendous boost they give to the productivity of labor. This results in mass production of consumer goods. But who absorbs all this new wealth? It is surely not all swallowed up by the fat capitalist. Nor can it all be exported. But then,

> Where does this mass of commodities go which is not consumed by the magnates and their stooges? If it does not go to the proletarians in one way or another, it must be absorbed by other classes. Either relative decrease in the number of capitalists and increasing wealth of the proletariat, or a numerous middle class—these are the only alternatives permitted by the continuous increase of productivity.[138]

And this conclusion, arrived at deductively, is proved by empirical investigations which show a wide diffusion of wealth.

Bernstein did not intend by this to write *finis* to social conflicts. They continue. Indeed, the rich grow richer faster than the poor grow less poverty-stricken. The distance between top and bottom of the social pyramid increases. Bernstein once likened capitalist society to an accordion which is being pulled upward at one end, but which has a weight attached to the bottom. Further, the people at the very top become ever more parasitic. Their social usefulness shrinks to zero.[139] Without saying so, Bernstein here reveals himself as an adherent of the "relative impoverishment" theory which relied on growing social distance to explain continued social tensions at a time in which the real wages of the proletariat were advancing. Bernstein was too perspicacious, however, not to recognize that such a process would never, unless powerfully countered by other events, lead to a revolutionary situation.

So much for the statement that the middle class was growing. But in what sense was it changing its character, as Bernstein so frequently insisted? Here, he particularly emphasized the rise of the "new middle class." This term had become

[138] *Voraussetzungen*, p. 90.
[139] *Der Revisionismus in der Sozialdemokratie*, pp. 33–34.

familiar to German social thought in the 1890s; it referred to the ever-increasing number of technical personnel, white collar workers, office and sales clerks, and government employees. These categories grew along with the mounting bureaucratization of monopoly capitalism. Their universal characteristic was dependence; in most cases, their incomes were little higher than those of the wage laborers, but their social standing and social pretensions definitely allied them with the bourgeoisie. Bernstein expressed confidence, however, that a large part of them felt "a strong community of interests with the workers," although he had to admit that this was by no means an unequivocal trend.[140] This group of personnel employed in industry, commerce, transportation, and agriculture had multiplied fourfold from 1882 to 1907. "The majority of them identify themselves more and more with the working class and should be added to it—along with their dependents," [141] wrote Bernstein hopefully.

But, Bernstein thought, this alliance between the strong new middle class and the workers will not be based on the realization of the white collar workers that they are sinking to the low level of the impoverished proletariat. The very opposite is true: the middle classes know that the worker's lot is improving and that his life is, in the best sense of that word, becoming more "bourgeois." [142] Bernstein made this expressly clear in his *Voraussetzungen,* and the point is of great importance for his thought:

> Nobody has any idea of destroying bourgeois society as a civilized, orderly social system. On the contrary, Social Democracy does not wish to dissolve this society and to make proletarians of all its members. Rather, it labors incessantly at lifting the worker from the social position

[140] *Der Sozialismus einst und jetzt,* pp. 64–65.
[141] *Wirtschaftswesen und Wirtschaftswerden,* p. 102. These lectures were first written in 1903.
[142] In this connection, Bernstein uses the word *bürgerlich* in the favorable meaning of "citizen." "Bourgeois society," then, is a system which recognizes every one as a full citizen and in which every one possesses certain economic minimum standards.

of a proletarian to that of a "bourgeois" and thus to make "bourgeoisie"—or citizenship—universal.[143]

Here again we see Bernstein's evolutionism at work: Socialism is the legitimate heir of liberalism; its mission is to improve the conditions of the population as a whole.

In rebuttal of these heresies, Kautsky followed a line of reasoning that is already familiar to us: social conflicts take an ever more virulent form, and Bernstein's statistics and theoretical arguments all have no validity. As a consequence, the proletariat can rely on nothing but itself.

If Bernstein says that we must not abolish classes because the forces of production have not yet developed sufficiently, Engels replies that we *must* abolish them because class domination has begun to act as a fetter on the development of productive forces.[144]

Kautsky had to admit that society was giving birth to a "new middle class." He even asserted that he had been one of the first to discover this group and call for study of the means by which it could be captured by Social Democracy.[145] Marx himself had described this group in his posthumously published *Theorien über den Mehrwert*.

This new middle class, Kautsky wrote, was created by the desire of the top exploiters to slough off clerical duties. The growth of enterprises, industries, and state functions accelerated the process. But "we would be committing a grave error if we merely added these people to the owning classes. The new middle class is based on entirely different foundations from the old, which is the firm bulwark of private property in the means of production." [146]

At the same time, it would be rash to treat the new middle class simply as proletarians: most of its number have been re-

[143] *Voraussetzungen*, p. 181.
[144] Kautsky, "Bernstein über die Werttheorie und die Klassen," *Neue Zeit*, XVII, 2 (1899), 77.
[145] *Bernstein und das sozialdemokratische Programm*, pp. 128–29.
[146] *Ibid.*, p. 130.

cruited from the bourgeoisie and many (such as the salaried employees) possess educational privileges not enjoyed by the workers.

Yet all this does not change the ultimate result, Kautsky concluded. Most of the new middle class is proletarized as a part of the general process of growing misery.

> As much as they cling to bourgeois appearances, the time will come for every one of the proletarized strata of the white collar groups at which they discover their proletarian heart. Then they will take an interest in the proletarian class struggle and finally they will participate in it actively.[147]

Bernstein's and Kautsky's interpretations of the middle class problem show some striking similarities. Both men considered the new middle class as an important social factor which was approaching ever closer to the working class; but the Marxist thought this would be caused by the proletarization of the middle class, while the Revisionist believed that the proletariat would grow bourgeois.[148] That is how it was possible that, in spite of the resemblances, the two men could come to opposite conclusions: Kautsky used his analysis as proof of the ever-growing bitterness of the class struggle, while Bernstein saw in it hope for future social peace.

We have now reached a crucial point in our analysis of Revisionist doctrine. In a sense, all the controversies about economic theory that have been discussed in this chapter go back to opposed sociological conceptions of the nature of

[147] *Ibid.,* p. 133. While a few top members of the new middle class may be counted as bourgeois, Kautsky said, we have a rather troublesome group in the center of the class in question. This group, too well off to be immediately proletarized, is uncertain and fickle; at one time it waxes indignant at the greed of capital, at another it looks down upon the bad manners of the proletariat. This group furnishes few allies to the working class but, on the other hand, it never constitutes a danger. *Ibid.,* pp. 134–35.

[148] Cf. Bernstein, "Wird die Sozialdemokratie Volkspartei?" *Sozialistische Monatshefte,* IX, 2 (1905), 669–70.

modern capitalist society. This divergence of thought reached its clearest expression in the conclusions concerning the middle class. For this reason it will be well to anticipate later history and ask, How closely did the Revisionist theory of class approach the truth? Was it an aid or a hindrance in the understanding of (and consequent social action in) the Weimar Republic?

First of all it must be said that the definite Marxist prediction that the middle classes would disappear was disproved by the facts. The development turned out to be far more complex than Marx had expected; the economic interpretation of history had been applied in such a way as to lead to incorrect results. Next, the modifications of this view, the "relative impoverishment" theory, and the Leninist theory of imperialism, are highly interesting but are not really theories of growing misery. The former (which was held, to some extent, by Eduard Bernstein) explains growing social distance between top and bottom, but does not deny that the position of the proletariat is improving. The latter is of great significance for the relations of one imperialist power to another or to backward areas, but, by explaining away the gains of the European worker as the profits of a "labor aristocracy," it gives up any pretense of a "growing misery" theory for the European proletariat. Finally, we may deal summarily with Kautsky: his theory, like the others, is not borne out by subsequent developments. It was, of course, true that the new middle class became more and more dependent on vast industrial and agricultural and commercial enterprises. It was equally true that its standard of living declined, in many cases, to that of the proletariat. But in spite of these events, the new middle class did *not* "discover" its "proletarian heart." And this is, of course, what matters.

Upon careful examination, we can hardly find a more satisfactory account of middle class behavior in Bernstein. He saw, correctly, that the middle strata were changing their character. He was equally sage in warning against a rigid economic interpretation of this development. "Above all, I fight against the conception," he wrote to Auer in 1899, "that there exists an automatic, self-executing process . . . of liquidation of those middle classes and professional groups." [149]

But beyond this conclusion his thought loses in definiteness. Bernstein certainly believed that the proletariat and the new middle classes would approximate in the sphere of economic interest as well as political action. This *rapprochement* was to occur partly through proletarization of parts of the middle class, partly through special factors such as family ties coupling both groups, partly through a lifting of the proletariat to a middle class level, a process which (to coin a terrible word) we might call "bourgeoization." The weight which was to be assigned to each of these factors was never specified.

At this point Bernstein breaks off. But we are justified in putting an additional hypothesis into Bernstein's mind, a hypothesis without which neither Revisionist middle class theory nor Revisionist political tactics would make much sense. We must assume that Bernstein believed that the new middle class, along with sizable sections of the old middle class, would join with the proletariat in voting Socialism into power. Further, these groups would have to acquiesce in the actions of the new Socialist regime and eschew a violent counterrevolution no matter how strongly opposed they might be to individual Socialist measures. It is perfectly evident that this assumption of a radicalized and democratic middle class is essential to Revisionism. For without it, how could the Socialists ever come to power legally and then hold it without violence? [150]

Anyone who knows anything about German history after

---

[149] Bernstein to Auer, in letter prepared for reading at the 1899 party congress, but never read. Bernstein Archives.

[150] This point remains valid in spite of Bernstein's frequently expressed skepticism of alliances with the bourgeoisie. Cf. Chapter VIII, Section 1. There is one ironic twist to the matter: If Bernstein had simply assumed that the whole middle class would be proletarized, he would not have needed this assumption analyzed above. For then the proletariat would have had a clear majority of the population. Geiger's statistics (*Die soziale Schichtung*, p. 73) actually give the proletariat a majority: capitalists 0.92 percent, old middle class 17.77 percent, new middle class 17.95 percent, proletaroids 12.65 percent, proletariat 50.71 percent. If this proves anything, it is that the proletariat was far from united.

World War I will recognize the fallacious assumptions of Bernstein's theory. Large groups within the German middle classes suffered severely in the inflation and the world depression.[151] These economic shocks added to their already strong sense of panic. Growing ever more dependent on huge and impersonal bureaucracies, both private and public, their cherished dreams of an independent existence in a shop or on a farm vanished as society became more inflexible. These people now had to face the bitter fact that their dependence was life-long, and that their "life-chances," to use Max Weber's phrase, did not differ substantially from those of the proletariat. The loss of income was severe enough, but the implied loss of status was ruinous.[152]

The Social Democrats, whether they followed Kautsky's or Bernstein's line of thought, expected these desperate people to become their allies. Nothing could have been more mistaken. Most members of the middle classes viewed the Social Democrats with fear and loathing and regarded them as little better than the Communists. What future did the impoverished white collar workers have in a Socialist state? That was their anxious question. The Social Democratic argument, that such a society would provide an acceptable social role to everyone, apparently did not impress them. They felt, with W. S. Gilbert,

> When everybody's somebody
> Then no one's anybody.

They believed that they would be reduced to being part of the masses, that they would be degraded into proletarians and lose the superior status due them as "brain workers." [153]

It did not matter in the slightest that this attitude rested on an irrational basis and that the Socialist term for the new middle class, "white collar proletariat" (*Stehkragenproletariat*), was a profoundly true characterization. These emo-

---

[151] Incidentally, while this is often overlooked, the German workers suffered greatly in these years, too.

[152] Of course, it need hardly be added that the generalizations in this and succeeding paragraphs are too sweeping to be accurate in every case. They are to indicate a widespread trend.

[153] The same view as presented here is expressed in Franz Neumann, *Behemoth*, p. 411.

tions were dangerous and unreasonable for they led the new middle class into political folly; but they were experienced vividly, and that is what counted.

If the Social Democrats could not attract these groups, there was one new party which seemed expressly designed to absorb them. Of course, there were many notable and honorable exceptions, but the large majority of the disturbed elements of the middle strata of the German population turned Nazi.

A glance at national election figures will show what happened: [154]

	(IN MILLION VOTES)				
				July	Nov.
Parties	1924	1928	1930	1932	1932
"Bourgeois" parties, except Center	13.2	12.9	10.3	4.0	5.3
Social Democrats and Communists	10.5	12.3	13.0	13.1	13.1
Center Party	4.1	3.7	4.1	4.5	4.2
National Socialists	.9	.8	6.4	13.7	11.7

The Nazis, then, recruited their millions from the middle class parties as well as from the nonvoters. Among their most active supporters were those young people who had never worked but had stepped straight from school into what appeared to be permanent unemployment. Obviously, it was very hard to organize these men and women into trade unions.

The appeal which the Nazis had for the disaffected groups was strengthened once the Nazi Party abandoned its attempts at infiltrating the Free Trade Unions and relied exclusively on terror against them. The decision to give up all remnants even of its fraudulent Socialism came when it became apparent to such leading lights as Hitler and Goebbels that they could make no inroads on the Social Democrats. Now the Nazis

[154] Taken from Evelyn Anderson, *Hammer or Anvil*, p. 141. Her conclusions, identical with the ones presented above, are to be found on pp. 140–41. They are fully confirmed by Geiger, *Die soziale Schichtung*, pp. 96, 109, 111–12.

were free to espouse doctrines which satisfied the irrational cravings of the middle groups. Their aristocratic "philosophy" offered social prestige and recognition to impoverished "brain workers" of all sorts and was taken as a promise that the Nazis would "rescue" these workers from proletarization. It was this fantasy of a graduated society with white collar workers above labor which served as the bridge between the new middle class and the Nazis.[155] At the same time, the Nazi Party enlisted the support of most of those Germans who were still burning with shame at the thought of the *Versailler Diktat*. Hitler promised to restore "national honor" and steer Germany away from the weak-kneed internationalism preached by the Social Democrats.

But let no one believe the Nazis' claim that their program conclusively demonstrated the superiority of ideas over "base" economic interests. The Nazis were sufficiently shrewd to appeal to divergent economic groups with frequently contradictory pledges. As Geiger well says:

> The history of the growth of the Nazi Party shows that, in reality, it did not overcome the disparities in economic outlooks by national (*völkisch*) ideals. . . . One might say that disappointed, hopeless, helpless, or at least uncertain materialists had begun to mistake their own desperation or perplexity for idealistic enthusiasm.[156]

A glance at the organizations of the new middle class will confirm this general thesis. Of the salaried employees, well over 650,000 were organized in the Allgemeiner Freie Angestellten Bund, an ally of the Socialist trade unions. That was in 1923. Nearly ten years later this organization had lost almost 200,000 members. During the same period, the Gesamtverband Deutscher Angestellten-Gewerkschaften, which

---

[155] Cf. Geiger, *Die soziale Schichtung*, p. 121. He writes that the chief elements in the "old middle stratum have this in common: they are at present (1932) on the defensive. It seems to me that the defense against economic pressure is basically . . . not as decisive as the defense of social prestige of the group as such." *Ibid.*, p. 87. Cf. also Ignazio Silone, *The School for Dictators*, pp. 75–79, 85–88, 94–95.

[156] Geiger, *Die soziale Schichtung*, p. 118.

started as a conservative body and became Nazi, grew from 460,000 to 590,000. Finally, the Gewerkschaftsbund der Angestellten, which contained many National Socialists, increased its membership from 300,000 to 400,000.

This ominous trend was duplicated in the organizations of the civil servants. The Socialist Allgemeiner Deutscher Beamtenbund had 350,000 members in 1923. After ten years it had shrunk to half its former size. On the other hand, the Deutscher Beamtenbund, organized right after the 1918 Revolution on a platform of political neutrality, pointed with pride to an increase of about 200,000—from 825,000 in 1920 to over a million in 1932. By the latter date it had abandoned all pretense of neutrality and had revealed its nationalist and reactionary face.[157]

The lack of appeal of the SPD became ever clearer as the Weimar Republic approached its disastrous end. How to attract these hostile groups was the subject of prolonged debate in Socialist journals from 1930 on, but by then it was too late to correct the faulty analysis of class relations which had guided the actions of German Social Democracy.[158] With the superior analytical tool of hindsight we can now see just where Social Democracy went wrong in its middle class theory. The orthodox Marxists had been too mechanistic, but in a curiously twisted fashion the same fault appears with the Revisionists. Bernstein had once wisely pointed out that to be anti-Manchester was not identical with being anticapitalist. He overlooked the equally pertinent truth that a man disillusioned with capitalism did not necessarily become a So-

[157] These figures are based on Emil Lederer and Jakob Marschak, "Der neue Mittelstand," in Vol. IX, Part 1, of *Grundriss der Sozialökonomik*, pp. 134–35, 139; and on Rudolf Küstermeier, *Die Mittelschichten und ihr politischer Weg*, pp. 44–45. The figures have been rounded off.

[158] Cf. especially Küstermeier, *ibid.*, and articles in the magazine *Die Arbeit* by Theodor Geiger and others. Note that the Social Democrats were not the only ones to go wrong. Cf. Lederer's and Marschak's conclusions in "Der neue Mittelstand," p. 141. They write that position between classes has become impossible and that the collapse of the new middle class and the strength of the trade unions will remove all inhibitions of the middle class from joining the unions. The conflict between employer and worker becomes ever more drastic, etc. . . .

cialist. However closely developments in England may have followed the Revisionist scheme, Bernstein's analysis proved woefully inadequate in the case of Germany. If we may say that one of the chief tasks of political sociology is to determine what certain groups will do under certain circumstances, we must conclude that Revisionist sociology was extraordinarily weak in this vital sector. The ignorance or, at least, undervaluation of irrational factors, the inability to add psychological insight to economic analysis, led to tragedy.[159]

Revisionist theory scored a number of brilliant triumphs and suffered from grievous errors. Its most consequential failure lay in the superficiality and narrowness of its analysis of the fate of the middle class.

[159] This is, of course, not to maintain that modern class politics is to be viewed from a predominantly psychological framework. Such a vantage point frequently leads to an overemphasis on irrationality and, consequently, to reactionary conclusions. (See Pareto's work.) But we cannot afford to overlook the insights of group psychology and psychiatry. Cf. Erich Fromm, *Escape from Freedom,* especially Chapter VI, "Psychology of Nazism." He writes, p. 208: "In our opinion none of these explanations which emphasize political and economic factors to the exclusion of psychological ones—or vice versa—is correct. Nazism is a psychological problem, but the psychological factors themselves have to be understood as being molded by socio-economic factors; Nazism is an economic and political problem, but the hold it has over a whole people has to be understood on psychological grounds." Silone is right, when he writes (*School for Dictators,* p. 126): "It is, of course, true that the Socialists, with their eyes fixed on the class-struggle and practical politics, were taken by surprise by the savage irruption of Fascism, failed to understand the reasons and consequences of its strange and unheard-of words and symbols, and did not for one moment imagine it possible that a movement of such a primitive nature might gain control of and manage a mechanism as complicated as the modern state. The Socialists were unprepared to understand the efficacy of Fascist propaganda because their doctrine was formulated by Marx and Engels in the 19th century, since when it has not made any great advances. In a passage in *The Eighteenth Brumaire* Marx rightly wrote that 'the tradition of the dead generations hangs like an incubus over the brains of the living,' but he could not anticipate the discoveries of modern psychology concerning the structure of the human mind."

Chapter 8

The Politics of Revisionism

The Inevitability of Gradualism

> *If you do not have the serious intention of achieving the final victory, you are assured of defeat from the outset.*
>
> EDUARD BERNSTEIN

MARXIST CRITICS HAVE professed to see in the antirevolutionary tactics of Revisionism a reflection of its dread of violence or the rationalization of a cowardly "parliamentarism at any price." Bernstein and his followers, on the other hand, were fond of describing their tactics as a logical outgrowth of their philosophy and their economic theory.

It is, in any event, certain that there exists a close relationship between Revisionist theory and practice: Bernstein's analysis of capitalist development was bound to lead to gradualist, nonviolent tactics. The Revisionists had substituted their conception of linear evolution for the Marxist view of dialectical conflicts. To them, capitalism was stabilizing itself, increasingly able to ward off depressions, and distributing the national product to all classes. In addition, they believed parliamentary government to be in the ascendant. Their study of contemporary Europe (particularly England) seemed to prove the growing political power of the proletariat. In some states it was already enfranchised and was beginning to participate in the formation of national policy. It was inevitable —or so it seemed to Bernstein—that this must become a general movement.

Revisionist parliamentarism was further strengthened by two tactical doctrines which may be called "Socialism-in-capitalism" and "organic evolutionism."

The first of these, "Socialism-in-capitalism," was chiefly a Fabian heritage. Socialist institutions, so the theory runs, begin to permeate capitalism even while the latter system is at its height.[1] The area of communal action is steadily increasing in size and significance. This is cause for great hope, for it demonstrates that the transformation of capitalism into Socialism can proceed in gradual and nonviolent fashion. The Fabian concept of "municipal Socialism," according to which city-owned gas and water works are milestones on the road to Socialism, is one expression of this doctrine.

This gradual process is, of course, not automatic. Its eventual success depends largely on the unity and energy of working class action. With a strong Social Democratic Party directing the fight, the proletariat may take advantage of tendencies already inherent in capitalism. Then "legislation . . . comes to dominate more and more areas which had earlier been at the mercy of the blind struggle of particular interests. This is the growing freedom of society over against economic factors." [2] Bernstein treated the subject quite specifically: "It is my firm conviction," he wrote in 1898,

that the present generation will see the realization of a great deal of Socialism, if not in the patented form then at least in substance. The steady enlargement of the circle of social duties and of the corresponding rights of the individual to society and *vice versa;* the extension of the right of supervision over the economy exercised by society organized either as nation or as state; the development of democratic self-government in community, county, and province; and the enlargement of the tasks of these bodies —all these signify for me growth into Socialism or, if you wish, piecemeal realization of Socialism. The transfer of economic enterprises from private to public management will, of course, accompany this development, but it will proceed only gradually.[3]

[1] Marx had, of course, held to such a view in his belief that the future society exists, in outline, in the contradictions of present-day society. One example: the coexistence of social production and private property in capitalism. Again we see how Marx and Bernstein could take the same idea and make it serve opposite ends.
[2] *Zur Geschichte und Theorie des Sozialismus,* p. 335.
[3] *Ibid.,* p. 233.

The very advance of capitalism, Bernstein held, paves the way for Socialism; trusts and cartels are already organized in such a manner that all the Socialists need to do is expropriate the shareholders and run the corporations for the benefit of society.[4] Human society is not static. Workers are steadily growing in numbers, power, and social importance. "They claim ever more citizenship rights and, if these should be withheld, they will fight for them." [5]

In a significant speech, the 75-year-old Bernstein applied the Socialism-in-capitalism doctrine to the Weimar Republic: The task of the Social Democratic Party regarding the realization of Socialism, Bernstein said, lies in the realization of what Lassalle had called the "idea of the working class." A glance at the German state was enough to show that the country was approaching that goal. It would be absurd to call Weimar Germany a "capitalistic republic." The working class had compelled acceptance of its "idea" in the most varied areas of legislation. The classical concept of capitalism usually refers to three distinctive areas: forms of production, modes of distribution, legal relations. Only the first had not been fundamentally modified in recent times; the other two had been altered greatly, partly as a result of legislation enacted under the pressure of the labor movement, partly as a consequence of direct action by the organized workers. The capitalist employer no longer could dictate the terms of employment; he was compelled to negotiate. Wage determination no longer was a private contest in which the larger amount of reserves acted as the final arbiter. Wages were becoming a social matter, even a subject of legislation. Strong labor organizations had set limits to the dictatorship of the capitalist employer. Finally, the development of cartels and monopolies had brought about an increase in public control and would lead to their eventual metamorphosis into public corporations. But the actual realization of Socialism—and this must be stressed—depends finally on the will, the moral strength, and the political ability of the working class. It can

[4] Bernstein, *Wirtschaftswesen und Wirtschaftswerden*, p. 36.
[5] *Ibid.*, p. 39. Cf. also *Von der Sekte zur Partei*, pp. 39–50.

be a result only of incessant political labor.[6]

While this, the first of the two tactical doctrines under discussion, derived from British experience, the second was a direct result of Bernstein's speculation about evolution.[7] Bernstein advocated what he called "organic evolutionism." He defined it as a concern with construction. It is opposed by another attitude toward evolution which is destructive in nature.

> The first appears as utopian, sectarian, peaceful, evolutionist, the second as conspiratorial, demagogic, terroristic. The closer we have come to the present time, the more decisive has become the formulation: on the one hand emancipation through economic organization, on the other hand emancipation through political expropriation.[8]

Marxism, Bernstein said, sought to combine both approaches, and had never really emancipated itself from the second. He characterized this reliance on revolutionary violence as "Blanquism." [9]

[6] Paraphrased from the much abbreviated concept of a speech delivered on June 16, 1925, at Berlin University. Bernstein Archives.

[7] Cf. pp. 143–51 above.

[8] *Die Voraussetzungen des Sozialismus und die Aufgaben der Sozialdemokratie,* p. 64.

[9] Undeniably, Marxist evolutionary philosophy was profoundly revolutionary. While Marx admitted specifically that certain countries, such as Great Britain and Holland, might achieve Socialism without violence, his philosophy still stressed the pain that would attend the birth of the new order. Man may shorten the birthpangs, but he cannot eliminate them. History has no anaesthetic; as Hegel had remarked, "Gangrene cannot be cured with lavender water." But it is questionable whether Bernstein's charge against Marx—that he overestimated the effectiveness of the creative power of violence—was well taken. Marx was no irrationalist *à la* Sorel and never preached violence for its own sake. He had well realized that tactics had to be adjusted to strategic situations. In his studies of revolutions, Bernstein saw with concern that irresponsible elements among revolutionaries inevitably attempted to take over the direction of the upheaval and drive it further to the left. This seemed especially true to him of the terrible confusion

Now, Bernstein sought, early and late in his career, to demonstrate the futility of force. It seems in retrospect that his case would have been far more clear-cut if he had simply divided tactics into nonviolent and violent without charging the advocates of a forcible revolution with being imbued with irrationalist Blanquism. Bernstein himself was compelled to admit that violence and conspiracy might be necessary tactics for a labor movement shackled by a controlled press and crippling police regulations.[10] Certainly there are situations in which the use of force may be defended on *rational* grounds —most obviously in a country in which peaceful methods of bringing about social change are doomed to failure. Bernstein's concentration on Blanquism prevented him from facing fully the crucial question: Was a nonviolent revolution possible in Imperial Germany?

Bernstein's own answer to this question was a cautious affirmative. Socialism was to be "emancipation through economic organization"; it required a persistent economic and political struggle on a wide front. To carry on this fight, the Revisionists strove to mobilize four distinct social groups: the Social Democratic Party with its active members and its satellite voters, occasional non-Socialist allies, trade unions, and cooperatives.

The German Social Democratic Party, Bernstein wrote, would lead its allies in the fight for Socialism. Bernstein was fond of citing Engels's Preface to *The Class Struggles in France* as proof that Engels had envisioned a similar role for a legal Socialist party. The German Socialists, Engels had written, had shown their comrades of all countries "how to use universal suffrage." More, "It was found that the state institutions in which the rule of the bourgeoisie is organized, offer still further opportunities for the working class to fight these very institutions." [11]

German Social Democracy, Bernstein wrote in full assent

---

of Paris in 1848. Here Bernstein saw the activities of the left-wing Blanquists as destructive of the real aims of the Revolution. Cf. his *Wie eine Revolution zugrunde ging, passim.*

[10] See *ibid.*, p. 56.

[11] Marx, *The Class Struggles in France,* Preface, pp. 20 f.

to these quotations from Engels, must "organize the working class politically and educate it for democracy. It must fight for all those reforms which are designed to raise the working class and to give the state a more democratic form." [12] The party must be content with unspectacular activity; it must not strive for the grand collapse that will give it a chance to take complete power, but it must perform its day-to-day tasks with energy and patience. The party

> does not fight for political power in the delusion that it will gain control overnight, but in the endeavor to secure for the working class an ever stronger influence on legislation and public life. . . . It is nonsensical to view the struggle for political power merely as the struggle for complete and exclusive domination within the state.[13]

But Bernstein insisted that the SPD could be an effective tool for the liberation of the working class on one condition only: it must free itself from outworn slogans and dare to recognize its true nature. He recalled Schiller's words:

> And what she is, that dares she to appear.[14]

The influence of the party would be far greater than it is, Bernstein wrote in a celebrated sentence, if "it found the courage to emancipate itself from a phraseology which is actually obsolete. and if it were willing to appear what it really is today; a democratic-Socialist reform party." [15]

The Revisionists thought that the effects of such an admission—which would have to find expression in a new party program—could be nothing but beneficial. "The bourgeoisie," Bernstein said, "is a highly complex class which is composed of a large number of strata with very divergent . . . interests. These groups stick together for long only if they feel either equally oppressed or equally menaced." [16] Now, if they

[12] *Zur Geschichte und Theorie des Sozialismus*, p. 234.
[13] *Ibid.*, p. 247.
[14] Quoted in *Voraussetzungen*, p. 198.
[15] *Ibid.*, p. 230.
[16] *Ibid.*, p. 196.

all feel the threat of Social Democracy they will form a united mass—a mass of enemies to Socialism. Bernstein denied that this was necessary, for "Social Democracy does not threaten them all equally strongly and offers no danger to anyone personally. It has no enthusiasm whatever for a violent revolution against the whole nonproletarian world." [17] It follows that "the more clearly this is expressed and reasoned out, the more promptly will that united fear disappear." [18] Many members of the bourgeoisie have other enemies (who are also the enemies of the workers), and they would much rather side with the workers against the common exploiters than side with the exploiters against the workers. But Socialism will hardly acquire these groups as allies if they are told: "We want to help you to swallow the enemy, and right afterwards we shall swallow you." [19]

This analysis of the function of Social Democracy as a candidly reformist and parliamentarist party brings the question of alliances in its wake. Bernstein expressed the opinion that the radical bourgeoisie could be counted on to support a Social Democratic program if it could be made to understand the peaceful intentions of the Socialists. However, we must note that side by side with this call for alliances on the basis of common interests, there goes a certain skepticism. On the one hand, Bernstein could write at the turn of the century:

> The victorious struggle for democracy, the formation of political and economic organs of democracy, are the indispensable preconditions for the realization of Socialism. If you reply that the chances for achieving this aim without political catastrophe are exceedingly small—indeed, almost nonexistent—in Germany, since the German bourgeoisie is becoming more and more reactionary, then that may be true for the moment, although there is some evidence to the contrary. But this state of affairs cannot last.[20]

And it will change precisely when German Socialism gives up its hollow cries of revolution and proletarization. In a per-

[17] *Ibid.*, pp. 196–97.
[18] *Ibid.*, p. 197.
[19] *Loc. cit.*
[20] *Ibid.*, 196.

ceptive early article Bernstein had pointed out that there was nothing shameful about compromise, that a great compromise had made a united Social Democracy possible in the first place.[21] This optimistic attitude towards the possibility of successful alliances between a candidly reformist Social Democracy and the radicalized, oppressed wing of the bourgeoisie informed most of the Revisionist thinking on tactics. As has been shown in the preceding chapter, this was a logically indispensable part of the Bernsteinian class analysis. Thus Bernstein converted the Marxist slogan. "The liberation of the proletariat can only be the work of the proletariat itself," into: "The liberation of the proletariat must be *primarily* the work of the proletariat itself."

Yet, on the other hand, Bernstein was pessimistic as to the possibilities of the very collaboration he advocated. He hoped that German bourgeois radicalism could follow the lead of English and French left liberals who, recognizing that most of their aims remained unfulfilled in present-day society, had frequently made common cause with Socialist parties. But he knew that this could happen only if German radicalism continued to move to the left—a most unlikely eventuality.[22] True, a number of German radicals claimed Bernstein as an ally—a fact which horrified his Marxist friends. Friedrich Naumann, founder of the National Soziale Partei, had called Bernstein "our most advanced post in the camp of Social Democracy." [23] But the National Sozialen were hardly ideal

[21] "Klassenkampf und Kompromiss," in *Zur Geschichte und Theorie des Sozialismus*, pp. 149–62.
[22] Bernstein, *Wesen und Aussichten des bürgerlichen Radikalismus*, pp. 35–36, 42–43.
[23] Quoted in *Voraussetzungen*, p. 260. In 1899, Naumann hailed the *Voraussetzungen* in a public lecture as a great contribution and concluded his speech with these remarkable words: "I do not believe that we will be able to acquire many voters from Social Democracy for a national ideal within a short time. I do believe, however, that a large segment of Social Democracy will be compelled by Bernstein and those who think like him (*Gesinnungsfreunde*) to rethink carefully the question of the relation of the national to the social. And I believe that this mental labor will lead them in due course of time to the realization that two words belong together which we National Sozialen have already coupled: NATIONAL and SOCIAL." Bernstein Archives.

companions in arms. Nor was Bernstein optimistic about the prospects for a coalition with other elements of the bourgeoisie. In 1907 he participated in a debate in the Hungarian newspaper *Pester Lloyd*. The German liberal, Theodor Barth, had written that German liberalism could not achieve its aims without the Social Democratic Party. Jaurès had added that German Social Democrats should aid liberalism in their country, to which Kautsky replied that all attempts at democratizing German liberalism must end in complete failure.

Bernstein, although less emphatic than Kautsky, substantially agreed with his orthodox colleague. The Social Democratic Party, he said, was sympathetic toward Barth's endeavors but considered them hopeless at the time. Jaurès's demand for an understanding between the German bourgeoisie and Social Democracy rested on an incomplete knowledge of German conditions. A political party should not be overly sensitive, but German liberals had shown beyond doubt that they wanted nothing to do with Social Democracy, and the latter should not forget that. The liberals' behavior in the 1907 Reichstag elections, in which they allied themselves with the worst of reactionaries, was unforgivable. Of course, if they should want an understanding with the Socialists, the SPD would not oppose it on doctrinal grounds. But what was needed above all was a thoroughgoing revision of liberal policies. A truly democratic policy of the liberals would be fully supported by the Social Democratic Party. Acts, not pious professions, count, and whether the liberals would change their ways was a question which only the future could answer.[24]

---

[24] Paraphrased from the newspaper article. Bernstein Archives. Bernstein himself was defeated in the Reichstag elections of 1907. At another place, Bernstein wrote concerning coalitions: "As far as the coalition with the liberals is concerned, that would be nothing unheard-of in the history of Social Democracy. Nor would it violate any principles or basic theories of Socialist doctrine. Everything depends on the details of the assumptions, the arrangements and the performance [of the alliance]. . . . I will not go so far as to call the question of coalitions exclusively a question of opportuneness. As a matter of fact, I am of the

This realistic attitude toward the German liberals conflicted with the theory of class alliances, and the contradiction between the two continued to prevent Revisionism from acquiring a clear view of its tactical principles. Bernstein was far more consistent in his treatment of the third and fourth members of the envisaged grand coalition: the trade unions and the cooperatives.

Both types of organization were perfect instruments for the piecemeal progress which Bernstein stressed. Their social function, which Lenin was to characterize contemptuously as "Economism," consisted chiefly of the struggle for the gradual improvement of the workers' and the consumers' living conditions. As we have seen, many Socialists, such as Lassalle and the Blanquists, had opposed trade unions.[25] We have also noted the aid which German trade unions gave the Revisionist movement without any real interest in theoretical questions. From the Revisionist point of view trade unions were, of course, a crucial weapon in the peaceful class struggle. Their victorious fight for favorable contracts gave them a stake in the nation's economy. Indeed, "we may regard a genuine contract won by a strong trade union as a real kind of part-ownership (*Teilhaberschaft*) in the industry." [26] Trade unions tend to "break the absolutism of capital and secure for the workers direct influence over the conduct of industry." [27] We may, therefore, call trade unions, "the democratic element in industry." [28]

Trade unions, then, help the party do the immediate, day-to-day work that will eventually lead to Socialism. This is true not only in the economic but also in the ethical sphere,

---

opinion that there are some alliances into which Social Democracy must not enter under any circumstances." "Der Kampf in Belgien und der politische Massenstrike," *Sozialistische Monatshefte,* VI, 1 (1902), 416.

[25] "The trade union struggle of the worker is the vain struggle of the commodity 'labor' to act as a man," Lassalle once said. Quoted in Bernstein, *Sozialismus einst und jetzt,* p. 70.

[26] *Ibid.,* p. 73.

[27] *Voraussetzungen,* p. 174.

[28] *Loc. cit.*

for the moral ideals of equality and freedom from wage slavery are embodied in labor organizations.[29]

The same may be said of cooperatives, which Bernstein discussed in detail. The neglect of cooperatives, Bernstein felt, was due to the overly political orientation of Marxist doctrine.[30] The pronounced state Socialists, such as Lassalle, had regarded cooperatives as petty concerns. Bernstein pointed out that producers' cooperatives had indeed been failures, but consumers' cooperatives had demonstrated astonishing vitality. Producers' cooperatives, Bernstein wrote in agreement with Beatrice Webb, were fundamentally individualistic.[31] Consumers' cooperatives, however, with their equal shares in profits, are democratic in character and might easily be transformed into the main agencies handling distribution in the Socialist state. Not only do they train the proletariat in organizing their buying power, but they are more immediate aids in counteracting commercial exploitation and in protecting the workers in times of strikes and lockouts.[32]

Bernstein's conception of an alliance among the Social Democratic Party, the radical bourgeoisie, the trade unions, and the cooperatives stressed the variety of the class struggle. The Socialists worked toward their goal within parliament and on the economic front. More votes meant greater political power, higher wages and standards of living among workers meant greater economic power for Social Democracy. The more power the Socialists acquired, the sooner Socialism would be realized. Then why fight a revolution?

Revisionists drove parliamentarism to its logical limits. Two controversies which divided German Social Democracy in the first decade of the twentieth century will further illuminate the length to which Revisionism was prepared to go.

In the Reichstag elections of June 1903, the SPD scored a great victory. Over three million votes (as against two millions in 1898) gave the party 81 mandates (as against 56 in the previous election). Bernstein assessed the consequences

[29] Cf. Bernstein, *Die Arbeiterbewegung*, pp. 118–40.
[30] *Voraussetzungen*, pp. 142–43.
[31] *Ibid.*, p. 148.
[32] *Ibid.*, pp. 149, 157, 169.

of this triumph, which exceeded all expectations, in an article
in the *Sozialistische Monatshefte*.[33] It created nearly as much
of a sensation in German Social Democracy as had his earlier
defection from Marxist orthodoxy.

If German Socialism wishes to assert its power, Bernstein
argued, its parliamentary party must be granted those digni-
ties which its strength deserves. Specifically, one of the vice-
presidents of the Reichstag should be a Social Democrat. The
occupancy of such an official post by a Socialist, Bernstein
wrote, will give the party a fairer share in the management of
parliamentary business. As an example of its importance he
cited the tariff measure, adopted in 1902 without the thoroughgoing debate it deserved.[34] What reasons have the Social
Democrats for refusing a post that is rightfully theirs? Merely
an old custom which dictates that, as a sign of protest against
monarchy, Socialists shall not pay homage to the Kaiser. It
was customary for the president and vice-presidents of the
Reichstag to call formally on the German emperor. But would
a formal visit to the Kaiser represent an abandonment of Socialist principles? asked Bernstein. Certainly not. Of course,
a Socialist "will not participate in a demonstration which aims
at glorifying the monarchic principle. But a visit to the German emperor cannot be characterized as such. . . ." [35]

That was too much for the party leadership. After a heady
victory, marked by such rhetorical generalities as "A great
victory lies behind us, greater victories face us!" the Bernstein proposal seemed a cowardly gesture. "Comrade Bernstein," wrote Franz Mehring editorially in the *Neue Zeit*,
"wants to translate the mighty and heroic fight of three millions into a courtesy bow to the monarchic form of government." [36] Bernstein's plan, which was the delight of the
anti-Socialist press, the editorial went on, was a slap in the
face of a fighting movement.[37] In a front-page statement in
the *Neue Zeit*, Bebel called on the forthcoming party congress

[33] "Was folgt aus dem Ergebnis der Reichstagswahlen?" *Sozialistische Monatshefte*, VII, 2 (1903), 478–86.
[34] *Ibid.*, p. 480.
[35] *Ibid.*, p. 479.
[36] *Neue Zeit*, XXI, 2 (1903), 418.
[37] *Ibid.*, p. 419.

to deliver a ringing declaration that "our representatives have better things to do than to indulge in tearful lamentations over the defeat of bourgeois liberalism and to woo the bourgeois parties." [38] Before that congress, Bebel published a lengthy article in which he pointed up the importance of the issue.[39]

If it had not been for Bernstein's proposal and its intemperate defense by Vollmar and others, the question of Revisionist tactics would probably not have arisen at all at the Dresden congress. But now it occasioned a debate that dwarfed all the earlier Bernstein debates. Bernstein himself only spoke once, and made it perfectly clear that he had never advocated compromise with monarchy. Nor had he ever desired to make Social Democracy *hoffähig* (that is, fit to be presented at court). He was concerned with parliamentary tactics only: "If I made the suggestion that we claim the post of vice-president and thus accept the usages of the Reichstag, no one can conclude from this that I have abjured our political principles in any fashion." [40] It had nothing to do with theoretical heresies, nor was it a sign of a "boundless overestimation of parliamentarism." "Our movement has been driven by experience to give parliamentarism an ever greater significance. . . . Should a situation arise in which the post of a vice-president would show itself to be really useful and valuable for the party, Bebel would be the first [to alter his stand]." [41]

[38] *Ibid.*, p. 449.
[39] *Ibid.*, pp. 708–29. Bebel's earlier declaration, with its sharp wording, had called forth bitter protests within the party. Bebel now wrote that of all his opponents—Heine, Vollmar, Kolb, and others—Bernstein had been by far the most objective. Bernstein's reply to Bebel in the Breslau *Volkswacht* had taken a form for which Bebel was grateful. Bebel said that the reactionary majority would never permit a Socialist vice-president to perform his functions. Besides, to dress up in the required knee breeches with long stockings and buckle shoes would be an insult to the whole labor movement. The enthusiastic reception of the proposal by the bourgeois press is an indication of this. Nor would the acceptance of the post increase the power of the SPD by one iota.
[40] *Protokoll über die Verhandlungen des Parteitages der SPD, 1903*, p. 392.
[41] *Ibid.*, pp. 397, 399. Cf. also Bernstein, "Der neue Reichstag und die Aufgaben der Sozialdemokratie," *Sozialistische Monatshefte*, VII, 2 (1903), 641–49.

Bernstein's attempt to bring the discussion back to the utility of practical parliamentarism, where he felt it really belonged, was in vain. The debate ended with an overwhelming victory for the Bebel-Kautsky orthodoxy.[42]

The second controversy arose five years later, in 1908, over the relation of Social Democratic parliamentary parties to the budget. Socialists had, as a matter of principle, always voted against the budgets submitted to the federal as well as state parliaments. The act had acquired symbolic significance, but it had had its opponents in Socialist ranks from the beginning. As early as 1894 the Bavarian Social Democrats, under Vollmar's leadership, had approved the Bavarian budget. In the same year the national party had condemned this action. It had reiterated this position at the Lübeck congress of 1901. But in 1908 the Social Democrats of Württemberg, Baden, and Bavaria—all South German strongholds of Revisionism —approved the budgets in their states. They were forthwith accused of violation of fundamental party principles and breach of party discipline.

At the congress of Nürnberg, in 1908, the South Germans defended themselves vehemently. They characterized the budget vote as a tactical step which ought not to be discussed in terms of abstract theory. "I have the feeling," cried delegate Timm of Munich, "that our party comrades who possess theoretical training have too little contact with the masses. . . . When science is remote from practice, it must lead to one-sided results." [43] Workers, not academicians, had urged the Bavarian Socialists to accept the budget.[44] It had contained a number of social improvements for which Bavarian Social Democracy had fought for years. Why jeopardize these gains? Why refuse to acknowledge the obvious fact that a

[42] Viktor Adler's comments are of interest. He wrote, rightly, that the problem was much less significant than all the noise would make it appear. But "Bernstein unfortunately demonstrates again and again that he has lost touch with the inner soul of his party or, let us say, that he has not yet regained it." Once more Bernstein had shown his "uprightness" and lack of "tactical adroitness." Gustav Pollatschek, ed., *Viktor Adlers Aufsätze, Reden und Briefe*, VI, 247, 250.

[43] *Protokoll über die Verhandlungen des Parteitages, 1908*, p. 298.

[44] *Ibid.*, p. 303.

powerful Social Democracy is having its impact on the class state? [45]

Delegate Ludwig Frank of Mannheim continued this line of argument. He pointed out that the party orthodoxy, best represented in the Reichstag by Bebel and Singer, had frequently collaborated with the state, whose right to exist they denied. It was easier for Prussians to talk: the three-class electoral law made it impossible for Prussian Social Democrats to get into the Landtag. "Your delegates to the Prussian parliament have been spared the outer and inner struggle: you haven't got any delegates!" [46]

A violent three-day debate followed and resulted in the adoption of a resolution which was an expression of the orthodox views of Bebel and Kautsky. "The vote in favor of the complete budget is to be viewed as a vote of confidence for the government," it ran in part. "The refusal of the budget fully accords with the class position of the property-less masses of the population which necessitates an implacable opposition to the existing state power that is subservient to capitalism." [47]

Bernstein, who was not a delegate to the congress, regretted the debate. He agreed with the South Germans that the problem was chiefly a tactical one, but he did not deny that the orthodoxy was right in raising the question of principle. The Kautsky-Bebel wing, he said, had an "absolutist" conception of the state, one which holds that the state must be overthrown first and reformed afterwards. Its suppressed premise was that economic and political conditions were deteriorating.[48]

> But this concept ought not to predominate. Never was the conscious orientation (*Selbstbesinnung*) toward the Revisionist viewpoint (the organic evolutionary attitude which amounts to determined reformism in politics) as necessary for Social Democracy as it is today.[49]

[45] *Ibid.*, pp. 300–304.
[46] *Ibid.*, p. 320.
[47] *Ibid.*, p. 550.
[48] Bernstein, "Zum Reformismus," *Sozialistische Monatshefte*, XII, 3 (1908), 1398–1405.
[49] *Ibid.*, p. 1403.

To say in the resolution that "the state, as long as it finds itself in the hands of the owning classes, constitutes an organ of class domination and is a means of oppressing the propertyless classes" is to overlook the possibilities of historical development. Bernstein recalled, as so often before, that nine tenths of Social Democratic activity is reform activity. "To raise such practical questions to questions of principle is always a mistake." [50]

The Revisionists were by no means the only Socialists who recognized the importance of parliamentary work and day-to-day activity in the economic field. Orthodox Marxists, too, held that the revolutionary struggle must be carried on with many weapons, including those of participation in parliaments as well as wage negotiations. But the Marxists always came back to intransigence while the Revisionists put all their emphasis on the legal means of social change.

The logic of the Revisionist position was impeccable. When Bernstein demanded that the party recognize openly that it had turned reformist, he merely told it an obvious truth. More and more, German Social Democracy had a stake in the existing system and hoped to reform rather than overthrow the state. The growing size of the party vote, the increasing power within the party of go-slow bureaucrats and antirevolutionary trade unionists daily confirmed Bernstein's words of 1899. The party leadership, particularly Bebel and Kautsky, were prisoners of their own speeches and programmatic declarations. An honest appraisal of the situation, which Bernstein had demanded, would have compelled the party to rewrite its program along Revisionist lines.

But it must also be said that the Revisionist theory of power was, at best, sketchy. Frequently Bernstein drew the wrong conclusions from undisputed facts. A good example was his insistence that the number of the propertied was growing, as could be observed in the increasing numbers of shareholders. Bernstein never sufficiently emphasized the essential impotence of this group in a period of capitalism in which ownership and control were widely separated.

"The inevitability of gradualism" should not have been taken as an axiom that stood above dispute. Bernstein and his

[50] Cf. Bernstein, *Von der Sekte zur Partei*, pp. 59–63.

followers were doubtless right when they decried rigid revolutionism as foolish. But whether or not parliamentarism can work depends on the social structure and political institutions of a country. The change from capitalism to Socialism involves a drastic transfer of power from one social group to another. Whether that transfer can be accomplished without violence is a tremendously complex problem that allows of no dogmatic answer.

A correct appraisal of necessary party tactics was especially difficult in twentieth-century Germany, since the true nature of German society was disguised under ideological legal forms. This the Revisionists never fully understood.[51] Bismarck's Germany had openly been a class state. Therefore, Social Democracy rejected Bismarck's social legislation as "ransom legislation," even though it actually improved the proletariat's living conditions. But in the last years of the Empire and even more in the Weimar Republic it became increasingly difficult to locate the true seats of power. It was possible to assume, for example, that the new middle class would ally itself with the proletariat. It did not. It was equally plausible to believe that a large Social Democratic delegation in the Reichstag of the Empire could help to transform Germany into a parliamentary monarchy on the English model. That, too, did not happen.

The tactical bankruptcy of the SPD, in which the supposedly orthodox Marxists had a share, showed itself most glaringly in the Weimar Republic. The Revolution of 1918 was almost literally forced on the Social Democrats, and once they were in power they did not know what to do with it. They mistook form for substance—Bernstein's speech of 1925, quoted above, is an excellent instance. It will be recalled that the aging Revisionist leader had argued that Germany could no longer be called a "capitalist republic" since organized labor had enforced higher wages and social legislation and since the dictatorship of the employer was coming to an end. But to talk that way was to misunderstand the nature of German society and to fail to see that the old centers of power—the army, the bureaucracy, the judiciary

[51] For one notable exception, see the section on the general strike immediately below.

—were rapidly regaining their former prominence and that big business was actually consolidating its hold on society.[52]

There is nothing inherently wrong with a Revisionist theory of social change. But to establish it without correctly analyzing the society to which it is supposed to apply can only lead to disaster.

"General Strike Is General Nonsense"

> *Behind universal suffrage there must stand the will to the general strike.*
>
> RUDOLF HILFERDING

Eduard Bernstein's parliamentarism, although his chief tactical weapon, was not a "parliamentarism at any price," as his radical opponents claimed. While, in general, he advocated nonviolent methods which were nearly identical with professed trade union tactics in Germany, he parted company with his union allies on one important point—the political mass strike.

On this issue, the trade unions stood massively against the party theoreticians. To the trade union leadership, tactics was a most practical matter: wages and hours negotiations, strikes if negotiations failed, united defense against lockouts, Social Democratic votes at general elections—these were the weapons in their arsenal. Party leaders, in contrast, felt that the labor movement needed to exert pressure in other ways as well. To give one example: Several international Socialist congresses had asked the proletariat to celebrate May 1st with parades and speeches to demonstrate its unshakable solidarity. Many trade union leaders agreed with such a plan in principle, but they opposed a complete cessation of work for a whole day, as demanded by the Socialist congress of Amsterdam in 1904. They feared that such a step would give occa-

[52] Cf. Franz Neumann, *Behemoth,* p. 32: "It was the tragedy of the Social Democratic party and trade unions to have had as leaders men with high intellectual qualities but completely devoid of any feeling for the condition of the masses and without insight into the great social transformations of the post-war period."

sion to lockouts; some stigmatized it as a one-day general strike to be avoided at all costs. The opportunists, always strongly entrenched in the movement, carried the day: the weasel words of the resolution of the 1905 Social Democratic Praty congress at Jena are proof of their triumph. "The party congress imposes the duty upon workers and workers' organizations . . . to cease work [on May 1st] wherever this is possible." [53]

Still stronger was the opposition of the trade unions to the political mass strike. The idea of a general strike for the achievement of certain noneconomic goals was an old one to German Social Democracy. Such a strike, sometimes called the "class strike," is to be distinguished from a work stoppage that concerns itself with problems of wages, hours, and working conditions. The political mass strike had been advocated by the so-called "Young ones," whose anarchist line had threatened to disrupt German Socialism in the early 1890s. Eduard Bernstein, encouraged by a successful mass strike in behalf of universal suffrage in Belgium in 1893, had called attention to the strike as a political weapon as early as 1894.[54]

The subject was reopened about ten years later. One close observer has listed five reasons for the reappearance of the general strike debate at that time. First, German Social Democracy possessed far less political influence than it had expected to obtain after its great electoral victory of 1903. The Prussian three-class electoral system still condemned the Socialists to political impotence in the very heart of Germany, and everywhere there appeared storm signals of a threatening assault on the civil and political rights of the working class. In this situation tacticians were apt to turn to nonparliamentary methods, largely in a defensive spirit. Secondly, German Socialists had before them the example of victorious political strikes in other countries—the Austrian workers had achieved important electoral reforms by means of mass walkouts, and the Swedes had secured universal suffrage by the same methods. Of even greater impact was the Russian Revo-

[53] Resolution quoted in Otto Heilborn, *Die "Freien" Gewerkschaften seit 1890*, p. 119.
[54] "Der Strike als politisches Kampfmittel," *Neue Zeit*, XII, 1 (1894), 689–705. Cf. also Bernstein, *Der Streik*, pp. 112–13.

lution of 1905 (an event followed with intense interest in Germany), which had begun with a series of strikes. Thirdly, international Socialist congresses, to which German Social Democracy frequently sent its top representatives, had repeatedly passed resolutions favoring mass strike action. In the fourth place, there existed a small but highly vociferous minority of anarcho-syndicalists in German Social Democracy. To them proletarian mass action was an end in itself and was to serve as a substitute for parliamentarism. Finally, and of greatest importance in this list, there were the academic discussions of the mass strike by party intellectuals. These men and women, far removed from the pedestrian concerns of managing trade union affairs, saw the general political strike as an extension of parliamentary and regular trade union activity. They, unlike the syndicalists, were not interested in the irrational aspects of strike action, but considered it a practical necessity in some strategic situations. This group of thinkers contained members of all wings of the party. Kautsky, Hilferding, Parvus, Liebknecht, Roland-Holst, and Bernstein were the leading names in the pro-strike movement.[55]

Bernstein's approach to the political mass strike was remarkable for its realism: it recognized the obvious limitations of parliamentarism in a nondemocratic country.

The Utopian mass strike, intent upon starving the bourgeoisie into submission, Bernstein argued, is nonsense. Equally absurd is the Sorelian view of the general strike as the supreme myth of the working class. The political mass strike is a straightforward tactical weapon. It may be used in special circumstances, both offensively and defensively.

How can we recognize the strategic moment? asked Bernstein. When mere talking can no longer accomplish anything, when even a whole party of eloquent Mirabeaus is unable to effect desired changes. What occasions are important enough to justify the calling of a strike? Bernstein replied by pointing to the obvious fact that Socialists can no longer win battles by fighting on the barricades—modern armies and techniques

[55] Cf. Elsbeth Georgi, *Theorie und Praxis des Generalstreiks in der modernen Arbeiterbewegung*, pp. 58–63; Bernstein, *Der Streik*, pp. 112–16.

of warfare rule out the street fight for Socialists. "But if this is so, the question arises, Which other methods are available to a people whose rights are obstinately denied, or if the attempt is made to withdraw rights which had been previously granted?" [56] The "other methods" consist chiefly of the political strike, which has the great advantage of being a familiar weapon, since it is closely related to the economic strike— a generally accepted form of the class struggle.

The political mass strike, free from Utopian elements, is the "means of putting the strongest pressure upon government and public opinion." [57] Its chances of success are small, and that is why it must be used sparingly. Like a revolution, the mass strike cannot be manufactured and cannot be called into being spontaneously; its only hope for success exists at critical moments, particularly when the ruling class is clearly in the wrong. This moral element is of great tactical importance, since it is reflected in public support for the strike. That is why Bernstein could define the mass strike as "an economic weapon with an ethical object." [58]

This analysis left no doubt as to the difficulties in the path of a victorious political strike in Germany. There the bourgeoisie, whose sympathy Bernstein considered imperative if the strike was to succeed, looked upon Social Democracy as its great enemy. Bernstein pointed to the paradox that the very size of the German Social Democratic Party made it unlikely that it could win a political strike for the simple reason that it could count on but little outside aid.[59]

Whatever its risks, the political mass strike remains a live option for German Social Democracy: Bernstein knew that the phrases "mass strike" and "must be fought under certain conditions" were vague and needed greater precision. This he attempted to give them: the mass strike need not be a universal work stoppage. It should involve workers in certain vital categories whose failure to show up for work could

---

[56] "Der Kampf in Belgien," p. 416.
[57] Bernstein, "Ist der politische Streik in Deutschland möglich?" *Sozialistische Monatshefte,* IX, 1 (1905), 33.
[58] "Politischer Massenstreik und Revolutionsromantik," *Sozialistische Monatshefte,* X, 1 (1906), 19.
[59] "Ist der politische Streik in Deutschland möglich?" p. 35.

paralyze the whole economy. Bernstein mentioned transport and communications, light and power, and food distribution establishments as key factors in any modern industrial society. He warned, however, that the strike must be prepared with the greatest care and that its organizers must see to it that workers' families do not suffer more in the general disorder than the ruling groups.[60]

The "certain conditions" under which mass action was imperative involved curtailment of (or, possibly, refusal to extend) the suffrage. That Bernstein, who wanted to arrive at Socialism by parliamentary means, felt the suffrage to be the most sensitive of all indicators of the state of the workers in a given society should not surprise us. Nor need we wonder that he was willing to overcome his strong distaste for violence and risk possible bloodshed in a situation in which the parliamentary rights of the workers were to be limited.[61]

"In a thoroughgoing democracy," he wrote, "the political strike will be an outmoded weapon. But how far removed are we in Germany from such a democracy!" [62] Take the shameful electoral law and the inequities in the Reichstag suffrage. "Should things go on like this forever? And how do you think we shall be able to change it one of these days? From which supernatural power is help supposed to come?" [63] True, universal suffrage is not the millennium. True, a political strike will be hard. But what if workers' action through legal channels should be frustrated?

> What should be the attitude of Social Democracy and of the German working class if the attempt is made to curtail the Reichstag suffrage? Can it—*dare* it—be content with Platonic mass meetings? To ask the question is to answer it. In full recognition of the difficulties which a political strike would face in Germany and especially in Prussia I

---

[60] *Ibid.*, p. 32.
[61] *Der Streik*, p. 117. As we shall see in Chapter X, Bernstein in his last years went so far as to wonder out loud whether a strike against German participation in World War I would not have been a good thing.
[62] "Der Kampf in Belgien," p. 416.
[63] *Loc. cit.*

do not hesitate to declare: we cannot do otherwise, it *must* be, resistance *must* be attempted.[64]

While Bernstein envisioned the mass strike as a peaceful although powerful demonstration which was to be used chiefly as a defensive measure, most of his allies in the mass strike debate took a somewhat more radical view. Hilferding, in a much-discussed article in the *Neue Zeit*, recalled to the proletariat its key position in modern production:

> It is this indispensability of the proletariat which is the foundation of its irresistible might and the necessity of its final victory. . . . To prevent our opponents from making parliamentary tactics impossible to us (after they have led us from success to success), the proletariat must be willing to defend universal suffrage with all means at its command. . . . Thus the general strike must be the regulative idea of Social Democratic tactics. "Regulative" in the sense that every proletarian must become aware that all his achievements, all his rights, all his aspirations can be protected and realized only if he is willing to defend them when necessary by the side of his comrades with the only method at his command—his power over the life process of society as a whole.[65]

Kautsky took a similar line, first in two articles in the *Neue Zeit*[66] and later in his preface to Henriette Roland-Holst's *Generalstreik und Sozialdemokratie*, a book which this Dutch Socialist had written upon Kautsky's suggestion.

Bernstein had favored a discussion of the political strike. In 1905 he had voted for Bebel's mass strike resolution which had considered the strike largely as a defensive weapon against "suffrage stealing." But the enthusiasm of the left

[64] "Ist der politische Streik in Deutschland möglich?" p. 36.
[65] Rudolf Hilferding, "Zur Frage des Generalstreiks," *Neue Zeit*, XXII, 1 (1904), 141. He was careful to point out that the strike was not to take the place of parliamentarism, but to make parliamentarism possible once more.
[66] "Der politische Massenstreik," *Neue Zeit*, XXII, 1 (1904), 685–95, 732–40.

wing alarmed him. He sharply criticized Mrs. Roland-Holst for basing her discussion of the general strike on the orthodox assumption that the class struggle was sharpening and that parliamentarism was "illusionism." [67] He was far unhappier with the group around Rosa Luxemburg, whom he accused of "romantic revolutionism" for desiring to transfer Russian conditions to Germany. Such procedure he condemned as sheer folly. A general strike, he said, must be called "as a last recourse (*Zufluchtsmittel*) of the working class, when the weapons which are today available to it fail, but not for romantic reasons." [68]

But even Bernstein's moderation caused great consternation among trade union leaders. These solid citizens were incensed at what they described as the irresponsibility of party intellectuals. After all, who would have to be in the front lines in a political strike, conducted for God knows what obscure aims—the ivory tower intellects or the working man? And why talk of revolutionary action when things were going so well? This was just another example of what happened if you allowed theoreticians to talk about practical affairs. At the fifth Trade Union Congress of Cologne in 1905, nearly all speakers echoed Bömelburg, who said that the anarchist general strike was beneath notice and that the Marxist political mass strike was a pernicious idea to be opposed at all costs as an impractical adventure. "Those who talk so glibly today of the political mass strike have generally no conception of the practical labor movement." [69] The only major union leader to dissent was the Revisionist von Elm, the president of the cigar sorters union. His point of view closely approximated that of Bernstein. All the others agreed with Auer's famous quip that, after all, "General strike is general nonsense." [70]

Indirectly, the mass strike discussion led to a clarification of power relations between the Socialist trade unions and the

[67] *Dokumente des Sozialismus,* V (1905), 394–95.
[68] "Politischer Massenstreik und Revolutionsromantik," p. 19.
[69] Quoted in Heilborn, *Die "Freien" Gewerkschaften,* p. 125.
[70] For von Elm's viewpoint, cf. his frequent articles in the *Sozialistische Monatshefte,* especially in the years 1905 and 1906.

Social Democratic Party, and ended with the total victory of the former. Bebel was compelled to negotiate secretly with the union leadership and surrender to their terms. The mass strike resolution of the 1906 party congress at Mannheim tried to save the party's face by reiterating the mass strike resolution of the previous year. But, it now added, "the decision of the Cologne Trade Union Congress [strongly condemning the mass strike] does not contradict our 1905 Jena resolution." [71] Happy are those who possess the dialectical skill to reconcile the irreconcilable!

For Bernstein's theory of political tactics his approach to the mass strike was a refreshing amendment. It recognized that nonviolence may be supremely desirable but also completely impossible when certain line-ups of social forces exist and when the machinery for peaceful social change is but a disguise for enforced social standstill. It is to be regretted that he never fully integrated this insight with his constitutionalism. Had he done so, he would have been in a far stronger logical position against both the intractable revolutionists of the left as well as the feverish legalists on the right who preferred the destruction of their movement to defensive action that might violate the sacred principles of law and order.

Democracy and the Socialist State

> *The material fate of the modern proletariat is for modern Socialists inseparably bound up with the cause of liberty.*
>
> IGNAZIO SILONE

In its fully developed form, Revisionism held to two final values—Socialism and democracy. These two principles were so thoroughly intertwined in Bernstein's thought that they can be considered separately only for purposes of analysis. Eduard Bernstein was a "Social Democrat" in the exact sense of that word.

"Democracy," Bernstein said, "is at the same time means and end. It is the means of the struggle for Socialism and it

[71] *Protokoll über die Verhandlungen des Parteitages, 1906*, p. 305.

is the form Socialism will take once it has been realized." [72]

Now, democracy may be defined as "the absence of class rule; . . . a state of society in which no single class enjoys privileges over against the rest of the community." [73] This definition, Bernstein felt, properly emphasized minority rights. "Equality of rights of all members of the community" countenanced majority rule but suggested that the "tyranny of the majority" was not democracy.[74] While "democracy is synonymous with the greatest possible freedom for all," it does not mean the absence of laws: anarchy and democracy are fundamentally different concepts.[75] Of course, democracy affords no absolute protection "against laws which some may feel are tyrannical." But "in our era there is almost complete assurance that the majority of a democratic community will not make laws which will permanently interfere with personal liberties." [76] For, after all, "the majority of today may always become the minority of tomorrow," and history has shown that "the longer a modern state has operated with democratic institutions, the greater the respect and consideration for minority rights and the smaller the spitefulness of party contests." [77]

While democracy insists on the abolition of class rule it does not—at least not at first—abolish classes themselves. But as the "university of compromise," democracy teaches social classes to cooperate with one another.[78] Bernstein thus saw democracy as an educational and a moral institution: "The democratic suffrage makes its possessor virtually a partner in the community, and such virtual partnership must eventually lead to actual partnership." [79] When a working class is still immature, universal suffrage may actually be only the right to pick your own executioner, but in the long run such suffrage will be to the lasting benefit of that working class. Bismarck's attempt at manipulating universal suffrage, which

[72] *Voraussetzungen,* p. 178.
[73] *Ibid.,* p. 176.
[74] *Ibid.,* p. 177.
[75] *Loc. cit.*
[76] *Ibid.,* p. 178.
[77] *Loc. cit.*
[78] *Ibid.,* p. 180.
[79] *Loc. cit.*

served his own ends for only a short time, is a good example.[80]

The political institutions of democracy must correspond to this theory. Democracy means freedom compatible with other freedoms—self-determination based on equality of rights and freedom of expression. Coercion cannot disappear but must be embodied in a democratic state machinery. Social Democracy, Bernstein felt, must lay great stress on self-governing municipalities. More and more power should be put into the hands of local communities—democracy is federalist in structure, dispersing its centers of power. But a national central government is indispensable for an efficient carrying on of public business; to dissolve all its institutions and to delegate its functions to local communities would be sheer Utopianism.[81]

It would be equally Utopian, Bernstein concluded, to rely exclusively on direct popular legislation. "The so-called coercive associations, the state and the communities, will retain their great tasks in any future I can foresee." [82] Democracy is representative, not direct; parliamentary, not plebiscitarian. Its bureaucracy is permanent and professional. The cure for the excesses of parliamentarism lies in local self-government, but that is not a cure-all.[83]

The strands of thought which underlie this philosophy are readily identifiable. They stem, more or less directly, from liberalism, from the utilitarianism of James and John Stuart Mill, the common-sense equalitarianism of the British Fabians. Therefore, Bernstein's philosophy of democracy is to be distinguished from Lassalle's, which despises liberalism, and from the movement initiated by Rousseau and echoed by such diverse figures as Robert Michels and G. D. H. Cole, which sees representation as the ultimate negation of democracy. Bernstein never made a secret of his heritage; he called on Social Democracy to acknowledge its indebtedness to the liberal philosophy: "It is of course true," he said, "that the great liberal movement of recent times has chiefly benefited

[80] *Ibid.*, pp. 180–81.
[81] *Ibid.*, pp. 189–98.
[82] Bernstein, *Wie ist wissenschaftlicher Sozialismus möglich?* p. 42.
[83] *Der Sozialismus einst und jetzt*, pp. 111–12. Cf. also Bernstein, *Parlamentarismus und Sozialdemokratie*, pp. 55–60.

the capitalist bourgeoisie, and that the self-styled 'liberal' parties were or became purely the bodyguards of capitalism." But "as far as liberalism as a world historic movement is concerned. Socialism is not only temporally but spiritually its legitimate heir." [84]

Democracy, according to Bernstein, is both means and end. This implies, as we have already seen elsewhere, that a majority of the population must desire Socialism before it is instituted, and that the hostile minority must be willing to accept the measures proposed by the new regime. Revisionists believed, with their customary optimism, that such a state of public opinion could be achieved: a gradualist reform program which would bring about Socialism almost imperceptibly would undoubtedly carry the support of the proletariat as well as most of the middle classes.

Speaking like a true Marxist, Bernstein refused to specify the exact nature of Socialist society. But several generalizations are possible, both on the basis of the theory of democracy just discussed and of some independent evidence.

1. Unlike the right-wingers who controlled German Social Democracy in the 1920s, Bernstein definitely aspired to Socialism as a final goal. He foresaw a lengthy period of transition, characterized by a minimum of violence and a maximum of rational planning. Nationalization was to proceed in piecemeal but effective fashion.[85]

2. The dictatorship of the proletariat was a barbarian idea. For one thing, the working class would not achieve victory by itself but with non-proletarian allies. Should one ally terrorize the others after the battle? "In spite of the great progress which the working class has made since the days in which Marx and Engels wrote," said Bernstein, "I do not consider it even today as sufficiently developed to assume political power alone." [86] Furthermore, democracy could be achieved only democratically. The dictatorship of the proletariat is an "atavism" which "belongs to a lower culture."

[86] *Voraussetzungen*, p. 252.
[84] *Voraussetzungen*, p. 184.
[85] Cf. *Der Sozialismus einst und jetzt*, pp. 133–42.

Is there any sense in holding to the phrase "dictatorship of the proletariat" at a time in which Social Democracy has in practice put itself on the basis of parliamentarism, equitable popular representation, and popular legislation, all of which contradict dictatorship? [87]

Marx's call for a dictatorship of the proletariat (made only in one or two places of his work) reminded Bernstein of irrational Blanquism of which he had already accused Marx in another connection.

3. The success or failure of the new society must be judged on utilitarian standards; its aim is "the greatest possible economic, political, and moral well-being of everyone." [88] It is difficult to determine just how much of the national economy Bernstein wished to see under public ownership. To socialize everything—the ideal of a "nebulous" communism—would be unwise. Socialization should proceed where justifiable on the basis of economic criteria. "Where the state operates less efficiently than private industry it would be un-Socialist to give preference to the state over private management." [89] A partial, pragmatic collectivism, it seemed to Bernstein, was the answer.

4. Implicit in Bernstein's writings on the subject of the Socialist society was the idea of growing equality. This equality was to extend citizenship to all. It required an economic base, and Bernstein's proposed social policies—nationalization, social insurance of all sorts, housing and food distribution programs—looked toward a shift in the distribution of the national income and a leveling of differences in living standards.[90]

5. Equally clear was Bernstein's opposition to the "absoluteness of property." Socialism would set boundaries to the rights of disposal over property through social legislation. In some cases, of course, the Socialist state would resort to ex-

[87] *Ibid.*, p. 182.
[88] Bernstein, *Zur Frage: Sozialliberalismus oder Kollektivismus?* p. 7.
[89] Quoted by Erika Rikli, *Der Revisionismus*, p. 92.
[90] *Ibid.*, pp. 88–89.

propriation. This step, Bernstein noted in conformity with rational principles of legislation, was to be taken under *general* statutes.[91]

6. Bernstein's view of democracy envisioned great tasks for the state of the future. He, and his fellow Revisionists, therefore saw nothing but Utopian speculation in Engels's "withering away of the state." "Engels's definition of the state" as a purely repressive institution, Bernstein once wrote to Kautsky, "is in my opinion absolutely inadequate. It might apply to the state in certain stages of development, but it does not do justice to the role of the state in its more highly developed form." [92] To define the state, Bernstein felt, was a difficult matter.[93] Even Socialists fundamentally disagreed on their attitude toward it—ranging from the absolute condemnation of the anarchists to the exaggerated admiration of such writers as Lassalle. Bernstein noted with some surprise how close Marx's view of the state coincided with that of Proudhon and suggested that this anarchist conception was essentially a myth. It overrated the function of the state as an "executive committee for the bourgeoisie" and neglected its positive accomplishments in the field of beneficial control. While Lassalle, Bernstein wrote, had to be taken with several grains of salt, he was still right in encouraging the working class to take over the state. The state, after all, has a bureaucracy which will be needed under any conditions: "The administrative body of the visible future can be different from the present-day state only in degree." [94]

Of course, if Bernstein had meant no more by the state than a permanent bureaucracy, his conception could have been reconciled with the Marxist view, which saw the government of people replaced under communism by the administration of things. But Bernstein never departed from his idea of the state as a center of coercive power—over people as well as things. "The state is a product of development. Its form at any time is partly determined by the past. It is impos-

[91] *Voraussetzungen*, p. 225.
[92] Bernstein to Kautsky, December 16, 1927, Bernstein Archives.
[93] Cf., for a detailed discussion, *Der Sozialismus einst und jetzt*, pp. 75–90.
[94] *Zur Geschichte und Theorie des Sozialismus*, p. 212.

sible to jump out of the state: we can only hope to change it." [95]

With this conception of a representative democratic state, organized on the basis of social and economic equality, Bernstein made his final break with orthodox Marxism.

Bernstein's Summary

A few notes scribbled on an envelope which was found among Eduard Bernstein's papers may serve as a summary of the Revisionist theory, which has been analyzed in detail in the last three chapters. They run laconically as follows:

> Peasants do not sink; middle class does not disappear; crises do not grow ever larger; misery and serfdom do not increase. There *is* increase in insecurity, dependence, social distance, social character of production, functional superfluity of property owners. [96]

The fruit of this view of social development was a ten-point party program—written in 1909—which Bernstein hoped to put in place of the Erfurt Program. A shortened version may conveniently close our theoretical discussion:

1. Capitalist modes of production and exchange dominate present-day western society. Large-scale, well-financed enterprises force small business completely into the background, and the strata of small peasants, small-scale artisans, and small businessmen form an ever smaller proportion of the total population. In contrast, dependent wage workers and employees are growing in increasing measure.

2. For the mass of the population this dependence means growing insecurity. Technological factors and the speculative character of modern capitalism create business cycles which, in turn, exhaust the economy and bring mass unemployment and ruin.

3. Modern capitalist enterprises such as trusts and cartels seek to impose some order upon the chaos in production, yet

[95] *Der Sozialismus einst und jetzt,* p. 90.
[96] Bernstein Archives.

they do not do so for the general welfare but to keep prices and profits high.

4. Capitalist production has led to a tremendous increase in the wealth of society, but the growing wealth benefits only a minute part of the working class. The profits from surplus labor are appropriated in growing measure by landlords and capitalists. Unearned income increases, the distance between the capitalist aristocracy and the wage workers grows. Luxury corrupts public life.

5. Production and exchange take an ever more social character, but ownership is separated from control: shareholders, the camp followers of the monopolists, lead a parasitical existence.

6. Workers cannot fight single-handed against this overwhelming parasitism and monopolist pressure. Only political, trade-union, and cooperative associations can resist these tendencies. Freedom of association and an equal, democratic, universal suffrage are the necessary preconditions for the liberation of the workers in capitalist society.

7. Of all classes within capitalist society only the working class is a truly progressive force. Other anticapitalist strata are either directly reactionary or advocate half-way measures. As a class, the workers have the greatest interest in multiplying social wealth through perfection of techniques and full utilization of natural resources. They are equally concerned with the elimination of parasitic forms of enterprise and the expropriation of the parasitic elements within society.

8. The class interest of the workers demands the transfer of economic monopolies into the hands of society and their operation in the interest of society as a whole. Social control is to be extended to all fields of production. The political organization of the working class implies its organization as a distinct political party—Social Democracy.

9. Social Democracy fights for democracy in state, province, and community as a means of realizing political equality for all and as a lever for the socialization of the soil and of capitalist enterprises. It is not the workers' party in the sense that it accepts only workers as members—everyone who subscribes to its principles may belong to it. But its chief appeal is to the workers, for the liberation of the workers must prin-

cipally be the task of the workers themselves. The chief job of Social Democracy is to fill the working class with this idea and to organize it economically and politically for its historic fight.

10. The struggle of Social Democracy is not limited to a single country but includes all countries which have undergone modern development. Economically and politically, Social Democracy prides itself on its internationalism. Its aim is a free league of peoples on a basis of national self-determination within the framework of civilized humanity.[97]

This, then, is the naturalist, ethical, reformist Socialism which Bernstein worked out in the 1890s and which became, admittedly or not, the social philosophy of millions of thinking Germans before World War I.

Its impact upon German Social Democracy was decisive. It now remains for us to assess its and Bernstein's subsequent career.

[97] Quoted in somewhat abbreviated form from *Der Revisionismus in der Sozialdemokratie,* Appendix, "Leitsätze für den theoretischen Teil eines sozialdemokratischen Parteiprogramms," pp. 42–48.

BOOK THREE / THE IMPACT

Chapter 9

Champions and Critics

Bernstein and the Revisionists

> *Let us not forget that Marx and Engels were, in their time, Revisionists too. Indeed, they were the greatest Revisionists in the history of Socialism.*
>
> EDUARD BERNSTEIN

BY 1900, Bernstein had done his theoretical work. Events were to impose themselves upon him now, and his philosophy was to undergo the severe tests of war and revolution. The years that followed brought out his true stature: in courage, integrity, and devotion to democracy, Bernstein stood head and shoulders above his party colleagues.

Yet his position within the party was curiously ambiguous. He had left Germany as an unknown; when he returned to Berlin in February 1901, he was the intellectual leader of a sizable and influential group within German Social Democracy. His prestige was at its peak, yet his doctrine soon lost all distinctness at the hands of his followers and was melted down with antirevolutionary attitudes of all sorts. This development coincided with, and was greatly furthered by, the ascendancy of the trade unions and the bureaucrats in the Social Democratic Party.

As the newly returned leader of the controversial Revisionists, Bernstein was in heavy demand as a public speaker and journalist. One of the first of his lectures, "How Is Scientific Socialism Possible?" given in May 1901, created a storm of indignation among the orthodox and led to another Bernstein debate. At the Lübeck congress of 1901, Bernstein was able to defend his position in person for the first time, and he emerged unscathed.[1] Another speech, which he delivered in Breslau on October 30, 1901, had a very different result: it

[1] Several strongly condemnatory resolutions were passed over in favor of a rather mild resolution of Bebel's which criticized Bern-

landed him in the Reichstag. Bernstein had agreed to address the Breslau SPD club on "Social Democracy during the anti-Socialist Law." Shortly before the meeting, a telegram brought news of the death of Bruno Schönlank, incumbent member of the Reichstag for Breslau-West. Bernstein spoke movingly of the deceased, and then turned to a modest account of his own activities in exile. When, in December, Breslau Social Democracy sought a candidate to fill the vacancy in the Reichstag, Bernstein's speech was recalled and he received the nomination.[2] Once the party had united behind his candidacy, important party leaders, including such anti-Revolutionists as Bebel and Singer, supported his campaign. He achieved a brilliant victory in the elections of March 1902: he received 14,700 votes, over three thousand more than all other candidates put together.[3]

Bernstein's new sphere of activity did not diminish his pro-

---

stein for the "one-sided manner with which comrade Bernstein has conducted self-criticism in recent years." *Protokoll über die Verhandlungen des Parteitages der SPD, 1901*, pp. 99, 186–87. For the 1901 controversy, see pp. 156–60 above.

[2] The club nominated three men: Oscar Schütz, a Breslau radical, who got 183 votes on the first ballot; Karl Liebknecht (44 votes); and Eduard Bernstein (203 votes). In the run-off, Bernstein won out over Schütz with 223 to 210 votes. Paul Löbe, "Eduard Bernstein als Breslauer Abgeordneter," in *Grundsätzliches zum Tageskampfe*, p. 8.

[3] *Loc. cit.* Among Bernstein's papers there is an anonymous pamphlet which was distributed to the voters during the 1902 campaign. It runs: "Is Eduard Bernstein a Social Democrat? Shall he be sent to parliament as a representative of German Social Democracy? No!!! 1. Eduard Bernstein is a monarchist. In 1897, when the British Crown Prince visited his city of residence, Bernstein put an English flag in his window. When the Queen of England died, he wore mourning. 2. He boasted in England to have descended from a Polish royal family. . . . 3. When Bernstein's stepson founded a company for the exploitation of an electrical invention, an English lady subscribed £ 200 (4,000 marks), apparently in the Queen's name. 4. Bernstein has connections with the Pall Mall Gazette, the most notorious jingo paper in London, which called for the extermination of the Boers. 5. As is known, he applied for a position with Transvaal financiers. 6. He slan-

digious journalistic output. From his maiden speech onward, his rare statements in the Reichstag dealt primarily with economic and tax questions. He was a widely respected figure, but he did not advance into the parliamentary limelight until after 1912, when he turned his attention to foreign policy.

From the day Bernstein returned to his native land, he found himself surrounded with supporters who called themselves, defiantly, "Bernsteinians" or "Revisionists." Their bible was the *Voraussetzungen,* their publication was the *Sozialistische Monatshefte,* capably edited by Joseph Bloch.[4] But once we try to define a "Revisionist," we run into considerable difficulty. If we wish to describe the group that rejoiced over the *Voraussetzungen,* it will be well to distinguish between all those German Social Democrats who inclined toward reformism and those who consciously identified themselves with Bernstein's views and made an effort to propagate or refine them. In this fashion we establish a useful distinction between reformists and Revisionists.

A glance at the proponents of Revisionism reveals the extraordinary role that Bernstein played in his movement. With the possible exception of Conrad Schmidt (of whom more below), Eduard Bernstein was the only Revisionist who reflected to any extent on theoretical problems. Before Bernstein's series of articles in the *Neue Zeit,* Probleme des Sozialismus, and before his *Voraussetzungen,* a revision of Marxist doctrine had been but a vague idea, cautiously expressed by the few German Social Democrats. After the

---

dered Marx and Engels by claiming that they left illegitimate children without support. . . . 7. Bernstein declared it to be his mission to dethrone Bebel and to chase Kautsky and Mehring from the *Neue Zeit.* Does Eduard Bernstein deserve to represent German Social Democracy in parliament? Comrades! Judge for yourselves! Do not be trapped by reformist phrases! Bernstein seeks only influence, money, and power. He is indifferent to everything else. England has corrupted him!" Bernstein Archives. This curious document, evidently designed to woo the radicals away from the party candidate, had no effect, to judge from the number of votes Bernstein received.

4 The *Monatshefte* were Bernstein's most regular outlet until 1914.

appearance of the *Voraussetzungen,* Revisionism was a social movement with a creed and a direction.

Of course, Revisionism had precursors—among whom we may mention F. A. Lange, Bernstein's mentor Höchberg, and Georg von Vollmar. The last, a Bavarian Socialist, was typical of the support that South German Social Democracy brought to Revisionism. Vollmar had been a radical in the 1880s, and the first editor of the *Sozialdemokrat;* he had, however, turned his back on revolution in the early 1890s and later became one of Bernstein's staunchest defenders.[5]

The point has repeatedly been made that Revisionism was most truly at home in the South German states, which had no three-class electoral system and in which collaboration between Social Democrats and bourgeois liberals was a live option. There can be no question that South German reformism was, in effect, congenial to Revisionism, but we would be underrating the latter if we described it as a merely local reform movement. True, several of the key Revisionists came from the southern part of Germany: Vollmar, probably the most representative of them; David, the agrarian theorist, member of the Reichstag and later president of the National Assembly at Weimar; Ludwig Frank, the idealist and patriot who volunteered for active service at the outbreak of the

[5] See Georg von Vollmar, *Über die nächsten Aufgaben der deutschen Sozialdemokratie,* which contains his famous Eldorado speeches. At the 1891 Erfurt congress he argued that the working class was improving its situation and that Social Democracy must pursue its quest for political power through peaceful means. His treatment of tactics foreshadows Bernstein, even in terminology: "Beside the general or ultimate goal we see a nearer aim: the advancement of the most immediate needs of the people. For me, the achievement of the most immediate demands is the main thing, not only because they are of great propagandist value and serve to enlist the masses, but also because, in my opinion, this gradual progress, this gradual socialization, is the method most strongly indicated for a progressive transition. Thus, the path of calm, legal, parliamentary activity in the widest meaning is given, for change in popular feeling will bring about a corresponding change in the Reichstag." Wilhelm Schröder, ed., *Handbuch der sozialdemokratischen Parteitage,* p. 522. Three years later he drew the consequences of this point of view by leading the Bavarian Socialist parliamentary party to defy Socialist tradition and vote for the state budget.

World War and was the first Reichstag deputy to be killed
at the front; Kurt Eisner, a brilliant literary man and ethical
Socialist, who became Prime Minister of Bavaria after the
1918 Revolution and was assassinated in February 1919. But
Revisionism had far wider scope: it attempted to furnish an
explanation of capitalist development in all countries and
under all political conditions.[6]

Most leading Revisionists were intellectuals. This is not to
claim a monopoly of intellect for the right wing: the party
radicals, too, could point to an impressive array of educated
men and women. But their predominance among outstanding
Revisionists is nevertheless striking. Bernstein, of course, must
be counted as one even though he lacked university training.
His years of independent study more than made up for the
absence of formal higher education. Eduard David, Conrad
Schmidt, and Paul Kampffmeyer were other prominent examples. Conrad Schmidt was an able economist who first
became known through his correspondence with Engels. His
chief concerns were value theory and the philosophical foundations of Socialism, and he arrived, quite independently, at
a position substantially similar to that of Bernstein.[7] Kampffmeyer, too, adopted his Revisionist position independently of
Bernstein[8] and grew into one of the most active writers on
social reformism after 1900.

Every Revisionist who had any literary pretensions made
his appearance in the pages of the *Sozialistische Monatshefte*.
The articles, reviews, and notes, although dealing with a wide
variety of issues, were marked by a common attitude: opposition to violence, stress on ethics, and emphasis on day-to-day

[6] As one German Social Democrat expressed it in Bernstein's
obituary: "[Bernstein's] Revisionism was not empirical and did
not have a Bavarian, provincial stamp, as did Vollmar's. Bernstein's Revisionism was not based on the political situation in one
state, it was total and philosophical (*weltanschaulich*). Nor did it
have a trace of agrarian coloring, as was true with the leaders of
South German and Southwest German Reformism—Vollmar,
David, Frank, and Kolb." Alexander Schifrin, "Eduard Bernstein,"
Deutsche Republik, VII (1933), 431.
[7] Cf. Kampffmeyer, "Die Lebensarbeit Conrad Schmidts," *Sozialistische Monatshefte*, LXXVI, 2 (1932), 897–904.
[8] Cf. his book, *Mehr Macht!*

reform work—the strengthening of cooperatives, the emancipation of women, the encouragement of trade union activities, the improvement of education. The united front which it represented was broken only in the somber days of August 1914.

Revisionism, then, may be separated from general reformism through its emphasis on intellectual criticism of Marxism and its attempt to establish an ethical Social Democratic world view. But this distinction became ever more difficult to maintain after the turn of the century. For after 1900 a number of reformists, whose interest in an unremitting drive towards Socialism was questionable, began to ally themselves with the Revisionist movement. They blurred the sharpness of outline which reformism had preserved in Bernstein's and Schmidt's writings.

The men who now ranged themselves around Bernstein reduced Revisionism to a reformist interest group within the Social Democratic Party. The right wing thus gained in influence but abandoned any claim to theoretical definiteness. The new men who took over the reformist wing of the party from what might be called the "real Revisionists" were distinguished largely by their mediocrity and paucity of social vision. No wonder, then, that Bernstein had to turn his back on all his former disciples when the war broke out. Most of them had never really fully understood Bernstein's devotion to international Socialism.

Among these latter-day pseudo Revisionists three groups stand out. First, there were the trade union officials, such as Legien, Leipart, Timm, Umbreit, von Elm, and others. Their natural interests made them sympathetic to the Revisionist movement, but, with the possible exception of von Elm, their horizons were bounded by trade union politics and their interest in social theory was, at best, polite. While their frequent identity of outlook with Bernstein cannot be denied, these men underlined the faults of Revisionism while possessing but a small part of its virtues.

The same may be said of the party functionaries, such as Friedrich Ebert. "Most of them," writes Erika Rikli, worked as editors, many were members of the Reichstag and other official bodies. In their professional activity they learned to appreciate positive, small day-to-day labor. Daily they observed the growth of labor organization and saw the successes of the inevitable policy of compromise. Through their work they grew into the reformist attitudes of the aging, advancing labor movement.[9]

She adds, wrily: "This narrow, daily contact with Socialist politics held certain dangers. Here were the roots of optimism, and of the inclination to overestimate the possibilities of growth of labor organizations." [10]

The third group, whose relation to even the mildest form of Socialism was still more doubtful, consisted of protectionists. A number of Social Democrats, such as Schippel, Calwer, Hildebrand, began by advocating selective tariffs and ended up by siding with the most extreme social imperialists during the World War. It should be obvious that neither protectionism nor social imperialism were necessary consequences of Revisionist thought. Bernstein vigorously rejected both,[11] and many of the Revisionists who supported the war did not make joint cause with the imperialists.[12]

The extreme difficulty of delimiting "Revisionists" should now be apparent. Bernstein's own career and writings clearly demonstrated the compatibility of reformism with Socialism and internationalism. Other reformists, however, less steadfast than he, equated the abandonment of Marxism with the

[9] *Der Revisionismus,* p. 26.
[10] *Loc. cit.*
[11] Cf., for example, *Protokoll über die Verhandlungen des Parteitages, 1904,* pp. 229–30.
[12] It should be noted, however, that in 1909, the year in which Calwer left the SPD, Bernstein still considered him a Revisionist, although one who did not agree with Bernstein on the issue of the tariff. Cf. *Der Revisionismus in der Sozialdemokratie,* pp. 7–8. Hildebrand was excluded from the party in 1910, but Schippel, in spite of his extreme imperialism and his denial of most of the basic principles of Socialism, remained a most active contributor to the *Sozialistische Monatshefte* until his death in 1928. For an appreciation of Schippel, see Paul Kampffmeyer, "Max Schippel," *Sozialistische Monatshefte,* LXVII, 2 (1928), 587–94.

surrender of both Socialism and internationalism. Their actions and publications have served to confuse the very real contribution which Bernstein's Revisionism in its unadulterated form made to Socialist thought.

Rosa Luxemburg

> [*First we had*] *Bernstein's articles in the* Neue Zeit, *which he then had to interpret with a letter to the party congress* [*of 1898*], *whereupon he wrote a book to comment upon the articles and the letter; then there followed articles in the* Neue Zeit *and the* Vorwärts *which were to protect the book against misunderstandings—and after all that Bernstein is still completely misunderstood by his critics.*
>
> ROSA LUXEMBURG

Of the many Socialists who undertook to challenge the Revisionists, Rosa Luxemburg was undoubtedly the most effective and most profound. Her sharp intellect, which so frightened her German party colleagues, was employed to full advantage in her pitiless analysis of Bernstein's position. With biting sarcasm—far superior to Kautsky's casuistic argumentation—she laid bare the fundamental weaknesses of the Revisionist approach to the problem of power.

Rosa Luxemburg's first attack on Revisionism took the form of a detailed criticism of Bernstein's series in the *Neue Zeit,* the "Problems of Socialism." These articles had seemed inoffensive to all other Marxists, including Kautsky, until Bernstein had uttered those fateful words about the goal being nothing, the movement everything. But Luxemburg had been suspicious of them from the first. When Bernstein published his *Voraussetzungen,* she saw her worst fears fully confirmed, and she attempted to refute the whole of Revisionism in her second attack. Her two lengthy articles, later brought out under the title "Sozialreform oder Revolution," contain the most telling of the radical objections to Revisionism.[13]

Social Democratic thought, Rosa Luxemburg begins, intimately connects social reforms and social revolution—the former is a means, the latter the end.[14] Revisionism, however, "amounts in practice to the advice . . . that we abandon the social revolution—the goal of Social Democracy—and turn social reform from a means of the class struggle into its final aim." [15] Since its final aim is the very heart of Social Democracy, any attempt to give it up amounts to far more than a tactical modification; it involves the whole future of the German Social Democratic Party. The importance of Bernstein and of his *Voraussetzungen*, Luxemburg warns, must not be underrated. "The book is of great historical significance for the German and international movements—it is the first attempt to give a theoretical basis to opportunist streams of thought within Social Democracy." [16]

With this warning, Rosa Luxemburg's analysis gets under way. It may be resolved into two questions: On what assumptions does Revisionism rest? What tactics does it propose as a result of its philosophy?

On the first of these points—the basis of Revisionism—Luxemburg repeatedly emphasizes that Bernstein has abandoned scientific Socialism and returned to Idealism. To introduce the principles of "justice" and "fair distribution" is to give up all the scientific achievements of Marxist economics. "With how much greater force," Luxemburg exclaims sarcastically,

> with how much greater wit did Weitling advocate this kind of Socialism over fifty years ago! Of course, Weitling, the gifted tailor, was not then acquainted with scientific Socialism. And when today, half a century later, his viewpoint (torn to shreds by Marx and Engels) is happily

[13] In *Gesammelte Werke*, Vol. III: *Gegen den Reformismus*, pp. 35–100.
[14] *Ibid.*, pp. 35–36.
[15] *Ibid.*, p. 36.
[16] *Ibid.*, p. 96.

patched up and offered to the German proletariat as the last word in science—then, indeed, a tailor did that patching job, but not a gifted one.[17]

Bernstein's analysis of the capitalist system, Luxemburg maintains, is the chief prop of his Idealism. He discounts the anarchy of capitalism and substitutes for it the concepts of "adaptability" and "viability." But if we do not hold that the contradictions of capitalism drive it to its doom, we give up the Marxist tenet of the "objective necessity" for Socialism.[18] If we argue, as Bernstein does, that we cannot count on a capitalist collapse, we must give up all hope for a Socialist future.[19]

Of course, if Bernstein's theory of capitalist development were backed up by genuine empirical evidence, his case would be much stronger. But the Revisionist idea of capitalist adaptability is no more than a myth. In actuality, Luxemburg argues, the contradictions within capitalism grow ever more apparent. The increase and internationalization of credit,

[17] *Ibid.,* p. 80.
[18] *Ibid.,* p. 40.
[19] Rosa Luxemburg here advances a complicated, but characteristic, chain of reasoning: Without a collapse of capitalism the capitalists cannot be expropriated. Consequently, Bernstein gives up expropriation and substitutes a gradual realization of the principle of sociability (*Genossenschaftlichkeitsprinzip*). But that cannot be realized within capitalist production. Very well: Bernstein gives up socialization and substitutes the reform of trade and the strengthening of cooperatives. But this development diverges from the actual material development of capitalist society—so Bernstein, to hold on to his point, abandons dialectic materialism. Again, *his* conception of economic development does not agree with Marx's law of surplus value: Bernstein gives up all of Marx's economic theory. Yet without it we cannot objectively justify the class struggle: so Bernstein relinquishes the class struggle, too. But the class struggle is inevitable in a class society: so Bernstein is driven to deny the existence of classes. And if there is no class struggle—indeed, if there are no classes—Social Democracy can ally itself with bourgeois liberalism, in this best of all possible worlds. *Ibid.,* pp. 92–93. While this logical sequence appears somewhat contrived and reminds the reader of the battle that was lost "all for the want of a nail," it remains a far more forceful argument than Kautsky's subtleties.

cited by Bernstein as evidence of capitalist stability, in reality contribute to the downfall of capitalism by further separating methods of production from methods of appropriation, and production relations from property relations.[20] The same holds true of cartels and trusts; far from stabilizing capitalism, as Bernstein holds, these are symptoms of the last stages of capitalism, in which vast properties are controlled by the few.[21] Furthermore, Bernstein's claim that crises are a thing of the past is simply false—the relative prosperity of the 1890s cannot hide the shadows thrown by the great convulsions of the capitalist system that are yet to come. Nor can prosperity conceal the fact that the preconditions for the final contradiction between production and exchange already exist.[22]

Rosa Luxemburg makes equally short shrift of Bernstein's contention that the number of propertied is growing. The truth is that the growth of the shareholding company (one of Bernstein's favorite examples of the dispersion of property) is but one more proof of Marx's law of the socialization of capitalist production.[23] With irony, Luxemburg points to Bernstein's admission that capitalism does show "a little" anarchy: "Capitalist society—to speak with Marx—is like that foolish virgin whose child 'is only very small!' "[24] Partial, national crises lead to world crises of unlimited dimensions.

In defense of Marxist economic theory Luxemburg makes the shrewd point that the word "abstraction" is a *Schimpfwort* for Bernstein. Thus to the Revisionist Marx's law of value is an "abstraction" of equal validity with the marginal theory of value. But, Luxemburg exclaims, "Bernstein has quite forgotten that this Marxist abstraction is not an invention but a discovery. It exists not in Marx's head but in our commodity economy." [25]

The conclusion which Rosa Luxemburg draws from her

[20] *Ibid.*, p. 43.
[21] *Ibid.*, pp. 44–45.
[22] *Ibid.*, pp. 47–48.
[23] *Ibid.*, p. 69. This is actually one of Luxemburg's weakest arguments.
[24] *Ibid.*, p. 72.
[25] *Ibid.*, p. 73.

examination of the basis of Revisionism is that it is not a truly Socialist doctrine but a bourgeois reform movement with no philosophy other than eclecticism.

This closely reasoned attack on the fundamentals of Revisionism carries over into Rosa Luxemburg's analysis of Bernstein's tactics. The Revisionists want to introduce Socialism gradually through three agencies: trade union and cooperative activities, social reform, and the political democratization of the modern state. All three, Luxemburg contends, must fail; the Revisionist belief in their supposed power rests on an erroneous estimate of capitalist development.

In the first place, trade unions cannot destroy Marx's law of wages; they cannot abolish exploitation, and Revisionist optimism concerning the unlimited extension of trade union power is unjustified.[26] Try as they will, the trade unions cannot gain for the workers any influence over production policy: they can affect neither size of output nor technical methods.[27] Consequently, the unions will be unable to fill the aggressive role which they have been assigned by the Revisionists— their work must be looked upon "as the defense of labor power against the attacks of profit, as the defense of the working class against the depressive tendency of capitalist economy." [28] Their struggle, although indispensable, is and will remain a labor of Sisyphus.

Secondly, social reform is equally limited in its long-run effectiveness. The capitalists, Luxemburg argues, will allow just as many reforms as will be compatible with their interests, and no more. Social reforms are not, by any stretch of the imagination, a step toward Socialism; they do not grant the workers a share in the control of society. On the contrary, they tend to *protect* capitalist property. Social reforms "are not an interference with capitalist exploitation; they lend order and regularity to this exploitation." [29]

Finally, the Revisionists rely on growing democratization.

[26] *Ibid.*, pp. 51, 53.
[27] *Ibid.*, p. 77.
[28] *Loc. cit.* The trade unions cannot transform capitalism, and the cooperative movement, Luxemburg holds, is even weaker.
[29] *Ibid.*, p. 56.

Luxemburg denies that such a process is actually discernible. The capitalist state does not tend to identify itself with society as a whole. Two examples of this truth are tariff protection and militarism. The former no longer protects infant industries but powerful industrialists in their struggle against the consumer—feudal interests are here given capitalist form.[30] The latter does not serve the whole country but merely protects the capitalists of one country against those of other countries, as well as the capitalists within one country against the workers.[31] Democracy is permitted to exist only as long as it serves the ruling classes and may be scuttled whenever these groups are threatened. Indeed, Luxemburg maintains, the realities of international politics and the threat of the working class to existing property relations will inevitably throw the bourgeoisie into the arms of reaction.[32] "The Socialist labor movement is today the *only* support that democracy has—and can have." [33]

Rosa Luxemburg's conclusions concerning Revisionism, then, are twofold: its philosophical basis is nothing more than "vulgar bourgeois economics," and its tactics cannot lead to a Socialist victory. Such a victory can be achieved only through a revolutionary seizure of power by the working class. To eliminate revolution in favor of reform, as the Revisionists have done, is not to arrive at the Socialist goal more slowly—it is not just a question of timing. The Revisionist goal is far different from the final aim of the radicals, for Bernstein's tactics can never lead to more than insignificant modifications in the existing order.[34] Opportunism is therefore incompatible with Social Democracy; it has nothing to offer, and the SPD would be better off without the Revisionists in its ranks.[35]

Now, this outspoken critique undoubtedly touched the weakest spots in Revisionism. Luxemburg validly charged that Bernstein's emphasis on the viability of capitalism raised the

[30] *Ibid.*, pp. 57–58.
[31] *Ibid.*, pp. 58–59.
[32] *Ibid.*, pp. 82–83.
[33] *Ibid.*, 83.
[34] *Ibid.*, p. 86.
[35] *Ibid.*, pp. 97–100.

question, Why strive for Socialism at all? She was correct, too, in asserting that Revisionism reduced the "necessity for Socialism" to desirability. Her most effective hit was undoubtedly scored by her attack on Revisionist tactics—Bernstein himself was frequently doubtful whether the parliamentary methods he so earnestly advocated could be successfully applied in Germany.

But the merits of her critique should not obscure the very real difficulties in her own position. In the first place, she made far too much of Bernstein's "abandonment of Socialism." In actual fact, it was quite possible to remain a Socialist without being a Marxist. She did distinguish between Bernstein's criticism of theory and Schippel's questioning of the struggle itself, but did not make that distinction sufficiently clear.[36] Secondly, her theoretical arguments against improvement in the condition of the working class could not alter the fact that the proletariat was really raising its standards. Bernstein's theoretical structure may have suffered from serious weaknesses, but his sense of immediate realities was unexcelled, and his Revisionism helped to explain rationally a prosperity which extended to the workers. Thirdly, Luxemburg argued that Bernstein's theory was wrong not only for Germany, but for all other countries as well. It is a commonplace, she said, to charge Bernstein with viewing the world through "English glasses." But if that is to imply that he *correctly* describes British conditions and is in error only to the extent that he transfers his observations to Germany, then what would happen to Marxism? Luxemburg's rigidly revolutionary frame of mind compelled her to deny that the working class could peacefully attain power in England. She was forced to underrate the commitment to democracy of defending classes, and she was therefore just as mistaken about England as Bernstein was about Germany.[37] Lastly, her own advocacy of revolu-

[36] Cf. Rosa Luxemburg, "Miliz und Militarismus," in *Gesammelte Werke*, III, 141. Her categorical argument (either you are a revolutionary Socialist or you are no Socialist at all) attempts to prejudge the issue of whether parliamentary Socialism is possible without examining it carefully.

[37] Cf. Rosa Luxemburg, "Die englische Brille," in *Gesammelte Werke*, III, 104–14.

tionary tactics involved her in hopeless contradictions. She well understood that a proletariat cannot assume power unless certain conditions exist; a Blanquist *coup d'état* is likely to lead to serious reverses for the working class.[38] But when was the proletariat to seize power? Who was to act in its name? What *form* should the revolution take? To all of these questions her answers were equivocal.[39] In her thought—as well as in Bernstein's—the dilemma of the difficulty of revolution over against the difficulty of reform is never fully resolved.

Rosa Luxemburg and her allies demanded the expulsion of the Revisionists from the SPD. They got nothing of the sort. The 1903 Dresden debate over Revisionist tactics, precipitated by Bernstein's ill-considered demand that the SPD claim the post of first vice-president of the Reichstag, demonstrates to a careful reader how deeply Reformism had penetrated the party. The oratorical battle lasted for three days. Over fifty speakers entered the lists, well over a dozen resolutions were brought in and heatedly argued. The final outcome left everything as it had been: the center, under the leadership of Bebel and Kautsky, kept control of the party. The radicals, whose main object was the purge of the Revisionists, were repulsed —Rosa Luxemburg did not even speak. The Revisionists, on the other hand, were handed a severe rebuke in the form of a resolution sponsored by Bebel, Kautsky, and Singer. Yet most of the Revisionists, apparently under the impression that the resolution did not apply to them, voted *for* it.[40] In other

38 "Sozialreform oder Revolution," p. 91.
39 "I say that the only force that will lead us to victory is Socialist enlightenment of the working class in the daily struggle," she declared at the 1898 party congress. Quoted in *Gesammelte Werke*, III, 129. The editor, Paul Frölich, voices his approval through a parenthetical exclamation mark—but her statement does not fit in with her other views and sounds just like Bernstein.
40 "The party congress most decisively condemns the Revisionist endeavor to alter our time-tested and victorious tactics based on the class struggle. [The Revisionists] want to substitute for the seizure of political power through overcoming our enemies a policy of meeting the existing order of things half-way.
The consequence of such Revisionist tactics would be to change our party. *Now* it works towards the rapid transformation of the existing bourgeois order of society into a Socialist one (in other

words, the SPD continued to behave as a Revisionist party and, at the same time, to condemn Revisionism; it continued to preach revolution and to practice reform.

The debates were long but inconclusive. They were to be the last serious attempt on the part of the center to deal with the Revisionist menace. Most of the major figures took the floor—Bebel, Vollmar, Auer, Kautsky, Bernstein. Vollmar and Auer took the line that the term "Revisionist" really meant very little, since the so-called "Revisionists" were not united on all matters of theory or policy, and often voted with the radicals. While the argument had some merit, it served to obscure the very real differences which still prevailed between the right and the left wings on the issue of tactics. It was a device that Auer had once characterized in a letter to Bernstein concerning the latter's demand that the SPD openly confess its reformist character: "My dear Ede, you *don't* pass such resolutions. You don't *talk* about it, you just *do* it." [41]

In any case, the course of events was to reduce the right-wing left-wing split to shadow-boxing. When the World War broke out, the alignments within the SPD were formed not on the basis of loyalty to Marxist ideology but on the fundamental attitude toward the autocratic, aggressive German state.

---

words, it is a truly 'revolutionary party' in the best sense of the word.) [*Sic!*] It would become a party that is content with reforming bourgeois society [if the Revisionist policies were adopted].

Further, the party congress condemns any attempt to gloss over existing, ever-growing class conflicts for the purpose of making our party a satellite of bourgeois parties." *Protokoll über die Verhandlungen des Parteitages, 1903,* p. 103.

The resolution was adopted by 288 against 11 votes. The protocol records "amusement" at the affirmative vote of the Revisionists Auer, Heine, Kolb, Löbe, Peus, and Südekum. *Ibid.,* pp. 420–21.
[41] Eduard Bernstein, *Ignaz Auer,* p. 63.

Chapter 10

The War

Bernstein and Foreign Policy

> *Above all, nations want to live in peace.*
>
> EDUARD BERNSTEIN

THE INSTABILITY of the European states system with its complex multiple alliances became more apparent as the new century began. Germany's ambitious naval armament program aroused British suspicions and, eventually, brought countermeasures. The Kaiser's blustering pronouncements on international relations, Russian imperialist foreign policy, Germany's unqualified backing of the Austro-Hungarian Monarchy, and French mutterings of *revanche* plunged Europe into an atmosphere of gloomy apprehension. As early as 1908 Eduard Bernstein's good friend Graham Wallas hinted at the dreadful possibility of "the horrors of a world-war" between the German and the British empires.[1]

As international tensions mounted, Socialist parties all over Europe began to concern themselves seriously with the problem of war. A European conflict, all Socialists agreed, would be a capitalist folly that would be paid for with the lives of the proletariat. For the first time in history there arose the dream of preventing war by mass action of its potential victims.

The Second International at its several congresses attempted to formulate a policy of war against war, to be followed by all member parties. Two great difficulties stood in the way of a successful policy: one was the fear of the majority of Socialists that a general strike against war (as demanded by some radicals) would be suicidal for the labor movement. Thus the only weapon that could have given the ruling class pause was voluntarily laid aside. The other was the declared determination of the German Socialists to fight Rus-

---

[1] *Human Nature in Politics*, p. 285.

sia if the latter attacked its western neighbors. In this way the unanimity against any war whatever was watered down into opposition to most wars, and the way was cleared to similar reservations by other countries. The Stuttgart congress of 1907, under the influence of the Russian Revolution of 1905, made minor concessions to the Vaillant-Jaurès demands for a general strike and insurrection in case of war. But with some amendments it adopted Bebel's rather lame resolution calling upon Socialist parties in all countries to do their utmost to prevent a conflict or, if it did break out, to urge its prompt cessation.

The resolutions and speeches at the various congresses of the Second International betrayed an amazing optimism. They assumed that the disciplined mass parties of the workers would act as a check against a European conflagration. Of all Socialist parties the German SPD was by far the strongest, both in its intellectual heritage and in numbers. German Social Democracy, more than any other, therefore, was expected to act decisively to prevent war. There was only one important exception to this high regard for the German party: in a prophetic speech to the 1904 Amsterdam congress the great Jean Jaurès accused the SPD of political impotence: "You are a great and admirable party," he cried, amidst great commotion in the hall,

> . . . but you still lack two essentials: revolutionary action and parliamentary action. You were granted universal suffrage from above, and your parliament is but a half-parliament. . . . Yours will be the only country in which the Socialists would not be masters even if they were to obtain the majority in the Reichstag. . . . You hide your weakness and your impotence by trying to dictate to everybody else! [2]

These were grim sentences. August 4, 1914, tragically confirmed them.

The foreign policy of German Social Democracy was negative: it opposed imperialism, condemned the Kaiser's inept

[2] Quoted in Maurice Lair, *Jaurès et l'Allemagne*, p. 92.

utterances, decried militarism, and called for peace. But this policy lacked a grand design. Interest in international questions was limited by the Socialist dogma that foreign affairs were merely a function of domestic developments. Furthermore, as the party accepted the German state more and more fully as a going concern, it confined itself to opposing particular policies rather than German foreign policy as a whole. As the day-to-day improvement of working conditions became the most vital business of the party, opposition even to imperialism weakened within Social Democracy.[3] The failure of German Social Democracy to offer thoroughgoing criticism tended to give the bureaucrats in the German Foreign Office a free hand.[4]

Officially, the party pursued an all-European policy; that is, it attempted to overcome German-French bitterness and, at the same time, to maintain good relations with the British. Indeed, around the turn of the century, at a time when German industry and agriculture were joining forces in a "God-punish-England" campaign, the SPD called for a German-British alliance.[5]

In spite of this policy, carried through consistently by the party center, there was considerable anti-British feeling within the SPD. This "continental orientation" could be found most strongly among right-wingers in the party—Bernstein's ostensible allies—and this hatred of "perfidious Albion" grew so strong with some of them that during the war they declared defeat of Great Britain to be Germany's primary war aim.[6]

[3] Cf. Max Victor, "Die Stellung der deutschen Sozialdemokratie zu den Fragen der auswärtigen Politik, 1869–1914," *Archiv für Sozialwissenschaft und Sozialpolitik,* LX (1928), 147–79, esp. 173.
[4] Pauline Anderson, *The Background of Anti-English Feeling in Germany,* p. 117.
[5] Eckart Kehr, "Englandhass und Weltpolitik," *Zeitschrift für Politik,* XVII (1928), 500–526, esp. 508.
[6] An excellent example of this view was the Revisionist Karl Erdmann's *England und die Sozialdemokratie,* which argued that the British needed to start the war since capitalism leads to war and England is the classical land of capitalism. (Bernstein owned this volume.) The right-wing imperialists, well represented by Max Schippel, were even more virulent. Cf. Schippel, *England und wir.*

Now, on this crucial point Eduard Bernstein differed fundamentally from the right wing. His Anglophile sentiments, acquired in his dozen-odd years of residence in London, was basic to his reasoning and played a decisive role in his thought. It is true that Bernstein's common-sense approach led him to adopt a series of moderate positions in foreign policy. He opposed war but agreed with Noske and Bebel that a nation must have the means with which to defend itself.[7] He criticized imperialism but admitted that it might have a progressive function—as in the case of England—in bringing advancement to backward nations.[8] It would be a grave misconception, however, to assume that Bernstein compromised with the Social Imperialists and that, in his hesitant acceptance of some forms of imperialism he made any concessions to the group around Calwer. His qualified support of British imperialism was based partly on his Anglophile feelings, partly on such considerations as had induced the Fabian Society to endorse the Boer War in 1900. At that time, Shaw had explained to his startled Socialist audience that it was better for the natives to be governed by the British, who would at least bring some progress with them, than to remain under Kruger's obscurantist rule.[9] Further, the Fabians argued, colonies existed, and one must give a realistic answer to the question, What shall we do with them? Now Bernstein used similar arguments. They were a far cry from the excessive nationalism of Schippel, Hildebrand, and the later Haenisch and Lensch.

As war came closer, Bernstein found himself more frequently on the side of the party radicals. One striking example was his desertion of his parliamentary colleagues on the issue of new taxes for greater armaments in 1912–13. The SPD parliamentary majority, containing most of the Revisionists, had strenuously opposed the bill increasing the armed

---

Joseph Bloch, editor of the *Sozialistische Monatshefte*, was also anti-British.

[7] Cf. Bernstein, "Patriotismus, Militarismus und Sozialdemokratie," *Sozialistische Monatshefte*, XI, I (1907), 434–40.

[8] Cf. Bernstein, "Sozialdemokratie und Imperialismus," *Sozialistische Monatshefte*, IV (1900), 238–51.

[9] Bernard Shaw, ed., *Fabianism and the Empire*.

forces but had decided to vote for the tax that was to pay for it, on the ground that it was a federal income tax imposed by the Reich. Bernstein, agreeing with the radicals, voted in caucus to oppose both. "It seemed to me illogical," he said later, "and a serious deviation from the path of Social Democracy, to grant money for a purpose which we considered pernicious, merely because it was to be raised in the form of a popular tax." [10] Once more Bernstein saw more clearly into the meaning of events than his Revisionist friends.[11]

The most revealing contribution that Bernstein made to the foreign policy debate was a little book he published in 1911—The English Peril and the German People.[12] It maintained that the "English Peril" had been artificially created but that the existence of the belief was, in itself, a danger, since it increased suspicion on both sides and provided an excuse for the armament race. Conflicts there had been, especially on colonial matters, but they were not basic or beyond conciliation. Bernstein made a special point of disproving the popular "encirclement" theory, according to which Germany must arm defensively against a European coalition inspired by Great Britian and designed to encompass Germany with hostile powers. He showed in detail the efforts made by the British to come to an understanding with Germany, frustrated only by German blundering and ambition: "All the events [of the past few years] show that the stimulus for the so-called 'encirclement of Germany' is to be sought in Germany itself." [13]

Bernstein cited a number of pro-German voices in England ("I could fill *volumes* with pronounced pro-German articles and letters to the press"), and commented angrily that the German public had been left in ignorance of these sentiments.[14] He accused powerful German sources of running a

10 "Entwicklungsgang eines Sozialisten," in *Die Volkswirtschafts-lehre der Gegenwart in Selbstdarstellungen*, I, 44.
11 Cf. *Protokoll über die Verhandlungen der SPD, 1913*, pp. 169–72, 419–517.
12 *Die englische Gefahr und das deutsche Volk*. Bernstein wrote this book after consultation with party leaders.
13 *Ibid.*, p. 18n. Cf. also Eduard Bernstein, *Die Wahrheit über die Einkreisung Deutschlands*.
14 *Die englische Gefahr*, p. 29.

smear campaign against Great Britain and emphasized that the interests of the two countries did not clash. "Is it not insane that two nations which year after year peacefully exchange goods amounting to about two billions should be tortured by the fear that the other is only waiting for an opportune moment to attack it?" [15] He ended with a warning that continued German-English friction would encourage other nations to engage in irresponsible adventures and that the deliberate misleading of the German people would bring grave troubles in its wake: "He who has recognized that the German people have no greater enemy than those who constantly declaim 'Enemies, enemies everywhere!' must dare to fight persistently for the creation of a true peace-league of nations and for the realization of the one great peoples' republic." [16]

But his scoldings and warnings were in vain. Three years later Europe was at war.

The Policy of August 4

> The conduct of the leaders of the German Social Democratic Party of the Second International (1889–1914) who have voted the war budget and who repeat the bourgeois chauvinistic phrases of the Prussian Junkers and of the bourgeoisie is a direct betrayal of Socialism.
>
> V. I. LENIN, 1914

The story of how the German Social Democratic Party voted for the war credits has been told many times. Rightly so, for it was a stupendous event that had incalculable consequences. It broke up the Second International and permanently split the European labor movement. In the following pages we shall confine ourselves, mainly, to Bernstein's part in the tragedy.

[15] *Ibid.*, p. 41.
[16] *Ibid.*, p. 48.

The Sarajevo assassination found Eduard Bernstein on
vacation in Switzerland. On July 31 he returned to Berlin,
firmly convinced that Russia was responsible for the Serbian
crisis. On the same day, Jean Jaurès was murdered. Bernstein had loved and admired the French Socialist above all his
party colleagues, and the news of his death struck him like
a personal blow. While he had no exact information, Bernstein believed—falsely—that the assassination had been engineered by Russian agents. His mind was made up: war with
Russia was inevitable and even praiseworthy. His error,
cleared up soon thereafter, determined his attitude toward
the war credits.

The last days of July saw frantic antiwar activity on the
part of German Social Democracy. Mass meetings were held
all over the country, condemning Austria and pledging a fight
for peace. The party sent Hermann Müller to Paris to negotiate with the French Socialists, but Jaurès was dead and
events in Germany frustrated his mission. Ebert and Otto
Braun went to Switzerland on July 30 to continue to keep the
party alive if it should be compelled to go underground. On
that day it still seemed almost certain that the SPD would
vote against war credits. On August 1 Germany declared war
on Russia, and the government's anti-Russian propaganda,
consciously directed at the German Socialists, did not fail of
its purpose. On August 3, Germany declared war on France,
supporting its case with imaginary French bombings of
several German cities. Popular support of the government's
policy was enthusiastic; the seeds of hate, sown in previous
decades by German nationalists and imperialists, now came
into terrible bloom.

The Reichstag delegation of the SPD met in almost continuous session on August 2 and 3. On the latter date, the
group of 110 voted on the war credits. Only 14 opposed
them; Kautsky pleaded unsuccessfully for abstention. Bernstein, unhappy but convinced that this was a defensive
struggle against Russia, voted with the majority.[17] On the next

[17] Cf. Karl Kautsky, *Sozialisten und Krieg*, p. 454. On this whole
period, cf. *ibid.*, pp. 402–64; Edwyn Bevan, *German Social Democracy During the War;* Eugen Prager, *Geschichte der U.S.P.D.;*
P. G. La Chesnais, *The Socialist Party in the Reichstag.*

day, Chancellor Bethmann-Hollweg revealed the violation of Belgian neutrality but stressed the defensive character of the war and asked for approval of the military budget. Hugo Haase read a tortured declaration aligning Social Democracy with all other parties in the defense of the fatherland. The die was cast.

The controversy which the decision of the SPD aroused was bitterer than any other in the history of Socialism. The German Socialists were reviled by the whole Socialist world. The greatest of parties appeared to have failed abysmally. Lenin, in Geneva, refused at first to believe the news.[18] But, in retrospect, the vote seems a far less significant "betrayal of Socialism" than the continued support of the war by the SPD after the full truth was known. On August 4 the war seemed primarily a defense against tsarism, the enemy of democracy and progress; on that day, documentation was incomplete, and hysteria had reached fever pitch. As Noske admitted later: the SPD had approved the credits to avoid "being beaten to death in front of the Brandenburg Gate."[19]

But Bernstein soon conceded that "the policy of August 4" had been wrong, even though the provocation to adopt it had been great. In an article, written during the war but never published, Bernstein said that the fateful vote had made a prisoner of the party. "The evil from which we all suffer today [the split in the party] would probably not have come over us without that vote."[20] In another article, written in October 1916 for the *Neue Zeit*, but suppressed by censorship, Bernstein wistfully recalled Jaurès's championship of the mass strike against war at the 1907 Stuttgart congress:

> At that time he seemed to me to be suffering from an *idée fixe*. Today I ask myself whether this phrase could not have been better applied to our own attitude. It is not always the daring flight of imagination that leads astray; sometimes the lack of imagination is worse. . . .

[18] Bertram D. Wolfe, *Three Who Made a Revolution*, pp. 634–35.
[19] Quoted in A. Joseph Berlau, *The German Social Democratic Party, 1914–21*, p. 73.
[20] Bernstein Archives.

Jaurès had realized, Bernstein concluded, that the general strike alone would not have prevented the conflagration, but the moral effect of the demonstration would have been huge.[21]

This conviction became firmer as time went by. We have an eyewitness report of a speech that Bernstein delivered on the occasion of the tenth anniversary of the outbreak of the war:

In a thoughtful speech in Breslau . . . Bernstein confessed that he wished now that German Social Democracy and he himself had been able to bring themselves to call for the mass strike in August 1914. Such an action, he said, would certainly have been a failure, but at least it would have meant that the SPD had done its utmost to perform its duty.[22]

These ideas seem to us today courageous and profoundly true, but they were, after all, afterthoughts, and did not influence Bernstein's actions on the afternoon of August 4, 1914.

On the evening of that day, Bernstein was sitting at home, gloomily contemplating the future, when Gustav Mayer, the biographer of Engels, came to see him and brought news that Great Britain had declared war on Germany. This must have been the saddest moment of Bernstein's life. He was crushed by the news, and "like one of the Old Testament prophets" he broke into words that foresaw the doom of his own nation.[23]

One thing was clear to Bernstein now: he must rethink his attitude towards the war, and his Revisionism or his party loyalty would be of little help. He must do it alone, and, while frenzied patriots rushed to the colors, Bernstein painfully sought to find answers to a great puzzle: the truth about the war.

[21] Bernstein Archives.
[22] Immanuel Birnbaum, "Internationaler Syndikalismus," in *Grundsätzliches zum Tageskampfe*, p. 84.
[23] Gustav Mayer, *Erinnerungen*, p. 218.

The Truth About the War

> *Nowadays one lives from day to day and scarcely dares to think about the future. But sometimes I hope that when peace comes you and I may meet and shake hands, and tell each other that we have never had one thought of each other that was not kind, and then sit down to consider whether we can help in any way to heal the wounds of civilization.*
>
> GRAHAM WALLAS TO BERNSTEIN, 1915

The next few months were a time of inner turmoil for the leader of the Revisionists. The documents that became available shed light on the aggressive policy of the German and Austro-Hungarian empires. Letters reaching Bernstein from abroad through neutral channels revealed the extent to which German Social Democracy was hated and despised for its support of a regime that had invaded a neutral Belgium and was laying waste northern France. Worst of all, Bernstein was dismayed at the effect which the vote of August 4 was having on his own party.[24]

Within the SPD all was confusion. The attitude toward the war crossed all previous lines of demarcation; only the Social Imperialists ran true to form. Of the Revisionists, David was prominent in defending the war; Friedrich Stampfer, although forty years of age, volunteered for active service. Eisner, on the other hand, soon turned against the war and later joined the Independent Socialists. The radicals, however, presented the greatest surprise: Mehring, Liebknecht, and Luxemburg formed the hard core of the resistance to the war, but some of their closest associates deserted them to become intense patriots. Most notable among them were Paul Lensch, who had worked with Rosa Luxemburg on the ultraradical *Leipziger Volkszeitung*, and who now turned imperialist, and Konrad Haenisch, whose career paralleled that of Lensch.[25]

[24] Cf. Bernstein, "Entwicklungsgang," p. 46.
[25] Cf. their wartime books: Paul Lensch, *Die deutsche Sozialdemokratie und der Weltkrieg;* Konrad Haenisch, *Die deutsche Sozialdemokratie in und nach dem Weltkriege.*

Bernstein became ever more isolated from his Revisionist companions[26] and renewed contact with his old friend Karl Kautsky, to whom he had not spoken for several years. His first steps in the process of self-clarification, begun in September 1914, consisted of launching a series of attacks on chauvinism within the SPD. He published scathing articles denouncing sections of the party press and gave speeches opposing any annexations after the war.[27] As a result, he had to endure a deluge of letters from Revisionists urging him to reconsider his stand. Typical of these communications was one he received on September 2, 1914, from Ernst Heilmann, who was associated with Noske on the prowar *Chemnitzer Volksstimme:*

> We need not argue over the Belgian question. Practically there isn't a chance that Germany will move out again. Our party comrades who have shed blood in this war would have very little use for agitation against annexation. We will protest to save face, but we won't break a leg for Belgium. . . . True, the war does not excuse *every* illegality, but *this* was forced upon us by the emergency. The good feeling of the democracies isn't worth 300,000 German lives.[28]

Even more revealing than this missive was a letter from the Revisionist H. Peus, member of the Reichstag from Dessau:

[26] Cf. for example a letter from Eduard David to Bernstein, October 24, 1914: "Yesterday's conversation leaves me little hope for an understanding. . . . Reason and duty force us to support *that* direction in the government which wishes, at least, to take a step in the right path [democratization of the Prussian constitution]. We must avoid everything that would strengthen the enemy power." Bernstein Archives.
[27] Like everyone else, Bernstein assumed that Germany would win the war quickly. On his campaign against the press, cf. "Die Sozialdemokratische Presse und der europäische Krieg," *New Yorker Volkszeitung,* Dec. 13, 1914, Bernstein Archives. Earlier he had written articles in a similar vein in the *Leipziger Volkszeitung,* for which he was strongly attacked. But on Nov. 4, 1914, Adolf Braun, the historian of the German trade union movement, wrote Bernstein to thank him for his courageous campaign for truth. Bernstein Archives.
[28] Bernstein Archives.

I regret that you give speeches against the annexation of Belgium. Must it be "annexation"? Could it not be an "affiliation," similar to the manner in which Bavaria was affiliated to Prussia in 1870? . . . We are wedged in between Russia and England, and France aids them both. . . . We must at last begin to see the facts.[29]

Letters such as these helped Bernstein to "see the facts." Late in September 1914 he wrote an article for the *Sozialistische Monatshefte* in which he crystallized his feelings. It is an important document in Bernstein's development. It begins with the assertion that in no country had there been a strong popular drive toward war—a denial of the widely held thesis that the British and French had wanted the war. Now that the conflict had broken out, the slogan, "My country, right or wrong," was applicable in a limited sense only: As long as one's country's independence is in danger, it deserves to be defended. However, criticism of the regime during the war is essential, and the British have never fought a war in which they failed to have—and to tolerate—strong opposition. Without mentioning Germany by name, Bernstein vigorously criticized the political impotence in which the government held the people by preventing effective criticism through parliament and by withholding vital documentary information.

The article continues with a sharp attack on German intellectuals who turned back medals and honorary degrees granted them by British institutions with the reason that England had double-crossed Germany and allied itself with barbarian Russia. Is that the vaunted German culture, of which the bourgeois papers love to talk? asked Bernstein. Prussia, too, had been allied to Russia. The only forum before which these actions could be judged is European democracy, and that has declared overwhelmingly that German militarism is the great enemy.[30]

[29] Bernstein Archives. Considerations of space forbid fuller quotations. The quoted examples are but two of many such letters.
[30] Bernstein felt, however, that this was not a complete view, since Russian militarism was a grave danger to Europe. Summarized from the concept of the unpublished article in Bernstein Archives.

Joseph Bloch, the editor of the *Monatshefte*, who had never before turned down one of Bernstein's manuscripts, rejected this article with deep regret. "Germany is fighting in a just cause," he wrote Bernstein on October 3,

> in truth it desires nothing more than a chance to live. . . . It wants nothing from other nations, but others want to limit, or even to take away, our right to exist. In this state of affairs, I can see no higher duty than to do everything that will help the German cause.[31]

Wolfgang Heine, one of Bernstein's most consistent supporters in the prewar years, read the manuscript and agreed with Bloch in a letter almost as long as the article it criticized.[32] In the correspondence that ensued, Bloch did his utmost to conciliate Bernstein, to assure him that the rejection was not an interference with his freedom of opinion, but "nothing can appear in the *Sozialistische Monatshefte* that would show the attitude of the German government in an unfavorable, that of an enemy government in a favorable, light." [33] During the last months of 1914 Bloch wrote several pleading and respectful letters to Bernstein but remained adamant in his refusal to print the article. Accordingly, on December 10, Eduard Bernstein ended his collaboration with the *Monatshefte*:

> We have been politically estranged for a long time on the basic question of the attitude to be adopted by Social Democracy in international relations as well as on the practical problems of foreign policy. . . . For this reason I do not see any need for talking this matter out in person. . . . At present it would only give rise to a violent argument, since I would let myself be carried away by the passion of my feelings. . . . No one pushed us into this war but our own rashness.[34]

Bernstein had severed another link that tied him to his party.

[31] Bernstein Archives. The correspondence is most interesting, and it is to be hoped that the International Institute for Social History will reprint it in full.
[32] Oct. 2, 1914, Bernstein Archives.
[33] October 8, 1914, Bernstein Archives.
[34] Bernstein Archives.

The second opportunity to vote on war credits came on December 2, 1914. This time seventeen members opposed the credits in caucus, but only Karl Liebknecht dared to vote on the floor of the Reichstag against granting the government funds to prosecute a war which he stigmatized as imperialist and annexationist. At this point Bernstein still stood with the majority, although with a heavy heart; the process of self-clarification had nearly reached the point of action. During this winter, the first of the war, he published a remarkable article in a highly respected academic magazine, in which he thoroughly analyzed the attitude of the Socialist parties of Europe toward the war. The vote of August 4 came under careful scrutiny. Beneath the scientific detachment of Bernstein's words one could detect the question with which he was now plaguing himself: "Is it still the same war that we believed it to be on August 4?" [35]

Events rapidly drove him to answer in the negative. He established closer relations with Hugo Haase, one of the few radicals who had always been his friend, and he began to feel that, after all, Mehring had been right when he had written to Bernstein in September 1914:

> Regarding the war question I am not of your opinion; for the sake of its past and its future the party, in my view, should have refused the credits. . . . That the vote was difficult I will gladly admit. But it seemed to me that the reasons for voting "no" were overriding. I cannot get over the resolutions of our international congresses.[36]

In early February 1915 the Social Democratic parliamentary party met to discuss Liebknecht's breach of party discipline. Legien moved that Liebknecht be expelled, while Bernstein brought forward a resolution recognizing Liebknecht's good will. It was a harbinger of things to come. On March 20 the Reichstag voted on war credits for the third time; this

[35] "Die Internationale der Arbeiterklasse und der europäische Krieg," *Archiv für Sozialwissenschaft und Sozialpolitik,* XL (1914–15), 267–322.
[36] September 17 and 21, 1914, Bernstein Archives.

time they were included in the regular budget. Liebknecht again voted "no," along with Rühle, and thirty-one SPD members abstained by leaving the chamber before the vote. Bernstein was one of these men—the road to rebellion was now open.

From now on, Bernstein's pen was busier than ever. Starting in the spring of 1915, Bernstein engaged in a furious controversy with several of his party colleagues which, at times, consisted chiefly of mutual vituperation. Bernstein's erstwhile lieutenant, Eduard David, had become the spokesman and apologist for the German government, and Bernstein assailed this one-time "Bernsteinian" in article after biting article in the *Neue Zeit* and *Vorwärts*. If we reread his polemics in these publications today, we will not get the full flavor of Bernstein's outraged sense of justice: some of the most pungent paragraphs were cut by the censors and survive only in galley proofs in Bernstein's papers.

In June 1915, Eduard Bernstein published, in conjunction with Haase and Kautsky, the famous manifesto, "The Demand of the Hour." Bernstein was responsible for the original idea and the first draft; the final version was a joint product.[37]

Its burden, in brief, was that the war had clearly become an imperialist venture on the part of the German government. The three authors adduced weighty evidence for their claim and asked if a situation ought to be tolerated in which German Social Democracy was allowed to vote for the war credits and give lip service to peace while it was prevented from participating in important policy decisions and from really working for peace. German Democracy, the manifesto concluded, had always been known as the party of culture and peace. In view of the openly annexationist aims of the German government, the party was now free to take decisive steps toward peace.[38]

The manifesto, signed by three such respected Socialists, caused a sensation within the party. Even though the *Leipziger Volkszeitung*, in which it had originally appeared, was

[37] Bevan, *German Social Democracy during the War*, p. 60
[38] The manifesto is reprinted in full in Prager, *Geschichte der U.S.P.D.*, pp. 72–74.

banned for a week, and even though most party newspapers never reprinted it, its contents were soon widely known and served greatly to strengthen opposition to a war that was becoming intolerable and senseless.

On August 20, 1915, war credits were voted once more, and again Bernstein abstained, along with some thirty of his colleagues.[39] The debate within the party after the August vote raged ever more furiously. The majority, disregarding both the size and intellectual status of the minority, anxiously apologized for every governmental action, no matter how repressive, and shouted down every criticism by the minority, no matter how reasonable, as "aid to the enemy." [40]

On December 29 twenty members of the SPD voted against the fifth of the war credit bills, and Bernstein was one of the twenty. The open split of the party was now only a matter of time. It came on March 24, 1916, during a stormy Reichstag debate on the emergency budget. Haase, who had been compelled to read the party's declaration of August 4, 1914, now cleared his conscience with a vehement attack on the war. Amid catcalls and constant interruptions, he pledged the minority to an unending struggle against a war which benefited only the imperialists. The session was one of incredible confusion. David, of all people, shouted at Haase: "You represent . . . other countries! Your stand will prolong the war!" [41] In a ceremonious meeting of the parliamentary party immediately following the Reichstag session, Haase was ex-

[39] Sitting in a neighboring room while the vote was being taken, Bernstein reported later, the thirty felt that mere abstention was but a sorry farce. Bevan, *German Social Democracy During the War*, p. 61. The exact vote of that day is not clear, owing to the precipitancy with which it was taken. Liebknecht voted "no," Rühle intended to do so but could not reach the chamber in time. *Ibid.*, p. 60.

[40] One striking example of how low the party had sunk as early as 1915 was the book, *Die Arbeiterschaft im neuen Deutschland*, edited by Friedrich Thimme and Carl Legien. It contained twenty essays, ten by bourgeois intellectuals such as Meinecke, Tönnies, Troeltsch, and ten by Social Democrats such as Noske, Winnig, Scheidemann, Lensch. The latter were far more craven in their support of the war than the former.

[41] Quoted in Richard Berger, *Fraktionsspaltung und Parteikrisis*, p. 25.

pelled from the party. Seventeen others, including Eduard Bernstein, followed him out of the SPD and organized the Sozialdemokratische Arbeitsgemeinschaft. This informal body, which was hastily put together to protect the parliamentary rights of its members, was to serve as a transition to a new party, the Unabhängige Sozialdemokratische Partei Deutschlands (Independent Social Democratic Party of Germany), which was not formed until a year later.

If we look at the series of events that turned Bernstein from support of the policy of August 4 to his activities designed to split his own party, two questions arise: What motives changed his mind? Why did he wait so long?

As to the first of these questions: Bernstein had often been called a pacifist, and his opposition to the war has been explained with that term.[42] But the name pacifist does not fit him. Bernstein, like all civilized people, hated war, but he recognized its place in the scheme of things, especially a defensive war against barbaric opponents. Then, too, he would never have approved war credits, no matter how just, if he had been a pacifist. The simple fact is that Bernstein became convinced that this particular war had been precipitated by German stupidity and ambition. His early support of the war and his later opposition to it were perfectly consistent: above all, Bernstein was dominated by his concern for truth. It had been his honesty that had compelled him to abandon Marxism, a system he had greatly admired. Now the same sincerity forced him to leave his party.

But why had he waited so long? First, of course, he needed fuller documentation to understand the true course of events preceding the outbreak of the war. Then, too, there was his concern with party unity. As he saw it, his party had split into three warring camps: the Social Imperialists, who saw in the war a welcome opportunity for Germany to eclipse England; the party center, which found it necessary to furnish alibis for the government; and the radicals, who uncompromisingly opposed the war, but who hoped to turn it into a revolution at home. Bernstein regarded all these directions as unsatisfac-

[42] Cf. Waldemar von Grumbkow, "Sozialismus und Pazifismus," in *Grundsätzliches zum Tageskampfe*, pp. 54–61.

tory and wished to create a fourth, recruited from all segments of the party. This, to him, was the meaning of the Arbeitsgemeinschaft, a group that honestly advocated peace for the sake of peace, a group that would offer opposition to a party majority that had become the slave of the annexationists.

But to raise the question as to why Bernstein waited so long as a criticism is to underestimate the magnitude of the step he took on March 24, 1916: on that day he decided to break with a party to which he had dedicated his life from his early youth—for well over forty years. He had grown up with his party, had lived through the evils of Socialist disunity and actively fought for the merger of the Lassalleans and the Marxists. He had sought to keep the party united during the hard days of the anti-Socialist law; even in the controversy over Revisionism he had tried not to split Social Democracy. He understood the need for party discipline, and the step he took to violate it was dictated by his ever-active conscience. The party was his life, and the decision to leave it infinitely hard. He never rested until he could rejoin it.

The Independents formed into a party in April 1917, against the advice of Kautsky and Bernstein.[43] The latter felt that the Arbeitsgemeinschaft which, after all, was not a separate party, might keep open the channels for a possible settlement of disputes within Social Democracy. This was, no doubt, an unrealistic sentiment—even his Breslau constituents repudiated Bernstein [44]—but it was characteristic of Bernstein's overriding desire to reestablish party harmony.

Once the USPD [45] had been formed, however, Eduard Bernstein joined it, although he never took a prominent part in its deliberations. While his friends Kautsky and Haase were leading members of the Independents, Bernstein did not feel at home in the radical atmosphere of the new party. He continued his controversies with the majority Socialists and

[43] "Entwicklungsgang," p. 47.
[44] Richard Berger, *Fraktionsspaltung und Parteikrisis*, p. 64.
[45] The Unabhängige Sozialdemokratische Partei Deutschlands will be referred to in the sequel by those initials or as the "Independents."

attended the international Socialist conference at Stockholm in the summer of 1917. There, consonant with his passionate concern for truth, he brought up the question of war guilt, which, he said, should not be shelved (as the German majority Socialists had demanded) but be discussed frankly and honestly.[46] But in the main Bernstein's thoughts turned to the peace which was to repair the terrible ravages of the war. In a series of talks and articles of these years he dealt with the democratic conduct of foreign policy, the nonsense hidden behind such slogans as "vital national questions," and, above all, he developed the concept of a league of peoples which must be established after the war on the basis of freedom and equality.[47] His ideas on the league were remarkably similar to Woodrow Wilson's.

This literary activity helped Bernstein over the grim years of 1917 and 1918. He never abandoned the hope of being able to reunite the Socialist factions. When the German Revolution broke out in November 1918, sweeping away the monarchy and giving absolute power to the Socialists, the hour of *rapprochement* had come.

[46] Bevan, *German Social Democracy During the War*, pp. 170–71.
[47] Cf. Eduard Bernstein, *Sozialdemokratische Völkerpolitik* and *Völkerrecht und Völkerpolitik.*

Chapter 11

Noske's Republic

November 1918

> *Whoever undertakes to govern a people under the form of either republic or monarchy without making sure of those who are opposed to this new order of things, establishes a government of very brief duration.*
>
> NICCOLÒ MACHIAVELLI

THE BIRTH of the German Republic secured to the Socialists what they had been working for since the beginnings of their party: complete control. But this sudden access of power found the Social Democrats woefully unequipped to guide the social revolution that had to be carried through before the young republic could be safe. The majority Socialists, the Eberts and Scheidemanns, were obsessed by their fear of Bolshevism, their desire for law and order, and their timidity before the old bureaucracy and the general staff. Thus the new government entered into a number of deals with the representatives of the old order—particularly big business and the army—which thwarted the very social changes without which the republic could not survive.[1]

At the beginning, SPD and USPD governed jointly through a provisional cabinet, headed by six People's Representatives. Eduard Bernstein became Assistant Secretary (*Beigeordneter*) to Dr. Schiffer, Secretary of State for the Treasury.[2] He was to remain in that post until February 1919. Bernstein applauded the coalition and did his utmost, during these tense months, to keep it alive.[3] It proved an impossible task: the

[1] For an elaboration of a similar viewpoint, cf. Arthur Rosenberg, *A History of the Weimar Republic*, Chs. I, II.
[2] Cf. A. Joseph Berlau, *The German Social Democratic Party, 1914–21*, p. 223n.
[3] Cf. Hermann Müller, *Die November-Revolution*, p. 52.

two Socialist parties were irrevocably split over the ultimate aims of the revolution. Personal enmities created by the war years, disagreements over Germany's future form of government (parliament, or government by workers' and soldiers' councils?), disputes over nationalization—all these matters were difficult to reconcile. A series of bloody incidents soon grew into civil war, and all possibilities of peaceful cooperation between SPD and USPD vanished.

Still, Bernstein tried. In early December he submitted a resolution to the convention of the Berlin USPD, calling for collaboration between the two Socialist parties in naming joint candidates for the forthcoming National Assembly. It never even came to a vote.[4]

On December 22, 1918, five days before the Independents left the provisional government, Bernstein once more attempted to stem the tide with a speech before members of both factions. "Our quarrels must be buried," he said. "Disagreements over earlier policy do not matter now. In this hour let us recall Marx: Socialists of Germany, unite!"[5] His conciliatory words were soon drowned out by gunfire all over Germany.

Bernstein, while somewhat doubtful of their methods, agreed substantially with the majority Socialists that order must be maintained and that progress toward Socialism must be gradual.[6] He was critical, therefore, of the USPD resignations from the cabinet. In January 1919, well before the civil conflict was at its height, Bernstein tried one last desperate expedient to bring the warring factions together: he rejoined the SPD without dropping his USPD membership. With that

[4] Newspaper clipping (unidentifiable), Bernstein Archives.
[5] Quoted and paraphrased from Müller, *November-Revolution,* p. 238.
[6] Bernstein criticized Noske for his early recourse to the military but believed that no one who undertook the task of defending the republic against internal subversion could escape the decisions which Noske had to make and the reputation which Noske subsequently acquired. He was sharply disappointed in the behavior of the right-wingers on many occasions and condemned the murder of Luxemburg and Liebknecht in the strongest terms. Eduard Bernstein, *Die deutsche Revolution, passim,* esp. pp. 143, 158, 160.

symbolic move, which he hoped others would imitate, he attempted to demonstrate the fundamental unity of the German working class. The stratagem failed: the Independents prohibited Bernstein from holding dual membership, and he reluctantly gave up his USPD affiliation.[7]

Bernstein was now within the SPD fold once more, but since he had returned as an individual and not as the leader of a group of right-wing Independents he never regained the influence he had enjoyed in the days before the war. Had Haase, Kautsky, and other Independents of their persuasion joined Bernstein in his move, they might have served as a powerful counterweight against the right-wing elements that now had control—and were to retain control—of the Social Democratic Party.[8] But Bernstein had come back alone, and the party no longer paid much attention to him.

The Truth About the Peace

Not one of the readers of the Vorwärts *knows anything about the International.*

FRIEDRICH STAMPFER TO BERNSTEIN [9]

During the war Bernstein's conscience had compelled him to leave his party rather than to abandon his views on the origin of the conflict. Now Bernstein was to risk ridicule and violent attacks from his party colleagues in his fight for the truth about the peace. Upon his return to the SPD (which came too late to permit him to be a delegate to the National Assembly at Weimar) Bernstein was appalled to find how widespread chauvinism was within his party and how willingly his colleagues lent themselves to anti-Allied propaganda, no matter how fraudulent.[10] Such eagerness to grasp at any lie that would absolve Germany from responsibility for the

[7] Müller, *November-Revolution,* pp. 260–61.
[8] Rosenberg, *History of the Weimar Republic,* pp. 58–59.
[9] Stampfer, editor of the *Vorwärts,* wrote this sentence in a letter rejecting an article by Bernstein.
[10] For examples of such chauvinism, see Berlau, *German Social Democratic Party,* pp. 285–318.

World War, Bernstein feared, would make Social Democracy into a satellite of the bourgeois and nationalist forces in Germany.

The first occasion to speak his mind came at the party congress of 1919, at which he delivered a courageous address on foreign policy. He began by pointing out that German Social Democracy no longer enjoyed the confidence of other Socialist parties. But without such confidence no international Socialist action was possible. Nor could confidence be re-established, Bernstein said, if the party took the viewpoint of Otto Wels (a member of the party executive) that the Versailles peace demands proved the correctness of the policy of August 4, 1914—the vote of that day, Bernstein exclaimed, could never be justified:

> I can only repeat what I said in the fall of 1914 in Berlin
> . . . : August 3 and 4 were the blackest days of my political life. . . . In my view, our vote was a disaster for our people as well as for the civilized world. Had we said "no," as we had every right to do . . . or had we abstained . . . the German people certainly would not be worse off than it is now. But millions of soldiers would not have been killed, millions would not have been crippled.[11]

The French and British governments, he added, had only wanted peace.

Then, against constant and hostile interruptions, Bernstein made his point:

> The peace conditions imposed upon us by the Allies are hard, very hard, and in part simply impossible. I say that openly and have said it in British newspapers, such as the *Daily Herald*. But—and Scheidemann has admitted this too: we acknowledge the necessity of a large part of them, hard as they are. Nine tenths of them are necessities. (Lively opposition.) Nine tenths of them are imperative necessities. (Stormy, continuous opposition and great unrest. Shouts of "scandal!") Do not forget: France has been

[11] *Prokotoll über die Verhandlungen der SPD, 1919,* p. 241.

hit harder by this war than Germany. Every expert will tell you that. (Continuous disorder.) Think of what happened in Belgium. (Calls of "Think of East Prussia!") I reject that point. . . . Who sacrificed East Prussia? We were told: the war is directed against Russia. And where was Germany's greatest strength concentrated? Germany's greatest strength was thrown against the West, against Belgium and France.[12]

These were hard truths, and the delegates did not want to hear them. Speaker after speaker arose to denounce Bernstein for hurting Germany at a critical moment in its history, for wanting to sacrifice German territory, for regarding the enemies of Germany as angels, and so forth, *ad nauseam*. But sensitive as Bernstein was to criticism, his devotion to what he considered the truth outweighed all other considerations and he persisted in his "antinational" opinions. In the budget debate of March 1921 Bernstein even dared to bring up the question of war guilt in the Reichstag, and to come to the conclusion that "the guilt for the outbreak of the war rested upon Imperial Germany." [13]

When reactionary circles began to spread the stab-in-the-back interpretation of Germany's collapse, blaming the loss of the war on homefront sabotage and "Jewish-inspired strikes," Bernstein fought this new nationalist myth sharply. He saw with dismay that such newspapers as the *Vorwärts* played into the hands of the nationalists by refusing to examine the facts and by spouting such clichés as "the honor and dignity of our nation." [14] He rightly recognized such propaganda as a grave danger to the republic.

Bernstein's papers contain numerous examples of his polemics on the origin and the end of the war. His point was always the same: the German Empire bore a grave responsibility for the outbreak of the conflict, and those who now

[12] *Ibid.*, p. 242.
[13] *Verhandlungen des Reichstages, Stenographische Berichte,* CCCXXXVIII, (March 3, 1921–March 19, 1921), p. 3097. Bernstein's speech is on pp. 3094–97.
[14] Eduard Bernstein to Eckstein, Nov. 19, 1925, Bernstein Archives.

denied it—and who denied, too, that the German armies were
beaten in the field in 1918—were undermining the Weimar
Republic in order to establish an authoritarian regime. He
firmly believed that it was the duty of his party and its press
to expose these lies and thus to discredit the reactionaries. He
was heartsick at the spectacle of the Social Democratic failure.[15]

In these active years Bernstein tilted his journalistic lance
not only against the right but against the left as well. His
favorite targets were those Socialists who advocated immediate wholesale nationalization, and the Bolsheviks. In true
Revisionist fashion, Bernstein inveighed against haste which,
he felt, was the besetting vice of many German radicals.[16]
He saved his heavy ammunition, however, for the Bolsheviks,
who stood for all the things he abhorred. The Bolsheviks,
Bernstein charged, rested their case for violence on a scholas-
tic, hair-splitting interpretation of several of Marx's early pronouncements. In their lust for power they had barbarized
Marx's evolutionary teachings. What is more, they ignored
Marx's economics in jumping to Socialism in Russia, a
country whose capitalist development stood on a far lower
level than that of any Western country. In short, Bernstein
concluded, the Bolsheviks had "brutalized" Marx's civilized
doctrine.[17]

In these last years, then, Bernstein acted as a sort of Cas-
sandra, warning against the dangers of a reactionary subversion of the Weimar Republic, warning against the Bolsheviks.

[15] Examples of his polemics: An article in the Breslau *Volkswacht*, September 29, 1927, calling Hindenburg a liar for declar-
ing at Tannenberg that the Versailles Treaty put on the German
people the whole guilt for the war. In an article dated August
20, 1926, entitled "Well-meaning Americans on the wrong way,"
he denounced Harry Elmer Barnes for concluding after a so-
called investigation that Russia and France bore the chief guilt
for the war. Bernstein felt that Barnes had been victimized by
propaganda and had allowed himself to become the front for
several reactionary organizations. Bernstein Archives. Bernstein
carried his valiant campaign into his very last years.
[16] Cf. "Entwicklungsgang eines Sozialisten," in *Die Volkswirtschaftslehre der Gegenwart in Selbstdarstellungen*, I, 55–56.
[17] Cf. especially *Der Sozialismus einst und jetzt*, pp. 113–25.

In 1928, upon his retirement from the Reichstag, he published a manifesto, prophetically urging the SPD to be on guard against the deadly enemies of the republic, who, he wrote, commanded huge financial resources and a powerful press: "And these people, behind whom stand above all the great landowners and the big captains of heavy industry, work cheerfully with the Communists." [18]

Bernstein lived his last years in increasing isolation. He belonged to an older generation and he was out of touch with the leadership of his party, which regarded itself as hard-headed and politically realistic but which only succeeded in following a self-destructive policy. From 1920, Bernstein again represented the SPD in the Reichstag, but his chief activity was now journalistic. He wrote articles and gave lectures before university audiences. His customary generosity now worked overtime as he devoted more and more of his energies to aiding young people. He helped foreign students to obtain residence permits in Germany, advised budding authors, gave financial aid to party members down on their luck.[19] His willingness to expend time, energy, and money for others became almost proverbial in the Socialist movement, especially after his wife's death in October 1923 accentuated his loneliness.

But the fact that he was widely beloved did not mean that he had any influence. The party remembered his birthday but did without his advice. In 1927 he could write to his good friend Kautsky that neither Hilferding's *Gesellschaft* nor Stampfer's *Vorwärts* would accept his articles; [20] he spoke gloomily of his "political death" and even hinted at suicide. The party was too busy with *Realpolitik* to listen to the aged Bernstein.

This is how Bernstein lived out his life: helpful to others,

[18] "Zum Wahlkampf, ein Mahnwort," manuscript in Bernstein Archives.
[19] His correspondence of these years is remarkable: letters of thanks abound, his relatives urge him to take care of himself, great names—Einstein, Rathenau—appear frequently as correspondents.
[20] Nov. 9, 1927, Bernstein Archives.

beloved by his friends and relatives, ignored by his own party, fearful of the future. In 1925 he had suffered two slight strokes, but he continued to serve in the Reichstag for three more years. His mind remained fresh until the very last. His last extant letter, written shortly after his eighty-second birthday, reveals his pessimistic outlook: "You are right," he wrote to Kautsky,

> we can only wish each other the strength to get through these miserable times without harm. What will be the outcome? Will that which we have worked for so passionately all our lives be preserved? We, as old fighters, cannot take such thoughts lightly in view of the serious situation. Since the great economic depression has created a general world crisis, our enemies may—as you say in your letter—make common cause at the decisive moment. However that may be, we must wait. Meanwhile I have full confidence in the energy of our party; it will carry on. . . .[21]

Eduard Bernstein died on December 18, 1932, six weeks before his last desperate hope was proved a delusion. The funeral was well attended, and the eulogies were eloquent. Willem Hubert Vliegen, historian of the Dutch Socialist Party, represented the Socialist International. The German Social Democratic Party chose Friedrich Stampfer, one of their most nationalist members, as its representative. His selection by a party which Bernstein had served so well was one of its last acts of ineptness. Surely the courageous leader of the Revisionists had deserved better.

[21] Jan. 23, 1932, Bernstein Archives.

Chapter 12

Who Shall Revise
the Revisionists?

> *Peasants do not sink; middle class does not
> disappear; crises do not grow ever larger;
> misery and serfdom do not increase. There is
> increase in insecurity, dependence, social dis-
> tance, social character of production, func-
> tional superfluity of property owners.*
>
> EDUARD BERNSTEIN

EDUARD BERNSTEIN was one of the most attractive personalities
produced by German Social Democracy. If he is remembered
less vividly today than, say, Bebel, this is due largely to his
lack of spectacular qualities upon which the popular imagination could fasten. Bernstein was the opposite of the dema-
gogue or the charismatic leader. He was a scholar—intelligent, widely read, patient, and above all, honest. His concern
with the truth had an almost obsessive quality: it drove him
into abandoning theories in which he had found security, giving up friends with whom he had found happiness, turning his
back on a party which had filled his life. He was nervous and
easily wounded by criticism, but when he felt that the truth
demanded it, he spoke fearlessly before hostile groups and
willingly made enemies.

Whatever the psychological mainsprings of his drive for
truth, it made him the great figure he was: it allowed him to
submit Marxist dogma to searching examination while not
surrendering the Socialist standpoint.

It must be said, however, this his doctrine made only a
negligible *theoretical* contribution to Socialist thought. Revisionism was not sufficiently clear on its underlying philosophy; its rationalist optimism was derived from common sense
and empirical observations of immediate facts. This had certain advantages: Revisionism was not shackled by dogma; it

298

could allow considerable flexibility in its description of the development of capitalism. That is what gave Revisionism its timeliness. While orthodox Marxists were offering tortured explanations of the prosperity of the 1890s and beyond, the Revisionists blithely admitted the general upswing and incorporated it into their theory.

On the other hand, Bernstein's optimism was not well founded; it took a short-run prosperity and converted it into the law of capitalist development. True, Marxism had underrated the true expansive powers of late capitalism and had not appreciated its capacity for distributing the growing national product even among the workers. Nor was Marxism later able to offer more than a crudely mechanistic explanation of the rise of Fascism. But Revisionism, too, was to run afoul of the developments of history: World War I severely shook its optimistic foundations, and the great depression disproved its hopeful assumption that the period of great crises was over. He who would revise Revisionism, therefore, ought to begin with its philosophic basis.

The contribution of Revisionism to Socialist tactics was equally problematic. As we have seen, Bernstein's whole position was predicated on the possibility of parliamentary action and peaceful transition to Socialism. Yet he realized— not always clearly—that the political structure of the German Empire would frustrate such tactics.

Nevertheless, the Revisionist position on tactics was of great value. It served as an antidote against the Leninists on the one hand and the Syndicalists on the other. It emphasized the *possibility* of parliamentary action and called attention to the value of democratic processes even in crisis situations. It was one of Bernstein's fundamental convictions that violence for its own sake was barbarian; his bitter and unremitting campaign against Bolshevism testifies to his devotion to liberal parliamentarism.[1] Bernstein was the antithesis of the dogmatic revolutionists; he would have refused to impose the will of

[1] He would have endorsed Albert Camus's dictum: "La violence est à la fois inévitable et injustifiable. Je crois qu'il faut lui garder son caractère exceptionnel et la resserrer dans les limites qu'on peut." *Actuelles*, p. 184.

his party upon a hostile country, and he was anxious to arrive at the desired end—Socialism—only with the proper means —democracy. In other words, he was unwilling to kill for the sake of logic.

This emphasis on parliamentary democratic Socialism, which is the keystone of Revisionism, is of the greatest significance. Of course, Bernstein was not alone in connecting these strands of thought—the Fabians had done the same. But Bernstein belongs in the very foreground of those who believed that it was possible to combine socialized means of production with parliamentary democracy, nationalized banks and transportation systems with civil liberties. In our time, in which the uninformed and the biased like to tax Socialists with lack of devotion to freedom, Bernstein's writings deserve much greater attention than they have hitherto received.

It will be admitted, then, that Bernstein's general political position is of great relevance to countries with genuine parliamentary institutions. What of his views on Germany? Here, as we have emphasized, Bernstein himself frequently doubted that an alliance with the more radical sections of the bourgeoisie would work. His theory, however, required such collaboration, and to this end Bernstein called upon his party to change its programmatic stand on tactics, to "appear what it really is today: a democratic-Socialist reform party." This standpoint has been criticized as unrealistic.[2] These critics hold that an open admission of its nonrevolutionary nature would not have won for the SPD any better treatment at the hands of the German government and would, in the bargain, have forced the radical left wing to break away from the party. This estimate appears to be valid for the short run: the Luxemburgs would no doubt have had to form their own party, and Germany would certainly *not* have become a parliamentary monarchy of the English type if the Erfurt Program had been rewritten in the manner Bernstein had demanded. But for the long run the split between revolutionary declarations and reformist practices served the party ill: the revolutionary goals were never reached anyway, and the

[2] Joseph Schumpeter, *Capitalism, Socialism, and Democracy*, p. 345; Julius Braunthal, *In Search of the Millennium*, pp. 196–99.

liberal segments of the bourgeoisie, which wanted nothing more than leadership into a democratic republic, could never bring themselves to support a party that marched under the revolutionary banner of the Erfurt Program. When the SPD switched to the reformist Görlitz Program in 1921, it was too late.

Another charge against Revisionist tactics that has frequently been leveled is that Bernstein's activities "emancipated the right wing of the party." [3] which strengthened the conservatives in the SPD and developed the philosophy which led to the party split during the war. However, as this study has tried to show, the reformists gained power in the party quite independently of the Revisionist theorists. No doubt, the *Voraussetzungen* hastened and rationalized the process, but it would have gone on anyway. The trade unionists, the party bureaucrats, for the most part did not bother with theory.[4] Nor can it be demonstrated that the Revisionist philosophy drove the party into voting for the war credits—the act which really caused the party split. The motives were mixed: the SPD had accepted the German state almost completely—an acceptance doubtless strengthened by the Revisionist theoreticians but caused chiefly by the needs of the trade unions and of the legal, parliamentary party. Further, we must list fear of bloody retribution, hatred of Russia, and the sudden discovery of patriotic sentiments. While many of the Revisionists were in the forefront of the patriotic tide among the Socialists, the orthodox Marxists contributed their share. If the Revisionist Heine's outpourings outdid the effusions of many bourgeois journalists, they were no more unfortunate than the chauvinistic publications of the ex-radicals Lensch and Haenisch. That the support of the war cannot be charged to Bernstein's Revisionism is best seen in Bernstein's own behavior during the conflict. His courageous stand has been underestimated and, instead, Revisionism has been judged by the attitudes of a David or a Heine. It is certainly true that Bernstein was unfortunate in his supporters—not one of them understood his democratic Socialism sufficiently to develop

[3] Alexander Schifrin, "Eduard Bernstein," *Deutsche Republik,* VII (1933), 432.
[4] Cf. pp. 130–40 above.

it further. Instead, they converted it into a fundamentally conservative concept which understood gradualism to be an admonition to do little and to do that slowly.

Bernstein's Revisionism was the child of its time: the logical expression of the belief in progress which motivated wide circles in Europe before it was destroyed by the war. Its advent, as has been shown, was inevitable: the Revisionists did not create the Reformist mood, but the mood, instead, called forth the theory.

From the outset, Revisionism faced a dilemma that confronts all democratic movements intent on radical social change: What methods shall be used to gain the desired end? The use of violence may overthrow the ruling class that bars the way—but is it not likely that the exigencies of the revolution will transform the movement into a repressive tyranny? Can the rule of terror not be established in the sacred name of the general will? On the other hand, if the parliamentary path is followed and the use of force eschewed, will the reformers ever gain the power they must have to put their theories into practice?

These questions allow of no dogmatic answer. In Germany, contrary to Revisionist expectations, a revolution was needed to dislodge the powers in control; however, that revolution was not prompted by any consciously revolutionary party. It was, instead, the by-product of defeat in the field and starvation at home. The Socialists who benefited from the revolution were far from initiating a tyranny; indeed, an excellent case can be made out for the contention that they failed precisely because they refused to crush the old centers of power and thus permitted the enemies of the Republic to gather strength.

In any event, Revisionist theory and practice form a chapter in the never-ending debate on political methods. It is a debate that cannot be easily resolved: how can a party safely navigate between the Scylla of impotence before the adversary and the Charybdis of betrayal of its cause? We know—as did Bernstein—that means and ends are intimately related and that rotten means may permanently disfigure a movement that uses them, no matter how dedicated it may be in theory to humane ends. But we know, too—and Bernstein had some idea of this—that a determined and ruthless opponent will not be cowed into surrender by speeches. A fanatic revolutionary movement does not face this problem, but a democratic theoretician must conscientiously grapple with it, patiently judging each great occasion by its peculiar and unique circumstances.

This political dilemma of means and ends is heartbreakingly difficult, but Eduard Bernstein never wavered in his conviction: "Democracy is at the same time means and end. It is the means of the struggle for Socialism and it is the form Socialism will take once it has been realized." [5]

[5] *Voraussetzungen,* p. 178.

Postscript, 1961

Since I wrote this book ten years ago, much has happened, both in the world of affairs and in the world of scholarship. Still, its subject remains as important as ever.

If that is so, appearance and reality are sharply at odds. Surely, Eduard Bernstein's brand of socialism appears less probable, and even less relevant, than it seemed to be in the first years after World War II. Democratic socialism is overshadowed by the double threat of nuclear diplomacy and the welfare state. Nuclear diplomacy has monopolized our attention and engrossed our best talents, confounded old-fashioned —i.e. Marxist—notions of exploitation or imperialism, and made preoccupations with matters social and economic seem trivial if not downright irresponsible. When life itself is at stake, what social theorist can concentrate on the standard of living, and even the quality of life?

On the other hand, the welfare state may be less horrifying than the bomb, but it is also more insidious: it suggests, although it has not proved, that it may be possible to have the benefits of socialism without socialism. Unemployment insurance, national health services, managed economies are now part of Tory platforms: thunder from the left has not been precisely stolen, but it appears to be on permanent loan. The result is what thoughtful Europeans like to call a crisis in socialism: few things are more disheartening to read than the theoretical pronouncements of socialist strategists. Everyone seems to agree that Marx is dead, although there is no agreement on how to bury him, and even less light on what prophet shall be put in his place.[1] The dilemma of democratic socialism with which this book is concerned was a dilemma of power; the new dilemma appears to be a dilemma of impotence.

One result, or symptom, of this new dilemma has been a

[1] Much the most interesting and sensitive obituary I have seen, giving due credit to Marx and distinguishing him clearly from the Marxists, is George Lichtheim's *Marxism, An Historical and Critical Study* (London, 1961).

rash of anxious self-diagnoses, not so much on the level of political theory but on the level of party politics. Why are we losing elections? is the theme of these examinations, implying the more rewarding question, How can we win? There are some exceptions, but most of these inquiries have led to remarkably predictable results: right-wing socialists have discovered that socialists should turn themselves into liberals, and steal back from the Tories the welfare planks purloined from socialist platforms; left-wing socialists have discovered that what their party needs to win is more socialism, not less.[2]

Another result, rather more depressing than these exercises in practical narcissism, is the writing of despairing sociology and weary history: the first retroactively superimposes the failures of the present upon the idealism of the past; the second projects contemporary tendencies upon an unpredictable future. Thus, one historian of the Second International has portrayed the Bebels and Jaurèses of the movement as windy, self-deluded rhetoricians; while among sociologists it has become fashionable to diagnose the fatigue of intellectuals, the blurring of issues, and the waning hope that material improvement will bring spiritual serenity as the "end of ideology."[3]

At the same time, there has been some useful scholarly work on the German socialist movement since this book was

[2] The most lively, and at the same time most intelligent tactical debate that is being carried on in socialist movements today is being carried on in England—the country in which Eduard Bernstein learned to be a Revisionist. The most persuasive spokesman for the right wing has been C. A. R. Crosland, in his *The Future of Socialism* (London, 1956), and his Fabian Tract, "Can Labour Win?" His views have received powerful support in the careful sociological survey by Mark Abrams, "Why Labour has lost Elections," *Socialist Commentary*, June, July, August 1960. The left wing reply has been carried by R. H. S. Crossman, and a group of young writers who published, under Norman MacKenzie's editorship, a little book of essays entitled *Conviction* (London, 1959). Meanwhile, in Germany, all is torpor.

[3] For the history see James Joll, *The Second International, 1889–1914* (London, 1955); for the sociology, Daniel Bell, *The End of Ideology: On the Exhaustion of Political Ideas in the Fifties* (New York, 1961).

published. Fortunately, there is a recent, up-to-date biblio-
graphical survey of this material, which saves me the trouble
of resurveying it here.[4] But there is one book, a brilliant one,
that I want to single out, for it is concerned with the same
issues I am concerned with, and from a different perspective:
Carl E. Schorske's *German Social Democracy, 1905–1917:
The Development of the Great Schism.*[5] As its subtitle makes
clear, Schorske's book analyzes the growing divisions within
the German socialist movement at a critical period. Bernstein was a central figure in the debates of those years, and
he appears prominently in Schorske's pages. In masterly
fashion, Schorske unravels the complex interplay of trade
unions, party bureaucracy, revisionists on the right and disaffected radicals on the left, both with one another and with
the great events of the day. He propounds, and, I think, ele-
gantly proves the thesis that it was not the voting of the war
credits on August 4, 1914 that split the party, but a deep and
incurable schism which preceded that fatal day. As long as
such books are written, obituaries on the subject, as distinct
from the movement, of democratic socialism, will be premature.

But it seems to me that even obituaries on the movement
itself are premature: even if it should be true that ideology
is dead, the need for radical thinking remains as great as
ever. To say this is not to advertise the relevance of my *Dilemma of Democratic Socialism:* I did not write that book as
a tract, but as a study in the history of political theory.

At the same time, I am troubled over the ease with which
intellectuals have proclaimed the irrelevance of socialism to
our world. To be sure, the reasons are cogent and the temp-
tations powerful: orthodox Marxism, once so secure a guide

[4] See William Harvey Maehl, "Recent Literature on the German
Socialists, 1891–1932," *Journal of Modern History,* XXXIII,
no. 3 (September, 1961), 292–306.
[5] (Cambridge, Mass., 1955). Schorske's book, along with Joseph
Berlau's book on *The German Social Democratic Party, 1914–
1921* (New York, 1949), and my own, was subjected to an extensive review by Klaus Epstein: "Three American Studies of
German Socialism," *World Politics,* XI, no. 4 (July, 1959), 629–
651.

to many, has been riddled by the harsh, irrefutable critique of reality; the easy old distinctions between right and left have been blurred by the irrationality or conservatism of the masses, and tainted by what we are, I think, entitled to call the betrayal of socialism by countries that call themselves socialist; the failure of social services to make the poor good, or at least rational, has given plausibility to the lamentations of the crisis theologians; the obtuseness of many intellectuals who continue to concentrate their spleen on American failings and excuse Soviet crimes has alienated many a thoughtful person from politics in general and left-wing politics in particular. The modern ex-socialist or ex-political intellectual is a tired refugee: so guilty about his youthful involvement and so proud of his belated discovery of "reality" that he has little time to look around him.

I put the word "reality" in quotation marks because I think the new realism is anything but realistic. What have we really discovered? That life is more complicated than Marx said it was, that politics cannot do everything, and that capitalist society can serve the general welfare better than was generally supposed before the Great Depression. Bernstein said much the same things half a century ago. Indeed, his social vision, far more complex than his rather flat, journalistic prose might indicate, has been confirmed in rather left-handed fashion by the welfare states of our time.

But this is not all that reality teaches us. Jane Jacobs, a refreshing, original critic of city planning, has told her readers that if they want to understand urban life they must go out and walk around. If we go out and walk around modern welfare states, we will discover, I think, not that they have done the socialists' job too well, but that they have not done it well at all. So far, this point has been made chiefly by left-wing English socialists—some of them highly trained economists[6]—but I submit that it is visible to the most unpolitical observer, so long as he observes.

The United States, wallowing in prosperity and vast wealth, is fair game for going out and walking around. Anyone who

[6] Among them some of the authors of *Conviction* (see note 2 above), and Richard Titmuss, the most accessible of whose writings in the Fabian Tract, "The Irresponsible Society."

has ever taken a small child to a public school in New York City and stayed to watch the senseless regimentation, the incipient hostility of the Negro child to the disdainful authority, the inadequacy of the plant, and the helpless, or vicious, methods of some of the teachers, will speak more cautiously about equal opportunities and open societies. Anyone who has ever visited friends in middle income housing projects (which most middle income people cannot afford) and observed the uniformed guards, the grim, asphalt-covered play space, the barrack-like buildings, will abandon any notion that project housing is adequate, let alone cheerful. And if he has any illusions left, let him walk past the rat-infested "Residence Hotels" that dot our richest cities like pockmarks, or read accounts of the rents paid by the ignorant and the exploited to slum landlords. Anyone who has ever read Congressional hearings on the cost of drugs or asked his less fortunate neighbor about the cost of medicine will read the leaflets of the American Medical Association with considerable skepticism. If we are to call this the Welfare State, surely the word "Welfare" is used in a Pickwickian sense.

As my examples suggest, the failures of the welfare state are by no means merely financial. They touch the quality of life as well as the standard of living. But this, too, makes socialism relevant, for writers like Eduard Bernstein argued long ago that while capitalism might conquer, or at least mitigate, economic crises, it could not furnish a life of dignity and self-respect to all. His laconic summary of the modern social question, which I have quoted in the text, is concerned as much with the feeling people have about themselves as with the amount of money in their pockets:

> Peasants do not sink; middle class does not disappear; crises do not grow ever larger; misery and serfdom do not increase. There *is* increase in insecurity, dependence, social distance, social character of production, functional superfluity of property owners.[7]

This paragraph sounds like the outline of the debate now going on among British socialists.

[7] See p. 250 above.

Of course, it is possible to fall into a rhetorical radicalism which grows tearful about the poor, a sentimental nostalgia which waxes lyrical about the past and myopically closes its eyes to the real achievements of the welfare progams of the last generation. There is indeed some evidence that such infantile left-wing thinking is not out of fashion, and that there are some writers and editors who mistake the struggle of generations for social criticism. It is precisely to escape such sentimentality that so many former socialists left socialist movements.

But it is also possible to be sentimental about how much has been done, and how little can be done: despair can be just as modish, just as unpolitical, as certain forms of Utopianism. All too many intellectuals have discovered that wealth does not make them easy in life but merely gives their neuroses wider scope, and they have concluded from this that the grosser miseries—associated with inadequate diet, housing, or medicine—do not deserve to be a target for extermination. This is giving up too easily. The interaction of environment to contentment, of childhood trauma to adult prosperity, of mother fixations to picture windows, is a complicated but also a fruitful subject for debate. Until recently, socialists have been suspicious of psychology, especially of psychoanalytical psychology. But once the barriers break down, the possibilities and the limits of social action will be defined more objectively than they have ever been defined before.

A Columbia College humor magazine once put out an issue dedicated to proving that Money Can't Buy Anything But Happiness. There is much in this *Jester's* jest. The relation between social services and happiness is neither automatic nor simple, but this not an argument against social services. The sad fact that most adolescent crime comes out of housing projects rather than old-fashioned run-down neighborhoods is not an argument against the rebuilding of cities. The observable truth that well-fed intellectuals are often personally wretched is not an argument against improving the general standard of living. All these, rather, are arguments for the application of humanity and intelligence to social problems. It may be that we must free ourselves from social worker's cant; but the anti-social-worker's cant, based on a misreading of Reinhold Niebuhr coupled with self-hatred for one's radical past, is far more dreary and far less constructive.

The role of socialism in this debate is not immediately obvious. Perhaps the programs needed to improve at once the standard of living and the quality of life will be undertaken without socialism, by a society devoted to private property and a mixed economy. But such programs will become realities only if existing governments are continuously and intelligently pushed from the left. It may be the fate of socialists to invent programs that non-socialists will carry out. It may be that democratic socialists will make their mark in history by thinking and criticizing rather than by governing. But even if that should be so, socialist thinking will become more rather than less necessary as the welfare state continues on its blithe, unideological path. The Bernsteins of this world may be so many Moseses, pointing to the promised land they cannot enter. But without their direction, the promised land would lie forever in obscurity. And it is not a bad fate to be a Moses.

BIBLIOGRAPHY

Bibliography

DOCUMENTARY SOURCES

The Bernstein Archives, housed in the International Institute for Social History at Amsterdam, Netherlands, contain a large number of letters from and to Eduard Bernstein, outlines of speeches and articles, newspaper clippings of articles by and about Bernstein, as well as clippings concerning matters which interested him. All this material was consulted by the author for this study.

BOOKS AND PAMPHLETS BY EDUARD BERNSTEIN

Die Arbeiterbewegung. Frankfurt: Rütten und Leonig, 1910.
Aus den Jahren meines Exils. Berlin: Freidrich Reiss, 1917.
Die deutsche Revolution. Berlin: Gesellschaft und Erziehung, 1921.
Die englische Gefahr und das deutsche Volk. Berlin: Vorwärts, 1911.
Ferdinand Lassalle as a Social Reformer. London: Swan Sonnenschein, 1893.
Ferdinand Lassalle und seine Bedeutung für die Arbeiterklasse. Berlin: Vorwärts, 1904.
Geschichte der Berliner Arbeiterbewegung. 3 vols. Berlin: Vorwärts, 1907–10.
Gesellschaftliches und Privat-Eigentum. Berlin: Vorwärts, 1891.
La Grève et le lock-out en Allemagne. Paris: Marcel Rivière, 1908.
Die heutige Einkommensbewegung und die Aufgaben der Volkswirtschaft. Berlin: Sozialistische Monatshefte, 1902.
Die heutige Sozialdemokratie in Theorie und Praxis. Munich: Birk, 1906.
Ignaz Auer. Berlin: Vorwärts, 1907.
Parlamentarismus und Sozialdemokratie. Berlin: Pan-Verlag, 1906.
Der politische Massenstreik und die politische Lage der Sozialdemokratie in Deutschland. Breslau: Volkswacht, 1905.
Der Revisionismus in der Sozialdemokratie. Amsterdam: Martin Cohen, 1909.
Sozialdemokratische Lehrjahre. Berlin: Bücherkreis, 1928.
Sozialdemokratische Völkerpolitik. Leipzig: Verlag "Naturwissenschaften," 1917.
Der Sozialismus einst und jetzt. Stuttgart: J. H. W. Dietz, 1922.

313

Sozialismus und Demokratie in der grossen englischen Revolution. 2d ed. Stuttgart: J. H. W. Dietz, 1908. This work was originally published in Vol. I, Part 2, of *Die Geschichte des Sozialismus in Einzeldarstellungen* (Stuttgart: J. H. W. Dietz, 1895) and has been translated into English as *Cromwell and Communism* (London: George Allen and Unwin, 1930).

Die Steuerpolitik der Sozialdemokratie. Berlin: Vorwärts, 1914.

Der Streik. 2 ed. Frankfurt: Literarische Anstalt, 1920.

Völkerrecht und Völkerpolitik. Berlin: Paul Cassirer, 1919.

Von 1850 bis 1872. Berlin: Erich Reiss, 1926.

Von der Sekte zur Partei. Jena: Diederichs, 1911.

Die Voraussetzungen des Sozialismus und die Aufgaben der Sozialdemokratie. Stuttgart: J. H. W. Dietz, 1920. The first edition of this work was published by Dietz in 1899; there also is an English translation, *Evolutionary Socialism* (New York: Huebsch, 1909).

Die Wahrheit über die Einkreisung Deutschlands. Berlin: Neues Vaterland, 1919.

Wesen und Aussichten des bürgerlichen Radikalismus. Munich: Duncker und Humblot, 1915.

Wie eine Revolution zugrunde ging. Stuttgart: J. H. W. Dietz, 1921.

Wie ist wissenschaftlicher Sozialismus möglich? Berlin: Sozialistische Monatshefte, 1901.

Wirtschaftswesen und Wirtschaftswerden. Berlin: Vorwärts, 1920.

Zur Frage: Sozialliberalismus oder Kollektivismus. Berlin: Sozialistische Monatshefte, 1900.

Zur Geschichte und Theorie des Sozialismus. Berlin: Edelheim, 1901.

BOOKS, MAGAZINES, AND NEWSPAPERS EDITED BY EDUARD BERNSTEIN

Die Briefe von Friedrich Engels an Eduard Bernstein. Berlin: J. H. W. Dietz, 1925.

Der Briefwechsel zwischen Friedrich Engels und Karl Marx, 1844 bis 1883. Edited in cooperation with August Bebel. 4 vols. Stuttgart: J. H. W. Dietz, 1913.

Dokumente des Sozialismus. A periodical. Berlin: Sozialistische Monatshefte, 1902–5.

Ferdinand Lassalle, Gesammelte Reden und Schriften. 12 vols. Berlin: Paul Cassirer, 1919.

Ferdinand Lassalles Reden und Schriften. 3 vols. Berlin: Vorwärts, 1893.

Grundsätze des Kommunismus. Berlin: Vorwärts, 1919. (Engels's original draft of the *Communist Manifesto*.)

Der Sozialdemokrat. A weekly publication edited by Bernstein from January 1881 until September 1890. Zurich and London, 1880–90.

ARTICLES BY EDUARD BERNSTEIN

In his long career, Bernstein wrote literally hundreds of articles and reviews. Only articles cited in this study are listed here.

"Allerhand Werttheoretisches," *Dokumente des Sozialismus,* V (1905), 221–24, 270–74, 367–72, 463–68, 555–59.

"Arbeitswert oder Nutzwert?" *Neue Zeit,* XVII, 2 (1899), 548–54.

"Die Bedeutung von Eduard Davids Agrarwerk," *Sozialistische Monatshefte,* VII, 1 (1903), 108–15.

"Carlyle und die sozialpolitische Entwicklung Englands," *Neue Zeit,* IX, 1 (1891), 665–73, 693–701, 729–36.

"Entwicklungsgang eines Sozialisten," in Die Volkswirtschaftslehre der Gegenwart in Selbstdarstellungen, I, 1–58. Leipzig: Meiner, 1924.

"Geschichtliches zur Gewerkschaftsfrage," *Sozialistische Monatshefte,* IV (1900), 376–88.

"Grundlinien des sozialdemokratischen Radikalismus," *Sozialistische Monatshefte,* XII, 3 (1908), 1511–19.

"Die Internationale der Arbeiterklasse und der europäische Krieg," *Archiv für Sozialwissenschaft und Sozialpolitik,* XL (1914–15), 267–322. Reprinted as a pamphlet (Tübingen: Mohr, 1916).

"Ist der politische Streik in Deutschland möglich?" *Sozialistische Monatshefte,* IX, 1 (1905), 29–37.

"Der Kampf in Belgien und die politische Massenstrike," *Sozialistische Monatshefte,* VI, 1 (1902), 413–20.

"Der neue Reichstag und die Aufgaben der Sozialdemokratie," *Sozialistische Monatshefte,* VII, 2 (1903), 641–49.

"Der neueste Vernichter des Sozialismus," *Neue Zeit,* XI, 1 (1893), 502–8, 534–39.

"Patriotismus, Militarismus und Sozialdemokratie," *Sozialistische Monatshefte,* XI, 1 (1907), 434–40.

"Politischer Massenstreik und Revolutionsromantik," *Sozialistische Monatshefte,* X, 1 (1906), 12–20.

Probleme des Sozialismus. This is the general title of a series of articles: "Allgemeines über Utopismus und Eklektizismus," "Eine Theorie der Gebiete und Grenzen des Kollektivismus," "Der gegenwärtige Stand der industriellen Entwicklung in Deutschland," "Die neuere Entwicklung der Agrarverhältnisse in England," *Neue Zeit,* XV, 1 (1896–97), 164–71, 204–13, 303–11, 772–83; "Die sozialpolitische Bedeutung von Raum und Zahl," *Neue Zeit,* XV, 2 (1896–97), 100–107; "Das realistische und ideologische Moment im Sozialismus," *Neue Zeit,* XVI, 2 (1897–98), 225–32, 388–95. These articles were incorporated into his book, *Zur Geschichte und Theorie des Sozialismus.*

"Revisionismus und Programmrevision," *Sozialistische Monatshefte,* XIII, 1 (1909), 403–11.

"Sozialdemokratie und Imperialismus," *Sozialistische Monatshefte,* IV (1900), 238–51.

"Der Strike als politisches Kampfmittel," *Neue Zeit,* XII, 1 (1894), 689–95.

"Technisch-ökonomischer und sozial-ökonomischer Fortschritt," *Neue Zeit,* XI, 1 (1893), 782–90, 819–29, 854–62.

"Was folgt aus dem Ergebnis der Reichstagswahlen?" *Sozialistische Monatshefte,* VII, 2 (1903), 478–86.

"Wird die Sozialdemokratie Volkspartei?" *Sozialistische Monatshefte,* IX, 2 (1905), 663–71.

"Zum Reformismus," *Sozialistische Monatshefte,* XII, 3 (1908), 1398–1405.

"Zur Würdigung Friedrich Albert Langes," *Neue Zeit,* X, 2 (1892), 68–78, 101–9, 132–41.

BOOKS AND ARTICLES BY OTHER AUTHORS

Adoratsky, V., ed. Selected Correspondence, Karl Marx and Frederick Engels. New York: International Publishers, 1942.

Anderson, Evelyn. Hammer or Anvil. London: Gollancz, 1945.

Anderson, Pauline. The Background of Anti-English Feeling in Germany. Washington, D.C.: American University Press, 1939.

Auer, Ignaz. "Partei und Gewerkschaft," *Sozialistische Monatshefte,* VI (1902), 3–9.

Bebel, August. Aus meinem Leben. 3 vols. Stuttgart: J. H. W. Dietz, 1910–14.

—— "Ein Nachwort zur Vizepräsidentenfrage und Verwandtem," *Neue Zeit,* XXI, 2 (1903), 708–29.

Beer, Max. Fifty Years of International Socialism. London: George Allen and Unwin, 1935.

—— A History of British Socialism. 2 vols. London: Bell, 1923.

Berger, Richard. Fraktionsspaltung und Parteikrisis. München-Gladbach: Volksvereinsverlag, 1916.

Berlau, A. Joseph. The German Social Democratic Party, 1914–21. New York: Columbia University Press, 1950.

Berlin, Isaiah. Karl Marx. New York: Oxford University Press, 1948.

Bevan, Edwyn. German Social Democracy during the War. London: George Allen and Unwin, 1918.

Binder, Hanni. Das sozialitäre System Eugen Dührings. Jena: Gustav Fischer, 1933.

Birnbaum, Immanuel. "Internationaler Syndikalismus," in Grundsätzliches zum Tageskampfe, pp. 83–94. Breslau: Volkswacht, 1925.

Bismarck, Otto von. Gedanken und Erinnerungen. 3 vols. Stuttgart: Cotta, 1921.

Blank, R. "Die soziale Zusammensetzung der sozialdemokratischen

Wählerschaft Deutschlands," *Archiv für Sozialwissenschaft und Sozialpolitik*, new ser., IV (1905), 507–53.

Böhm-Bawerk, Eugen von. Karl Marx and the Close of his System. New York: Augustus Kelley, 1949.

Bortkiewicz, Ladislaus von. "On the Correction of Marx's Fundamental Theoretical Construction in the Third Volume of *Capital*." Appendix to Böhm-Bawerk, *Karl Marx and the Close of his System* (see preceding entry).

Braun, Adolf. Die Gewerkschaften vor dem Kriege. 3d ed. Berlin: J. H. W. Dietz, 1925.

Braun, Lily. Memoiren einer Sozialistin: Kampfjahre. Munich: Lange, 1911.

Braunthal, Julius. In Search of the Millennium. London: Gollancz, 1945.

Brunhuber, R. Die heutige Sozialdemokratie. Jena: Gustav Fischer, 1906.

Brutzer, Gustav. Die Verteuerung der Lebensmittel in Berlin im Laufe der letzten dreissig Jahre. Leipzig: Duncker und Humblot, 1912.

Budon, Adrien. Socialdémocratie pratique; les idées d'Edouard Bernstein. Orleans: Imprimerie du Progrès du Loiret, 1903.

Camus, Albert. Actuelles. 7th ed. Paris: Gallimard, 1950.

Cassau, Theodor. Die Gewerkschaftsbewegung. Halberstadt: Meyer, 1925.

David, Eduard. Sozialismus und Landwirtschaft. Berlin: Socialistische Monatshefte, 1903.

Dawson, W. H. Bismarck and State Socialism. London: Swan Sonnenschein, 1891.

Dühring, Eugen. Capital und Arbeit. Berlin: Eichhoff, 1865.

———— Careys Umwälzung der Volkswirtschaftslehre und Sozialwissenschaft. Munich: Fleischmann, 1865.

———— Cursus der National- und Sozialökonomie. 4th ed. Leipzig: Reisland, 1925.

———— Cursus der Philosophie. Leipzig: Koschny, 1875.

———— Der Ersatz der Religion durch Vollkommeneres und die Abstreifung alles Asiatismus. 3d ed. Leipzig: Thomas, 1906.

———— Kritische Geschichte der Nationalökonomie und des Sozialismus. 4th ed. Leipzig: Naumann, 1900.

———— Sache, Leben und Feinde. 2nd ed. Leipzig: Naumann, 1903.

———— Die Verkleinerer Careys und die Krisis der Nationalökonomie. Breslau: Eduard Trewendt, 1867.

Elm, Adolf von. "Sozialdemokratie und Arbeiterschaft," *Sozialistische Monatshefte*, VI (1902), 241–45.

Engels, Friedrich. Herr Eugen Dühring's Revolution in Science [Anti-Dühring]. New York: International Publishers, 1935.

Erdmann, Karl. England und die Sozialdemokratie. Berlin: Kirstein, 1917.

318 / Bibliography

Flesch, Karl. "Rückblicke auf die sozialistische Bewegung in Deutschland," *Jahrbuch für Sozialwissenschaft und Sozialpolitik, I* (1879), 75–96.

Fromm, Erich. Escape from Freedom. New York: Rinehart, 1941.

Geiger, Theodor. Die soziale Schichtung des deutschen Volkes. Stuttgart: Ferdinand Enke, 1932.

Georgi, Elsbeth. Theorie und Praxis des Generalstreiks in der modernen Arbeiterbewegung. Jena: Gustav Fischer, 1908.

Gooch, G. P. English Democratic Ideas in the Seventeenth Century. 2d ed. Cambridge: Cambridge University Press, 1927.

Gray, Alexander. The Development of Economic Doctrine. London: Longmans, Green, 1931.

Gridazzi, Mario. Die Entwicklung der sozialistischen Ideen in der Schweiz bis zum Ausbruch des Weltkrieges. Zurich: Girsberger, 1935.

Grossmann, Henryk. Das Akkumulations- und Zusammenbruchsgesetz des kapitalistischen Systems. Leipzig: Hirschfeld, 1929.

Grumbkow, Waldemar von. "Sozialismus und Pazifismus," in Grundsätzliches zum Tageskampfe, pp. 54–61. Breslau: Volkswacht, 1925.

Grundriss der Sozialökonomik. Vol. IX, Part 1. Tübingen: Mohr, 1926.

Grundsätzliches zum Tageskampfe: Festschrift für Eduard Bernstein. Breslau: Volkswacht, 1925.

Haenisch, Konrad. Die deutsche Sozialdemokratie in und nach dem Weltkriege. Berlin: Schwetschke, 1916.

Hayes, Carlton J. H. "History of German Socialism Reconsidered," *American Historical Review, XXIII* (October 1917), 62–101.

Heilborn, Otto. Die "Freien" Gewerkschaften seit 1890. Jena: Gustav Fischer, 1907.

Helfferich, Karl. Deutschlands Volkswohlstand, 1888–1913. Berlin: Stilke, 1913.

Hertz, Friedrich Otto. Die agrarischen Fragen im Verhältnis zum Sozialismus. Vienna: Rosner, 1899. Preface by Eduard Bernstein.

Hilferding, Rudolf. Böhm-Bawerk's Criticism of Marx. New York: Augustus Kelley, 1949.

———. "Zur Frage des Generalstreiks," *Neue Zeit, XXII*, 1 (1904), 134–42.

Howard, E. D. The Cause and Extent of the Recent Industrial Progress in Germany. Boston: Houghton, Mifflin, 1907.

Kampffmeyer, Paul. "Die Lebensarbeit Conrad Schmidts," *Sozialistische Monatshefte, LXXVI*, 2 (1932), 897–904.

———. "Max Schippel," *Sozialistische Monatshefte, LXVII*, 2 (1928), 587–94.

——— Mehr Macht! Berlin: Sozialistische Monatshefte, 1898.

Kampffmeyer, Paul, ed. Friedrich Ebert, Schriften, Aufzeichnungen, Reden. Dresden: Reissner, 1926.

Kautsky, Karl. Die Agrarfrage. Stuttgart: J. H. W. Dietz, 1899.

———— "Bernstein über die Werttheorie und die Klassen," *Neue Zeit*, XVII, 2 (1899), 68–81.

———— Bernstein und das sozialdemokratische Programm. Stuttgart: J. H. W. Dietz, 1899.

———— "Bernstein und die Dialektik," *Neue Zeit*, XVII, 2 (1899), 36–50.

———— "Bernstein und die materialistische Geschichtsauffassung," *Neue Zeit*, XVII, 2 (1899), 4–16.

———— The Class Struggle. Chicago: C. H. Kerr, 1910.

———— Ethics and the Materialist Conception of History. Chicago: C. H. Kerr, 1907.

———— "Der politische Massenstreik," *Neue Zeit*, XXII, 1 (1904), 685–95, 732–40.

———— Sozialisten und Krieg. Prague: Orbis, 1937.

Kehr, Eckart, "Englandhass und Weltpolitik," *Zeitschrift für Politik*, XVII (1928), 500–526.

———— Schlachtflottenbau und Parteipolitik, 1894–1901. Berlin: Ebering, 1930.

Kleene, G. A. "Bernstein vs. 'Old-School' Marxism," *Annals of the American Academy of Political and Social Sciences*, XVIII (1901), 391–419.

Koch, Walter. Volk und Staatsführung vor dem Weltkriege. Stuttgart: Kohlhammer, 1935.

Kroner, Richard. Von Kant bis Hegel. Vol. I. Tübingen: Mohr, 1921.

Kuczynski, Jürgen. Löhne und Konjunktur in Deutschland, 1887–1932. Berlin: 1933.

Küstermeier, Rudolf. Die Mittelschichten und ihr politischer Weg. Potsdam: Alfred Protte, 1933.

La Chesnais, P. G. The Socialist Party in the Reichstag. London: T. Fisher Unwin, 1915.

Lair, Maurice. Jaurès et l'Allemagne. Paris: Librairie Académique Perrin, 1935.

Laski, Harold J. Communism. New York: Holt, 1927.

Lederer, Emil, and Jakob Marschak. "Der neue Mittelstand," in Grundriss der Sozialökonomik, Vol. IX, Part 1, pp. 120–41. Tübingen: Mohr, 1926.

Legien, Carl. Die deutsche Gewerkschaftsbewegung. 2d ed. Berlin: Sozialistische Monatshefte, 1911.

———— "Die Gewerkschaften als Organe des nationalen Wirtschaftslebens," *Sozialistische Monatshefte*, XXI, 1 (1915), 165–67.

———— "Die Neutralisierung der Gewerkschaften," *Sozialistische Monatshefte*, IV (1900), 369–76.

————— "Ziele und Mittel der deutschen Gewerkschaftsbewegung," *Sozialistische Monatshefte,* IV (1900), 109–16.

Leipart, Theodor. Carl Legien. Berlin: Verlag des Allgemeinen Deutschen Gewerkschaftsbundes, 1929.

Lenin, V. I. What Is To Be Done? New York: International Publishers, 1929.

Lensch, Paul. Die deutsche Sozialdemokratie und der Weltkrieg. 2d ed. Berlin: Vorwärts, 1915.

Lindsay, A. D. Kant. London: Benn, 1934.

————— Karl Marx's Capital. London: Oxford University Press, 1925.

Löbe, Paul. "Eduard Bernstein als Breslauer Abgeordneter," in Grundsätzliches zum Tageskampfe, pp. 7–13. Breslau: Volkswacht, 1925.

Lozovsky, A. Marx and the Trade Unions. New York: International Publishers, 1942.

Lukacz, Georg. Geschichte und Klassenbewusstsein. Berlin: Malik, 1923.

Luxemburg, Rosa. "Sozialreform oder Revolution," "Die englische Brille," "Miliz und Militarismus," in Gesammelte Werke, Vol. III: Gegen den Reformismus, pp. 35–100, 104–14, 132–49. Berlin: Vereinigung Internationaler Verlagsanstalten, 1925.

MacIver, Robert M. The Web of Government. New York: Macmillan, 1947.

Marck, Siegfried. Hegelianismus und Marxismus. Berlin: Reuther und Reichard, 1922.

————— "Die Philosophie des Revisionismus," in Grundsätzliches zum Tageskampfe, pp. 23–30. Breslau: Volkswacht, 1925.

————— Sozialdemokratie. Berlin: Pan-Verlag, 1931.

Marcuse, Herbert. Reason and Revolution. New York: Oxford University Press, 1941.

Marx, Karl. Capital. Vol. I. New York: Modern Library, n. d. Vol. II. Chicago: C. H. Kerr, 1933. Vol. III. Chicago: C. H. Kerr, 1909.

————— The Civil War in France. New York: International Publishers, 1940.

————— The Class Struggles in France. New York: International Publishers, 1935.

————— Critique of the Gotha Programme. New York: International Publishers, 1938.

————— The Poverty of Philosophy. New York: International Publishers, n. d.

————— Revolution and Counter-Revolution. London: George Allen and Unwin, 1891.

————— Theorien über den Mehrwert. 4th ed. Vol. II, Part 2. Stuttgart: J. H. W. Dietz, 1921.

Marx, Karl, and Friedrich Engels. Communist Manifesto. New York: International Publishers, 1932.

———— Gesamtausgabe. Third Division, Vol. IV. Berlin: Marx-Engels Verlag, 1930. (This work is cited in the footnotes as *Marx-Engels Gesamtausgabe.*)

Mayer, Gustav. Bismarck und Lassalle. Berlin: J. H. W. Dietz, 1928.

———— Erinnerungen. Zurich: Europa-Verlag, 1949.

———— Friedrich Engels. 2 vols. The Hague: Martinus Nijhoff, 1934.

———— Johann Baptist von Schweitzer. Jena: Gustav Fischer, 1909.

———— Lassalle als Nationalökonom. Berlin: Mayer und Müller, 1894.

Mehring, Franz. Geschichte der deutschen Sozialdemokratie. 8th ed. Vols. IV and V. Stuttgart: J. H. W. Dietz, 1919.

———— Karl Marx. New York: Covici-Friede, 1935.

———— Zur Geschichte der deutschen Sozialdemokratie. Magdeburg: Faber, 1877.

Michels, Robert. "Die deutsche Sozialdemokratie, Partei-Mitgliedschaft und soziale Zusammensetzung," *Archiv für Sozialwissenschaft und Sozialpolitik*, new ser., V (1906), 471–556.

———— Political Parties. Glencoe, Ill.: Free Press, 1949.

———— "Psychologie der antikapitalistischen Massenbewegungen," in Grundriss der Sozialökonomik, Vol. IX, Part 1, pp. 241–359. Tübingen: Mohr, 1926.

Müller, Hermann. Karl Marx und die Gewerkschaften. Berlin: Verlag der Sozialwissenschaften, 1918.

Müller, Hermann (1876–1931). Die November-Revolution. Berlin: Bücherkreis, 1928.

Nestriepke, Siegfried. Die Gewerkschaftsbewegung. 2d ed. Vol. I. Stuttgart: Moritz, 1922.

Neumann, Franz. "Approaches to the Study of Political Power," *Political Science Quarterly*, LXV (1950), 161–80.

———— Behemoth. 2d ed. New York: Oxford University Press, 1944.

———— Koalitionsfreiheit und Reichsverfassung. Berlin: Heymanns, 1932.

Neumann, Sigmund. Die deutschen Parteien. Berlin: Junker und Dünnhaupt, 1932..

Oncken, Hermann. Lassalle. Stuttgart: Frommann, 1904.

Pease, Edward. The History of the Fabian Society. New York: Dutton, 1916.

Perlman, Selig. A Theory of the Labor Movement. New York: Macmillan, 1928.

Petegorsky, David. Left-Wing Democracy in the English Civil War. London: Gollancz, 1940.

Phillips, W. L. Why Are the Many Poor? London: Fabian Society, 1894.

Plekhanov, G. "Bernstein und der Materialismus," *Neue Zeit,* XVI, 2 (1898), 545–55.

―――― "Conrad Schmidt gegen Karl Marx und Friedrich Engels," *Neue Zeit,* XVII, 1 (1899), 133–45.

―――― "Materialismus oder Kantianismus," *Neue Zeit,* XVII, 1 (1899), 589–96, 626–32.

Pollatschek, Gustav, ed. Viktor Adlers Aufsätze, Reden und Briefe. Vol. VI. Vienna: Wiener Volksbuchhandlung, 1929.

Prager, Eugen. Geschichte der U.S.P.D. 2d ed. Berlin: Verlag "Freiheit," 1922.

Protokoll des Kongresses der deutschen Sozialdemokratie, 1880. Zurich: Herter, 1880.

Protokoll über die Verhandlungen des Parteitages der SPD, for the years 1898, 1899, 1901, 1903, 1904, 1905, 1906, 1908, 1913, 1919. Berlin: Vorwärts, various dates.

Quessel, Ludwig. "Landwirtschaft und Industrie," *Neue Zeit,* XXI, 2 (1903), 450–56, 481–90, 513–19.

Renner, Karl. Die Wirtschaft als Gesamtprozess. Berlin: J. H. W. Dietz, 1924.

Rikli, Erika. Der Revisionismus. Zurich: Girsberger, 1936.

Robinson, Joan. An Essay on Marxian Economics. London: Macmillan, 1949.

Roland-Holst, Henriette. Generalstreik und Sozialdemokratie. 2d ed. Dresden: Kaden, 1906.

Roll, Erich. A History of Economic Thought. Rev. ed. New York: Prentice-Hall, 1946.

Rosenberg, Arthur. The Birth of the German Republic. London: Oxford University Press, 1931.

―――― A History of the Weimar Republic. London: Methuen, 1936.

Schifrin, Alexander. "Eduard Bernstein," *Deutsche Republik,* Vol. VII (1933).

Schippel, Max. England und wir. Berlin: S. Fischer, 1917.

Schorske, Carl. "German Social Democracy, 1905–1917." Unpublished dissertation, on deposit at Harvard University Library.

Schröder, Wilhelm. Geschichte der sozialdemokratischen Parteiorganisation. Dresden: Kaden, 1912.

Schröder, Wilhelm, ed. Handbuch der sozialdemokratischen Parteitage. Munich: Birk, 1910.

Schulze-Gaevernitz, Gerhart von. Der Grossbetrieb. Liepzig: Duncker und Humblot, 1892.

―――― Zum sozialen Frieden. Leipzig: Duncker und Humblot, 1890.

Schumpeter, Joseph. Capitalism, Socialism, and Democracy. 2d ed. New York: Harpers, 1947.

Shaw, Bernard. The Fabian Society, What it Has Done, and How it Has Done it. London: Fabian Society, 1892. Tract No. 41.

Shaw, Bernard, ed. Fabianism and the Empire. London: Grant Richards, 1900.

Silone, Ignazio. The School for Dictators. London: Cape, 1939.

Sombart, Werner. Die deutsche Volkswirtschaft im 19ten Jahrhundert. 2d ed. Berlin: Bondi, 1909.

Sweezy, Paul. Socialism. New York: McGraw-Hill, 1949.

——— The Theory of Capitalist Development. 2d ed. New York: Oxford University Press, 1946.

Thimme, Friedrich, and Carl Legien. Die Arbeiterschaft im neuen Deutschland. Leipzig: Hirzel, 1915.

Umbreit, Paul. 25 Jahre deutscher Gewerkschaftsbewegung. Berlin: Verlag des Allgemeinen Deutschen Gewerkschaftsbundes, 1915.

Veblen, Thorstein. Imperial Germany. New York: Viking, 1939.

Victor, Max. "Die Stellung der deutschen Sozialdemokratie zu den Fragen der auswärtigen Politik, 1869–1914," *Archiv für Sozialwissenschaft und Sozialpolitik*, LX (1928), 147–79.

Volkswirtschaftslehre der Gegenwart in Selbstdarstellungen. Edited by Felix Meiner. Vol. I. Leipzig: Meiner, 1924.

Vollmar. Georg von. Uber die nächsten Aufgaben der deutschen Sozialdemokratie. Munich: Ernst, 1891.

Vorländer, Karl. Kant und Marx. Tübingen: Mohr, 1911.

Wallas, Graham. Human Nature in Politics. 3d ed. Boston: Houghton, Mifflin, 1915.

Waltershausen, Sartorius von. Deutsche Wirtschaftsgeschichte, 1815–1914. Jena: Gustav Fischer, 1920.

Webb, Sidney. Socialism, True and False. London: Fabian Society, 1894. Tract No. 51.

Weber, Max. The Protestant Ethic and the Spirit of Capitalism. New York: Scribners, 1930.

Wittenberg, Max. "Ein Blick auf den wirtschaftlichen Aufschwung am Ende des 19. Jahrhunderts," *Volkswirtschaftliche Zeitfragen*, XXII (1900), 3–58.

Wolf, Julius. Sozialismus und kapitalistische Gesellschaft. Stuttgart: Cotta, 1892.

Wolfe, Bertram D. Three Who Made a Revolution. New York: Dial, 1948.

Zahn, Friedrich. Deutschlands wirtschaftliche Entwicklung. Munich: Schweitzer, 1911.

Ziekursch, Johannes. Politische Geschichte des neuen deutschen Kaiserreiches. 3 vols. Frankfurt: Frankfurter Societätsdruckerei, 1925–30.

INDEX

Index

shadow, 67 f.; relations with, and influence of, Fabians, 68, 104, 107 ff., 162, 182; one of Engels's executors, 68; transition to Revisionism: resulting pain and inner struggle: cooling of friendship with Kautsky, 73; study of Paris Revolution of 1848, 72n; beginning of his purge in Probleme des Sozialismus: resulting storm of discussion, 74 ff.; remark that the goal is nothing, the movement everything, 74, 164, 262; controversies between Kautsky and, 77 ff., 171, 174, 188, 196 ff.; *Die Voraussetzungen* the bible of Revisionism, 78, 257; fame as leader of the movement, 78; lapse of warrant against him, 78; return to Germany, 79, 81; expulsion from party a t t e m p t e d by leaders, 79 ff.; explanation and debates re alleged deviationism of, 80 f.; extent of indebtedness to, and dissent from, Marx and Engels, 85 ff., 143, 147-50; attitude toward Lassalle's economics and political philosophy, 89 ff.; ethical theories, 94; his Dühring discipleship, 101; disillusioned after visit to D., 103; circumstances that compelled modification of his philosophy, 110; called erudite by Michels, 119n; on class structure of party, 119 f.; attitude toward trade unions, 139, 140; view of the dialectical process, 143 ff.; men he most admired, 143; a common sense philosopher, 143, 160; substitution of unilinear progress for dialectical evolution, 146, 148; return to Lassalle, 150; extent of Kant's influence, 154-63 *passim;* "Scientific Socialism," an attempt to introduce Kantian concepts into

Social Democracy, 156 ff.; objections to his excursions into Critical Philosophy, 160; views re capitalism's collapse and the crisis theory, 188-98, 308; sociological scheme of class relations, 205 ff.; defeated in 1907 Reichstag election, 228n; one of leaders in pro-strike movement, 239; Revisionist theory summarized: proposed ten-point party program, 250-52; in demand as speaker and journalist: head and shoulders above party colleagues, 255; in Reichstag, 256 f., 296, 297; devotion to international Socialism, 260; Luxemburg's pitiless analysis of position of, 262-69; foreign policy, 274-76, 293; influence of his Anglophile sentiments, 274, 275 f., 279; changing attitude before and during World War I, 274-89; his Reichstag votes against armament tax, 275; for war credits, 277, 284 (abstained, 285, 286, against, 286); announced conviction that "policy of Aug. 4" wrong: effects, 278-89 *passim;* painful effort to find truth about the war, 279; isolated from Revisionists, 281; anti-war article rejected by *Monatshefte,* 282 ff.; end of their collaboration, 283; among those who left SPD and formed new party, 287; why changed from support of war to later opposition, 287; why waited so long, 287 f.; services to, and love of party: decision to leave it, hard, 288; in cabinet of Weimar Republic, 290; efforts to hold the governing parties together, 290 f.; rejoined Social Democrats: came back alone, 292; courageous fight for the truth about the peace, 292-95; influence and

Lassalle, Ferdinand, 38, 153, 157, 222; founded first independent workers' party, 20; book on Schulze von Delitsch, 24; Bernstein's attitude toward, 24n, 68n, 150; creation and leadership of the Allgemeiner Deutscher Arbeiterverein, 29-35, 90n; death, 31; theory of the state, 31 f.; 93, 249; view of political action by workers, 32; balance between views of Marx and, 32, 37; works edited by Bernstein, 67, 89n; personality, career, 89, 90n, influence, 89, 94; economic doctrines, 89-94; extent of Bernstein's criticism and acceptance of them, 89-94 passim; Iron Law of Wages, 91 f., 94, 133; ethical theories, 94; attitude toward unions, 133, 134, 229; toward operatives, 230; philosophy of democracy, 246

Lassalleans, 62, 69; conflict between Eisenachers and, 24, 25, 27; doctrinal differences, 34; personal rancor, 31, 35; after Lassalle's death, 31, 101; hostilities ended: emergence of a united party, 36 f.

Laterne, Die, 45

League of Nations, 276, 289

"Legal," why word dropped from Gotha Program, 49

Legien, Carl, 134, 260, 284, 286n; quoted, 135, 139; sincerity, service, 138n

Leipart, Theodor, 260

Leipziger Volkszeitung, 280, 285 f.

Lenin, V. I., 37n, 198, 229, 278; realization of differences between German and Russian parties, 113n; trade unions, 131 f.; on voters of war budget, 276

Lensch, Paul, 274, 280, 286n, 301

Leveller movement, 65, 66

Liberalism, awakening and revolutions of 1848: lack of power,

19; opponents, 19, 32 f.; distrust of 93; divergence or coalition of radicals and, 227 ff.; Social Democracy's indebtedness to, 246 f.

Lichtheim, George, 304n

Liebknecht, Karl, 256n, 280; vote against war credits, 284, 286n; breach of party discipline, 284; murdered, 291n

Liebknecht, Wilhelm, 23, 26, 27, 34n, 35, 38, 43, 49, 50 f., 53, 55, 256n; a leader of Eisenach party, 33; draft program, Gotha Congress, 38; founding of *Sozialdemokrat,* 45; visit to Marx and Engels, 46; exile, 52; attitude toward Dühring, 102; official interpreter of Marx's theory, 102n; quoted, 111; furthered trade unions, 132, 133

Lilburne, John, 65

Lindsay, A. D., on Marxian prediction, 188 f.

Lobe, Paul, 270n

Local communities, democratic, 246

Locke, John, 66, 94, 98, 100

London, publication of *Sozialdemokrat* in, 59; staff exiled to, 59n; Bernstein's life and activities, 60-81; Socialists in, 67 f., (*see also* Fabians); evidences of peaceful social change, 69; *see also* England

Lukacz, Georg, quoted, 144

Luxemburg, Rosa, 112, 150, 243, 280; views re capitalism, 185, 194; sharp intellect: sarcasm, 262; profound and effective attacks on Revisionism, 262-69; examination of its basis, 263 ff.; of Bernstein's tactics, 266 ff.; twofold conclusions, 267; difficulties in own position, 268 f.; rigidly revolutionary frame of mind, 268; murder of, 291n

MacDonald, Ramsay, 68

greatest, 272; but reviled for support of the war, 278, 280; war guilt discussed at Stockholm conference, 289; without confidence in Germans, no international action possible, 293
"Socialists of the chair," 69
"Socialitary system" of Dühring, 97 ff.
Social legislation, Bismarck's program, 52; Socialists' reaction, 53 f., 236; workers benefited, 128
Social reform, held limited by Luxemburg, 266
Sociological concepts of Marxism, 86 f.
Sorelian view of the general strike, 239
South German Social Democracy, 258, 259*n*; strongholds of Revisionism, 233; budget vote, 233
Sozialdemokrat, founding of, 45 f.; Bernstein's editorship, 47, 50 f.; declared the only official organ of the party, 50; Kautsky as collaborator, 51; party's best newspaper, 51; policies, 54-58 *passim;* why staff expelled from Switzerland, 57 f.; editor's refusal to alter basic character of: publication continued in London, 59; why Bernstein's editorship ended, 60; values he gave it, 60*n*; smuggled into Germany: role in party, 115; Vollmar first editor, 258
Sozialdemokratische Arbeiterpartei, 33 ff.; *see also* Eisenachers
Sozialdemokratische Arbeitsgemeinschaft, 287, 288
Sozialdemokratische Partei Deutschlands (SPD), party name changed to: reorganization, 115*n*; *see entries under* Social Democratic Party
Sozialismus und Demokratie in der grossen englischen Revolution (Bernstein), 64-67

Sozialismus und kapitalistische Gesellschaft (Wolf), 71
Sozialistische Arbeiterpartei Deutschlands, 37; *see* Social Democratic Party
Sozialistische Monatshefte, 136, 156, 231, 283; publication of the Revisionists, 257; subjects dealt with, 259 f.; Bernstein's anti-war article rejected, 282 f.; end of his collaboration with, 283
"Sozialreform oder Revolution" (Luxemburg), 262 f.
SPD, *see* Sozialdemokratische Partei Deutschlands
Stammler, Rudolf, 152
Stampfer, Friedrich, 280, 297; quoted, 292
Standard of living, effect of industrialism, 128
State, Lassalle's ideas, 31, 93; Marx's, 32; voluntary submission vs. force, 97; reform of, vs. overthrow of, 235; SPD accepted the German, 301; varied attitudes toward, 249; Bernstein's conception of a democratic, 249 f.
Staudinger, F., 152
Steamship lines, subsidies to, 55
Stocker, Adolf, anti-Semitism, 125*n*
Strikes, political mass strike, 237-44; opposition of trades unions, 238 f., 243; countries in which victorious, 238; five reasons for debate on, 238 f.; advocates, 238, 239, 242; realism of Bernstein's approach to, 239 ff.; defeat of party's resolutions for, 244; against war, 271, 278
Südekum, Albert, 270*n*
Suffrage, Prussian e l e c t o r a l system, 20, 234, 238; made farce of universal, 20; efforts to attain, 30; universal, in democratic state, 93, 245 f.; mass strikes in behalf of, 238 ff.

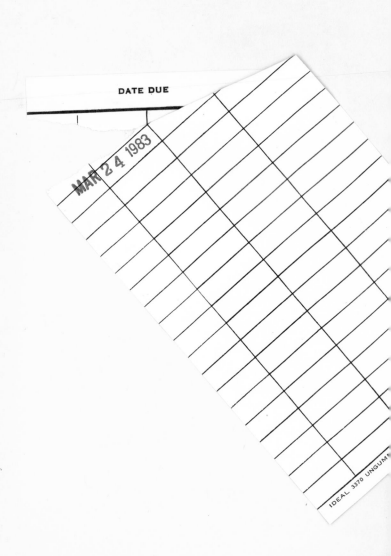

DATE DUE

MAR 24 1983

IDEAL 3370 UNGUM